THE DAMAGE
LIES CAN DO

THE DAMAGE LIES CAN DO

The psychological legacy of targeting and bullying

MICHAEL J A COLLINS

BROWN
DOG
BOOKS

First published 2024

Published under licence by Brown Dog Books and The Self-Publishing Partnership Ltd, 10b Greenway Farm, Bath Rd, Wick, nr. Bath BS30 5RL, UK

www.selfpublishingpartnership.co.uk

ISBN printed book: 978-1-83952-842-2
ISBN e-book: 978-1-83952-843-9

Cover design by Kevin Rylands
Internal design by Mac Style

Printed and bound in the UK

This book is printed on FSC® certified paper

MIX
Paper | Supporting responsible forestry
FSC® C013604

Contents

Chapter 1	My Reasons for Writing this Book	1
Chapter 2	Psychology	4
Chapter 3	How Did I End Up at Abbotts?	11
Chapter 4	Deliverance: Setting the Scene: Starting off at Abbotts	17
Chapter 5	Meeting my Nemesis	25
Chapter 6	The Leaving Do and Last Contact with Linda	39
Chapter 7	Dayshift and Events Leading up Until the Disciplinary Hearing	42
Chapter 8	Nicky Albert: The First Disciplinary Interview	48
Chapter 9	The DHL Document Debacle	54
Chapter 10	Linda's Rumours and Lies	56
Chapter 11	Linda's Witness	62
Chapter 12	Racism at Abbotts	64
Chapter 13	Good Management and the Not so Good	69
Chapter 14	Linda's Exploits	75
Chapter 15	Sexual Exploits on Site at Abbotts	78
Chapter 16	The Most Disturbing Case of All	82
Chapter 17	Gone Overboard	84
Chapter 18	The Shaun Smith Hearing	88
Chapter 19	The Verdict Hearing	91
Chapter 20	Thames Valley Police	95
Chapter 21	I Appeal to Les Muggeridge at the Abbott Gatehouse	103
Chapter 22	My Appeal Hearing with Pat and Les	106

Chapter 23	The Depression Really Sets In	110
Chapter 24	Les Lies	113
Chapter 25	The Tribunal in Brief	114
Chapter 26	I Receive the Judge's Summary	119
Chapter 27	The Alleged Letter from Richard	125
Chapter 28	A Case of Relevance for the Judge's Perusal	129
Chapter 29	Meeting Staff After My Time at Abbotts	136
Chapter 30	I Appeal to Senior Judges and the Ombudsman	138
Chapter 31	Your Honour and My Hypocrisy	142
Chapter 32	Reporting Shaun and Pat to Amanda White	148
Chapter 33	Abbott Policies	151
Chapter 34	I Take the Lie Detector Test	154
Chapter 35	Abbott's Reaction to my Polygraph Test Results Being Sent	156
Chapter 36	Get Up, Get Knocked Down Again, Jane Ingram	160
Chapter 37	Meeting Shaun Smith Again: Andy Payne	163
Chapter 38	So the Ball is Back in Andy Payne's Court	172
Chapter 39	Lie Detector Merits and Judicial Issues	176
Chapter 40	Meeting Shaun Smith Again in Salford	185
Chapter 41	Cutting Off Your Nose to Spite Your Face	187
Chapter 42	The Wisdom of Solomon	196
Chapter 43	Window Dressing	204
Chapter 44	This Paddy Never Let Britain Down	208
Chapter 45	Morals, Honesty and Grown-up Behaviour	220
Chapter 46	The Weak Authorities Who Look the Other Way	223
Chapter 47	The Ball is now in Abbott's Court	225
Chapter 48	Tangents and Sticking to the Subject.	227
Chapter 49	How to Finish the Book	229
Chapter 50	Postscript: Appeals	231
Kowtowards		240

Chapter 1

My Reasons for Writing this Book

For well over a decade I have been fighting for justice against an enemy much larger, more powerful and influential than myself.

There comes a time when you have exhausted every other possible avenue, and faced corruption at every turn that you must draw a line in the sand and reappraise your approach.

So now I'm putting it to the wider jury to see what they think.

I didn't want to have to do this, and gave the guilty every chance to put right their wrongs. Even after all these years, unequivocal proof and polygraph testing, I still haven't even heard the word 'sorry' from anyone involved.

For well over a decade I have fought the good fight. Now, apart from re-mortgaging my house only to meet another judge totally lacking in impartiality, representing a system I know to be corrupt, this is the only feasible option left open to me.

I have given all involved plenty of notice – in fact, well over a decade of notice – that I intended to write this book. They have not responded. Perhaps they thought I was bluffing. Well, I have stood up to be counted every time before and I won't give up, as I know the cause is right.

I have written many, many times what is actually in this book in search of justice.

I promise that in this book, everything I have written, however ghastly and unbelievable, is the truth and the whole relevant truth. There are obviously areas where I'm quoting what I believe beyond all reasonable doubt to be true, but mostly what I know absolutely to be true.

I say the whole relevant truth as the whole truth would be so many books in length.

This is just the highlights, although, I'm sure you will agree on reading, there are enough of those.

I'll be dead in few years anyway, and this book could hasten that event somewhat. With the depression and anxiety I suffer, that may even be a blessing.

I have rattled some very heavy cages along the way. This book will poke the bear a whole lot more.

Single-handedly taking on a multi-billion dollar, utterly corrupt, unscrupulous multinational pharmaceutical company and their legal influences seems a bit foolhardy: somewhat like taking on an army armed only with a pea-shooter.

I have challenged many in authority to stand up for the truth and justice.

Sadly, not one of these have I found to have a sense of decency and the will to act on it.

I have challenged police chiefs, judges, local MPs who were also Prime Ministers, Cabinet Ministers, a Second Sea Lord, Admiral and Knight Commander of the Bath, pharmaceutical CEOs and every relevant institution and organisation.

All the above will put the institution before truth and justice and believe they can do so with impunity: a belief in which it sadly seems they are right in adhering to.

Until someone changes and educates them, that is how it will stay. We live in hope.

I'm happy to one day face a judge far higher than all them and account for my actions.

If any 'friend' wishes to protect themselves or their interests by distancing themselves from someone they perceive disadvantageous to know, I fully understand.

Like those involved in the Post Office / Horizon scandal, I have to stand up against an evil and do all I can to get justice. This may save the next victim, and so on and so on. As many of them felt initially, 'I'm on my own.' This David will in all probability lose but he has to do so having given Goliath the best battle he can.

The size and influence of the enemy is overwhelming, but I'm up for it and on the side of right.

The toll that all this has taken on my mental health and my family has been far too great. I have written, written and written. If it were on paper it would reach the ceiling.

I heard it said at a workplace meeting once.

- Would you like your family to see your actions?
- Would you like your friends to see your actions?
- Would you like your actions to be printed in a newspaper?

If the answer is no, then you are a bully.

I'm still fighting the evil bullies well over a decade on.

There are those locally who possibly noticed that my once active social life totally stopped soon after our wedding. Perhaps reading this book you will understand the reasons why. Putting my family first, state of mind and finance were among the most obvious reasons for my decision.

When those you are loyal to would lie about you, and intentionally attack your character without just cause or remorse and will throw you under a bus as they did to me, then they deserve no further loyalty. To censure what happened would be to assist them to the detriment of my family and their next victim.

I know these bullies and how they try to censure the truth.

I'm going public because what these types fear most would be others seeing behind the facade.

I have mentioned the names of those in authority I have dealt with like management, police and the judiciary etc. I have not named others, except for a few complimentary exceptions.

Chapter 2

Psychology

Mental health – Why this book had to be written: my psychological problems in writing

I have made a promise for a number of years now to friends and enemies that I would write this book. The years of depression have taken their toll.

I have had so many failed attempts at writing this, only to end up with more material than when I started and no apparent resemblance of a book in sight.

Invariably my writing would focus on a point I've already written about and I would write about it all over again from a slightly different perspective, often inspired by some other outside injustice that I could clearly relate to myself.

Overthinking and tangents are the enemies of clarity and a stressful, unnecessary journey away from it.

Hardest battle I've ever fought, against myself, to write this

They say that often your toughest opponent is yourself. I have enough enemies to overcome without that, as you will hopefully see when reading this book.

I would just keep adding more and more instead of being concise and addressing issues.

There are clearly a number of inadequacies within myself that need addressing.

Has there been perhaps a subconscious, cowardly hiding and contentment with failure that is the reason this book has taken so long to materialise?

Have I subconsciously accepted being an underling for too long as it is the easier option?

Oh yeah, I'll write this book; I've promised. Well, when? And how are you going to do it?

There needs to be a destination and a plan and a framework for getting there.

This is what I had to educate myself to do. Another reason for writing this book was that it could be great positive therapy. It was a cathartic exercise battling my own inadequacies. I had to devise a framework for getting from start to end and stick to it.

Presenting a logical sequence when you have so much to wade through is a challenge.

Loser syndrome

I have failed a great many times to write this book. I suppose it is a contradiction in itself; but I have allowed the loser within me to win so many times.

So much of this is to do with conditioning; both of yourself and by others. It is also easier to find a way to not face your fears and biggest obstacles.

You can ask yourself: Once you have reached that finish line and climbed the mountain, so to speak, what goal do you then have? Will there be a void or, what seems more likely, so many more mountains to climb? The publication of this book may just be the end of a chapter, not the end.

Much as there have been successes, there are the everyday failures – the putting off until tomorrow what you can do today. I'm a great one for being overwhelmed by the whole picture before I look at the component parts that need to be addressed.

Subconsciously you can allow an acceptance of failure that goes unaddressed without admitting it to yourself. I'm sure most of us do this in our own individual ways.

Many of us work so many times harder than so many others and have so little reward to show. There is the old adage: *don't work harder, work smarter.*

Some, certainly myself included, allow themselves to be naturally unworthy and subservient, hence they work so hard for others. Some have the self-worth battered out of them. Even within a family, some children are destroyed and treated as serfs whilst others may be treated as princes or princesses. This conditioning can last a lifetime. Through life the royalty will always find other conditioned serfs to continue the pampering that they expect: their part comes mainly when taking the credit.

Self-effacing conditioned default position underlings often don't stand up to lies against them, and can even perversely and illogically invite more.

It is an incredible handicap to be conditioned to initially accept what people say on face value. It is also an incredible advantage, for others, to be able to lie without a conscience.

The former are generally the conditioned subservients. The latter can come from two camps: those who are accustomed to getting their way at all costs and those hurt so badly they live a life of denial.

At a tribunal or the like, those like myself are disadvantaged by a conditioned, meek, trusting, subservient position to begin with. We let too much go before reacting; then it seems too late. Others are professional liars.

The meek, subservient, honest and trusting then overwhelm themselves with seemingly pointless post-mortems whilst the liars move on without a thought for the damage caused.

Injustice in itself will not just destroy lives through the likes of family torment and suicides but can lead to all sorts of issues and self-destructive traits and dependencies. I know, for example, and can fully understand Sara Payne, who I will mention later; her husband Michael's losing and eventually fatal battle with alcohol and depression.

I know the real, positive and brave me and yet there can be this pathetic helplessness that is all-consuming and overwhelming. It can be viewed as an understandable escapism at best or a self-destructive, cowardly, self-pitying selfish denial that unfairly impacts others who care for you at its ugliest.

So often I am kicking myself, saying, 'Come on, this is so straightforward,' yet either it is so hard or do I just make it that way? I can make the simplest journey a trudge through treacle through overthinking, mental side-tracking and carrying unnecessary cargo.

During my mental health interviews I've had a lot of good dialogue with a lot of good people. One who stood out was a former GP. She was not actually a psychiatrist, but she had the potential to be a brilliant one.

On the one hand she empathised, but she also challenged me too: both are needed. We could have a good game of verbal tennis quoting lines from the Bible that are totally contradictory with one another, for example 'Blessed is he who hungers and thirsts for that which is right whilst blessed are the peacemakers.' Then, 'If struck on one cheek, offer the other.' Then, as Gandhi would put it, 'An eye for an eye and the whole world goes blind,' and so on.

Extreme panic and anxiety attacks after revisiting the events

I hear with so many wrongly accused victims of injustice that there is a totally debilitating trauma that takes hold – a sort of PTSD. It is not something that you can just put right. You have the insecurity of what others might be thinking or saying and it is impossible to know the right tactic to put this right, or even if it can be put right.

Through no fault of your own you are suddenly a completely different person. If I go here, I might now meet that person, and what might they have heard or be thinking about me? Part of your soul dies. You now have this new baggage, this darkness, like a cloud permanently over your head. Your happy and positive side is shattered.

Common sense dictates that what I'm doing is foolhardy, ill-advised and even stupid and that I can't ever win and will end up crucified. I know that to be the way the world is, yet the idealist in me says 'Stand up for that which is right. Overcome the fear and go ahead and do what you must do.'

I'm not one who has no sense of fear – fear in fact overwhelms me – but someone must be brave enough to stand up for right in the face of such obvious wrong. I tend to be that sort of someone.

I care about truth; I care about real justice. I have stood up for others, now is the time to stand up for myself, my family and perhaps others too overwhelmed to have a voice. I know that if this meets the corrupt one-sided authorities again that my chances of winning are not good, shall we say, but what else can I do? Justice matters to me.

It is so hard with all the mental pressures I feel, knowing I'm probably welcoming more rounds of torment against an unscrupulous enemy who, let alone being infinitely more powerful than myself, seem immune from the law and, indeed, in control of it. Sometimes a man just has to do what he has to do. Someone has to. Yes I am foolhardy, and perhaps even stupid.

In the dark and overwhelming times I will inevitably go on a long walk, add to the endorphins to pick myself up, and say, 'Keep going. We're only here once. Don't let the bastards grind you down.'

These issues began at a time where everything was positive, just after our wedding. Addressing someone else's psychology: did this make someone envious?

Without all the depression and focus on this over the years, I could have been a so much better husband and father. We must have missed out on so much and I feel guilty and sorry for that too, adding to the psychological baggage.

The hope is that this book ends this, and I give my family the positive time they deserve.

You can also take this mistrusting, cynical, battered mentality into everything else in life after a major trauma.

In this state of mind you can waste life so easily, focusing on other wrongs that so often do not even concern you.

There is also in my case a history of extreme anxiety attacks going back to childhood that manifest themselves in very overtly visible physical convulsions that I mostly manage to avoid performing in public, although remembering one of my nicknames as a kid, I wasn't always successful.

I've had so many of these intense attacks that occur so often whilst writing this book. I was winning the battle but since the events that led to this book I am now in 'full relapse with interest' mode.

Other visual manifestations are the periods where I don't do the stuff around the house, leave the letters unopened and all that sort of thing.

These are some of my demons and, if fully explained, they could fill another book.

Kicking myself up the ass

Understanding that there are these issues is important. It is also important to then correct these issues otherwise the torment is eternal.

As said before; it seems so straightforward to tell myself just to do it. But it's so easy, without the right focus, to just add more and more, get overwhelmed by the whole picture and create anxieties.

I'm so often finished and totally mentally overwhelmed leaning towards worst-case scenarios, before I've even got started.

I tell myself I don't want to leave a crucial piece out of the book; I don't want to do too many duplicates either. You need to just tell yourself, 'Tough shit baby, just get on with it. Perfection takes forever; you're far from perfect; shit happens.'

I've never given up. I'm always going to write the book, but I was never saying when.

Not so long back I took a year off alcohol. There were so many times in my life I would have had far more reasons to do this; perhaps that's another book in itself, too. On this occasion it was merely, just because as Bruce Springsteen would say:' Man, I'm just tired and bored with myself.'

Since the life-changing event and subsequent depression, I found that hangovers can be a trip to hell; which made such a decision a lot more appealing.

It was a bit like a lent; I just did it; but didn't set myself any goals whilst I did it. I wasted it really; just like I could waste so many weekends having a beer Friday & Saturday night, rendering myself pretty useless all weekend.

I'm very strong willed at giving things up, but not so clever when it comes to actually doing the extra things. That's my real test.

So I'm abstaining again. Well, most of the time; this time with a few targets and a deadline i.e. a specific relevant date and a clear objective.

It has got to be this time
I had given myself a deadline in which time if I don't write the book, then I'm never going to write it.

In trying to write this book I have been falling off the horse, getting side-tracked then getting back on but, one day, this horse has finally got to go somewhere other than in circles.

When writing this book, referring back and reading stuff you forgot was alleged nearly kills you, but you must get up again.

I would say to myself, 'In the time before this trauma you often achieved and exceeded with many targets.

Stand up! Be strong!'

If I get this monkey off my back then perhaps I can open the door for other life improvements.

I know too; it could re-open all the old wounds. But the guilty have walked away unscathed, and without a care, whilst I have been beating myself up and going through hell. I have to aim at closure. Hopefully with this book I can say, 'Everything is in there. That's the last I'm writing about this. Too many years have been wasted.'

I may have to take a few more hits after publication. The worst may be yet to come.

But I want to be able to draw a line.

I have only ever confided in very few outside of my family, the issues I have faced these last 15 years. There is so much to explain and you can jump from one bit to another, then go back because you missed a point, then think, 'Where was I again in what I was telling you?'

I can now say to anyone who may be interested, 'It's all in the book.'

One obvious hit during writing was when I hit the wrong key and lost a chapter.

Some days can be almost normal. You forget, or maybe delude yourself and try to ignore just how awful the lows are until you revisit them; or do they revisit you?

Justice must be served. It's the only cure in my case.

I may get justice via the printed word when those who intentionally tried to destroy me by making some ridiculous allegations will now have their deeds published. I hope that when they see this they might understand how I felt, reading the lies told about me. I may have a similar effect on them as they did with me, with the key difference being that I'm telling the truth – a truth that, because of their actions, needs to be told to correct an injustice.

The truth must be told and I didn't ask for, want or deserve this. It is just what I have to do.

Hobson's choice: Damned if you do and even more damned if you don't. You feel like a bit of a grass for writing the book, yet if you don't right the wrongs; only the wrongs will be on record.

Is it all worth it?

The simple answer is; probably not. I'm still mentally tearing myself apart writing these words.

15 years of torment but, like so many others who have faced injustice, you simply go on.

All those wasted years; all that pain and, so far at least, not a solitary gain. The only exception could be the brief euphoria after the polygraph test.

A conscience can be a real curse and disadvantage.

If I had killed myself or lost my wife, home and family, those who would facilitate that and who tried to destroy us wouldn't have cared a jot.

They might care about people seeing what they are really like.

Thinking of the day I meet my maker, I can at least now say, 'I tried the best I could.'

Chapter 3

How Did I End Up at Abbotts?

I had quite a good scientific job at a company in Milton Park. I was involved in precision technology clean rooms, making what was then cutting edge technology, photonic transceivers etching and depositing fine layers of materials including gold onto silicon wafers. After redundancy, I had to find work fast to pay the mortgage and put food on the table.

So before working at Abbotts I had the misfortune to work at the Asda Distribution Warehouse in Didcot, Oxon – an emergency fill-in job for a while. Most of the staff were OK, but let's just say it was not run with the good of one and all in mind; but hard work never scared me.

You have to wonder with these PC HR middle-management types whether they accept to undergo some sort of brain surgery whereby, in exchange for some minor power or authority, they accept undergoing an operation whereby a hamster is inserted into their tiny minds to operate the controls, as it is impossible to relate any sense to them which they can adequately compute.

On top of being as thick as shit these so-called middle managers were permanently intentionally rude, nasty and obnoxious way beyond what duty called for and without provocation or justification in the vast majority of cases. There was also a mutual self-help society very prevalent when it came to dishing out work and rewards, whereby those who kissed ass the most but worked the least were inevitably rewarded the most, at the expense of the honest.

This was a distribution warehouse. Apart from goods in and the office, goods out staff were divided into three main groups, not counting the downstairs office. There were the low-level order picker trucks (or LLOPs, known as lollops), the fork truck drivers and the HGV vehicle loaders.

The lollops were basically electrically powered trucks that carried two pallets of goods that were hand-picked from various aisles and shrink-wrapped to be sent to various Asda stores around the country. There were, of course, picking targets. A minimum to keep your job, with occasionally a bonus awarded like a bag of groceries or cans of beer, wine etc. for picking excess amounts.

Believe me, you had to earn your corn. Unless of course you were one of the favoured ones who might achieve this target by picking up a couple of pre-wrapped pallets that counted as a thousand items picked. Others would pick up four display stands that were one pallet each that would merely count as four items picked. Basically, the system was open to abuse.

The incident that led to my departure

Naturally there was competition amongst workers, particularly on nights where bonuses were on offer. There was enough competition in the first place to get a LLOP that ran smoothly and was reasonably charged. Such machines were the exception not the rule. You did, however, always test the brakes and forward and reverse motions and log this information on the machine log before use.

There were some workers who took this competition a little too far and decided to go down the intimidation route, and some would say, 'Why not?' It seemed to be the example of the managers and middle managers. At a neighbouring warehouse that supplied another supermarket chain, knives being pulled on staff and other intimidation was not uncommon.

So the scene is set. These trucks when loaded with two pallets and battery weight had all the destructive power of a loaded fork lift. When misused, they could easily maim and kill. There were many high-rise aisles to negotiate. There was a wait for fork lifts to reload stock pallets from above, and always competition to get round to achieve your target, but most of us played reasonably fair.

But then we got a new employee, a Turkish chap. To say this lad drove without due care and attention was an understatement. He was simply intentionally intimidating and would push his luck as far as he could. Never being one to cower or shirk, I told him off a few times regarding both his driving and littering. There was a fair amount of litter generated peeling stock tickets, for which we had a bag at the front of the truck, but his would just be tossed overboard whilst he intentionally played 'chicken' with anyone standing in the aisles or driving other trucks. In short he was a psycho, for want of a better description.

So, I am one of his least favourites as these sorts hate people with consciences and the courage of their convictions who challenge them and dent their egos.

Then one evening I am down an aisle picking an order, standing between my LLOP and one of the supporting girders for the high rise stock racks in a tight space, to leave room for other vehicles to pass and pick from the aisle opposite.

Then suddenly there is an almighty CRAAAASSSH! This guy has driven at top speed straight into the back of my LLOP; and without doubt intentionally. Did he apologise? Did he hell! He just said, 'Brakes don't work,' and carried on. He was not even picking stock from where I was, so should have passed me anyway. Today was my turn for his intimidation tactics.

He should also have checked his brakes beforehand and, if his brakes did not work, would have known not to continue his work with a faulty truck. He would also surely have slowed down before impact. All you have to do is not accelerate and a natural stop will soon occur.

So anyway, off he goes and I look around the area where I stand for a witness. The only person in the vicinity is an aisle sweeper. I said to him, 'You saw that, didn't you!' He just pointed to his tongue as he clearly did not have a command of English, or did not want me to think he did.

I was pretty unhappy and shaken and went straight to the office and told them what happened, and that the incident happened just two minutes ago and to review the camera evidence. There were multiple cameras that were always on and always working to prevent stock theft. I am immediately told that the cameras down that aisle aren't working, to which I remarked with astonishment, 'You haven't even checked; so how could you know? They would be working if I nicked something.'

So I take another manager to the scene of the crime. You can see the skid mark on the floor where my truck has been pushed forward by the impact. I point out that had the impact been a little off- centre the truck would have swung and that I would have been crushed between the truck and the girder and, at a minimum, would have been crippled for life and possibly even been killed.

I pointed out that I asked the cleaner, still nearby, but he does not seem to speak English. Then along comes our friend in his LLOP. I said, 'Why are you still driving a truck with defective brakes, and why did you not test your machine before use, and drive off from an accident?' He said, 'Brakes are OK now.' Well, how would he know that? Has he just got them fixed and tested in 2 or 3 minutes flat?

He then says, 'Cleaner says there was no accident.'

Oh, really! So why are there visibly marks on the floor where my truck, which I haven't moved since, has clearly been shunted along; and why do these marks clearly stop where my truck is now?

So I then remarked to him, 'Why are you asking a cleaner about an 'accident' that never happened? If nothing happened; then there would be nothing to ask the cleaner about.'

I also remarked that if you can converse with the cleaner then you must speak the same language, and we are relying on the guilty party's translation. He then says to the manager, 'He mentioned my language.'

Upon this the hamster working the controls in the manager's brain goes into one track overdrive. He just keeps saying to me on the way back to the office, 'You can't go mentioning his foreign language.' I reply, 'I never mentioned the word foreign; only the blatantly obvious fact that they spoke the same language. But that is not important; the fact that I was nearly killed is the important point; now get the camera footage and let's sort this out!'

I am then told to take an early tea break and a senior manager will talk to me soon. I think, 'Great. I may speak to someone with sense who will look at the footage.' If anyone had stolen stock, don't worry, there would be footage, no problem. And this was, after all, far more serious. An incident has clearly occurred, as can be seen from the shunt marks. I have complained instantly. I thought, the evidence is there, this will be sorted. But I was thinking logically. Management don't do that. Management cover up too.

I am then invited to the upstairs offices where I am sat down with four managers who wish to interview me. 'Great,' I thought; let's get this menace sorted out.

Do they, or will they address the issue? Do they hell! I keep trying to address the issue as I'm in shock and annoyed because I could just have been killed or crippled. I naturally think of the impact this could have had on my young family.

I clearly explain to them that I did not use the word foreign, that only the manager did. But that that is not the issue. My near miss is the issue. But if I tried to communicate with a cleaner who could not speak English, then that is part of the evidence. I said to these managers that if this chap and the cleaner spoke in a language that I did not understand, then it would logically be foreign to me but it is not a word I uttered at the time. More crucially, if they are both speaking about an incident, then an incident clearly happened. To me that is wholly logical.

Now can we get on with the main issue and let's look at my truck skid marks and the video evidence as, after all, he seemingly deliberately crashed into my truck and then carried on in a vehicle he himself said was not safe.

He is thus intentionally endangering more people by his actions, and breaking company rules.

But there was only one show in town as far as they were concerned. I said, 'I'm not happy and want to take this higher. I could have been killed or maimed and you are ignoring this.'

So later on in the night shift, in the early morning, I get to be interviewed by the site manager, the 'top dog'. We sit down either side of his desk. He starts by assuring me, 'Don't worry, it's all OK. I have spoken to the other chap and he is not going to take this any further.'

I will be diplomatic and say I was a tad visibly unhappy about this. I say, 'What sort of message does this send to all the staff?' I told many other staff what has happened as well; all of whom are on my side including the vast majority of decent ethnic minority staff who all know I'm genuine.

I suppose another very plausible explanation for the manager's actions was that during the night they did look at the footage from the camera that actually was working, and saw that I was telling the truth. But, rather than admitting their 'woke actions' were totally wrong and apologising, they tried to defuse the situation and defend their stupidity by saying, 'He is not taking this any further.' Why, after all, would I immediately after the event insist they looked at the irrefutable camera footage, if I wasn't telling the truth? I'd look pretty stupid if they did look, and I wasn't right.

For the record, I have no issue with Turkish people. My issue is with intimidating bullies. Some hamster-controlled brains are too dim to see that. I was the victim of institutionalised racism and it was someone else who instigated the incident and I was discriminated against for my ethnicity.

There is one member of staff who then privately tells me that before my incident the same chap had intentionally driven at him. So I say, 'Come on, let's go to the office, the management need to know. But he is too scared and afraid for his job. What a coward. I'd happily take a lie detector regarding this fact. I can't remember his name but he was a small chap, older than me, with glasses. He used to do a lot of work in other depots and annoy other staff with his journey times and mileage travel claims.

A few weeks later, while I'm serving notice, someone gets their legs crushed by an overseas worker who drove a LLOP into them. This chap's catchphrase was, 'Cracking.' Sadly this extended to cracking another employee's legs. I later learned that after a brief suspension he was back driving trucks.

Another chap used to regularly fall asleep, and not just the once either. Literally with a raised heavy load bound for the top racks. It was often a spectacle for an audience to behold. He was never once suspended or stopped long- term from driving lift trucks. (People falling asleep on shift endangering lives with machines active is another issue that will occur again later.)

As said, I was already serving my notice and in my final week when I heard of the leg smashing incident and then, later, the reinstatement. My disgust had not abated at my treatment but I did all I could and continued to voice my concerns in correspondence with the new manageress after leaving.

There was also, as I left, a new system being introduced whereby staff would wear a headset for 12 hours and be instructed in a digital computerised voice where to go and pick their orders from. No way was I working in an already unsafe environment with this in my ears, too.

This was unsafe for two reasons. Firstly, it would be like driving whilst using a mobile phone. The driver would be distracted. Secondly, 12 hours of mobile phone emissions in your ear and no information regarding the radiation levels. No thanks. At least it might have made the workload more even and random for all, hence fairer, but still. No thanks.

I then went to a local employment agency, Total Employment, Didcot, who had exciting night shift vacancies at a pharmaceutical plant in Witney Oxon. I live in between the two locations and thought that anything must be better than Asda.

So off I go to my new job at a pharmaceutical company with renewed optimism and relief.

They say history sometimes repeats itself and in my case this was so true.

As with Abbotts, the headliners in this book, I was with an American-owned company where one- trick pony, blinkered kiss-asses were promoted way beyond their capabilities and there was an incident where you could not talk sense to these dumber-than-dumb blinkered kiss-asses.

In yet another astonishing parallel to Abbotts I was driven at by a psychopath, and the use of technology would have shown the truth. Instead, these brain-dead PC-obsessed mindless morons viewed a minor politically correct point, that was a simple misinterpretation on their part anyway, as infinitely more important than killing or wilfully crippling an employee.

And, 'quelle surprise', what I predicted their neglect would lead to at Asda did occur.

This was to have another parallel in my new job, too.

Chapter 4

Deliverance: Setting the Scene: Starting off at Abbotts

Apologies: This is definitely not the most exciting chapter, but hopefully sets the scene, so to speak.

Deliverance: this is a strange title for a chapter. But if you imagine the film with the rednecks and the duelling banjos music and some very strange characters set in their ways that don't care for strangers in these here parts, then that is the sort of picture I'm trying to paint.

But to me it was a kind of deliverance, as I had got away from Asda.

My fellow inductee on the day I joined was a strange person who would prove to be a psychopath. There was another person from Abbotts in charge of our induction.

I felt a little odd straight away with these two, but these were my company for the first week whilst we signed off all the relevant pharmaceutical forms. This Abbott employee performing our induction struck me immediately with her appalling language. No one with Tourette syndrome would ever be half as bad, and her first week with us seemed to be like all her other weeks at the company whereby she was off more than on. She was obsessed with having a 'bay-bee' and her fertility treatment left her job a poor second, as she was only too keen to announce. But although almost entirely useless, she was shagging an engineer at the company and seemed to have the powers that be in the palm of her hand; and she went up and up in the company.

Her other half was also shagging another, larger lady from another shift at the time, but such was the way at Abbotts. This heavyweight ménage à trois was just one example among many of the extra-marital affairs that were so commonplace.

Such was the way at Abbotts. This girl was treated almost as a deity by the management although she hardly ever showed up for a full week whilst I was there, and her gob was just embarrassing.

One must wonder how, in such an allegedly professional company as Abbotts, such an obnoxious, vulgar, foulmouthed, uncouth, totally unreliable person was even tolerated, let alone lauded, pampered and cherished so much. But that was Abbotts. Their ability to judge an individual was always arse about face and always seemed to favour the nasty, vindictive, lazy and unreliable types, as I would ultimately find to my cost. Kiss the right backsides and you'll go far, regardless.

So that was kind of how it was; exceptions aside, most stabbed everyone else's back and to say it was a vipers' nest of cliques was taking understatement to the extreme. In many places this is true.

I suppose I must have seemed a bit of an oddball from the off, as I was only there to do a good job, earn my pay and go home again.

Although destined to crash and burn my co-starter, the mentalist, initially fitted in superbly well. She was vindictively competitive, kissed every butt in authority from the outset and, amazingly, fell head over heels in love with the shift boss on day one and couldn't help but tell everyone of her sheer amazement at this event, the like of which had never happened to her before. I bet it surprised her even more that in virtually no time at all the boss was indulging in anal naughtiness with her and relaying this to others, as well as expressing his disappointment in her performance.

The shift boss was someone who would serially misuse his position and would only come out of the office, from what I saw, to talk sex in the most grotesque, stomach-churning way. He would make your skin crawl. Eventually the relationship between these two and his relationship with another, whose marriage he destroyed and then shacked up with, was to lead to the dismissal of a third girl.

The two he was shagging did not like the third one. Much as she was also no angel, and perhaps as conniving as the other two, the cards were stacked against her due to the game of influence, spite, alliances and backstabbing that was prevalent across the board.

The mentalist would eventually crash and burn herself due to a shocking wine addiction and the shortest fuse and most violent temper, blatant nastiness and the tendency to fly off the handle and overreact when not getting entirely her own way almost daily.

The hungover, wine-induced, OTT theatrics and waterworks from this girl on the night of the 7/7 bombings was a sight to behold. She was hysterical because she knew someone who lived in London who had not contacted her since the incident. Well, there are only 10 million people in London and some of us grew up there. But anyway… that's enough ink for now on that one.

The cliques and unfriendliness to a virtually competitive level was quite unreal and unlike anything I had experienced before or, perhaps, since. The real super cliques were amongst teams on final packing machines called Sieblers. Around those there parts was real Deliverance country. Those there folks had been there a few years and that was their kind of locality and they were not really open to outsiders. Most were from remote parts and only came out in the dark of night.

Us newbies worked on three other initial production stages known as meshing; tape laying and row converting, which were all initial processes in making the diabetic test strips, along with printing and card cutting and strip sorting CCSS, the details of which I will not bore you with.

To cut a long story short, all these processes occurred before the product was finally delivered in rows of 50 strips to be cut individually into test strips and foil packaged by the good ole folks from Deliveranceville, in Mr David Cameron's constituency.

Had it been true, the nasty rumour that Rt. Hon PM and local MP David Cameron engaged in unusual ceremonies or rituals at Oxford, which he completely denies, he might just have fitted in at Abbotts, more so than at Oxford University. Now I'm just being bitchy. One male member of staff pointed out at Abbotts: Why should all male staff have to wear beard guards at the slightest sign of stubble, and Foul-mouth, with her blatant whiskers, be immune? Surely a fair point in these days of supposed gender equality.

Anyway, back to working at the factory. I was then to be trained on a few machines. The floor boss or team leader was not universally popular and a bit of a git. However, I did not mind him so much as others as he was quite a fair git and did tend to target the workshy more. I once described him to his face as a kind of necessary evil. I think he quite appreciated that; such was his nature.

As time went by I proved my worth, particularly on one machine called a row converter; the machine everyone else hated, as did I, yet I was soon constantly producing excellent output, shift in and shift out, and although still a temp, I was training most of the newbies.

Those who were struggling and failing to pick up the job with others, especially any of the Deliverance crew, were being successfully trained by me. When I came back from two weeks holiday I could not believe how pleased the process coordinators were that I was back. Output and training could now return to their former level.

One Kenyan girl called me an Angel to her process coordinators and said how cruel and unhelpful others had been while I was off. I did not do anything that amazing, to my mind. But what I did do was say to anyone I was training that no question is too silly – ask as many and as often as you like and, what is more, I am going to show you and explain everything, but let you press all the buttons and talk me through what you are doing until you feel confident and competent.

The Deliverance crew had a very different, intentionally clique-driven approach. To outsiders and newcomers it would be a case of pressing all the buttons themselves, whilst tutting and treating you like you are stupid if you asked anything, especially in front of their fellow rednecks. This was quite deliberate and I would experience this first-hand when I went on to my initial so-called Siebler training.

I seemed popular with all the temps, who were mostly African. Let alone was I helpful, and someone of whom they could ask things, but I would also ask the questions many wanted asking at staff meetings but were a little too timid and fearful to ask themselves. I was slowly noticing that this was serving to alienate me from the Deliverance crew who did not like someone new on their ranch with a conscience and the courage of his convictions. 'We just don't communicate with new folks round here and that's how it is in these here parts.'

One particular person I befriended was a lovely woman called Selina. She was Fijian and I think even bigger than me in stature, and with a larger than life, happy personality and outlook to match. Myself, a Nigerian 'praise the lord' happy clappy kind of guy and Selina hit it off well and had a lot of laughs. Selina and I were particularly close.

She then discovered she had breast cancer and attacked it in true Selina style, eventually having both breasts removed although one was fine. I did all I could to help, having internet access, and was a genuinely caring someone to talk to on the phone, as I thought the world of her and we clicked.

At the time of my wedding she had a relapse, so didn't attend or tell me at the time until she was better.

I lost contact with Selina since my torment started, as with her troubles I did not want to add mine to hers. After she left work through ill health we used to have lovely long phone chats where we would end up laughing our heads off, cheering each other up. I dare not phone now with the passage of time, perhaps partly through fear I may get bad news and not wanting to burden her with mine, but she remains in my heart. I also did not want to tell her my story as I felt she would want to stand by me, and I did not want to burden her in any way. This was exactly her way with me. Still love you, Selina.

Next on the agenda was the merger of two factories, 'Medisense' Abingdon, an older more established factory, with the Abbott Witney Rednecks. Firstly, Abingdon sent an advance posse who could not believe the inward-looking, hostile, unfriendly environment at Witney that had even changed the personalities of some former Abingdon souls who had moved previously.

Before the Abingdon lot moved over; I had always enjoyed overtime on B nights as there were people that were so much easier to get along with than the shift I belonged to. This also underlined that it was not my imagination. The folk on my shift were just simply bloody weird!

I learned, when the sites merged; the Abingdon shift, B nights had many relationships involving extra-marital affairs. It was said on that shift that you had your wife and your Medisense wife.

I was pleased to see lots of new staff suddenly coming in from Abingdon. Well how was I to know who was to be amongst them?

In some cases, these inter- staff relationships did affect the workplace.

Still being only a temp I was actively looking for permanent work elsewhere, especially with the new influx limiting my chances. I was at the second interview stage at a company in Wantage called McDermid Autotype. This was to cause me a few problems.

Firstly; being the honest and open type and confident in my work ethic at Abbott; I offered my managers' names at Abbott as a reference knowing McDermid Autotype supplied Abbotts with material .

Being the totally open type, I told my managers at Abbott I was looking for the security of full time work elsewhere also; especially now there were so many new full time workers suddenly here from Abingdon.

The main problem this gave me was that doing overtime on B nights and working in the inspection area; it introduced me to a woman; one of the new staff from Abingdon called Linda; who came and sat next to me; made my acquaintance and started talking to me about my application to McDermid's, as her husband; also a new member of staff from Abingdon; wanted to apply there also.

I had assumed that he was full time as he had been with the company years; but he had taken a redundancy and wangled his way back as a temp somehow. He and his wife were well known pains in the ass and trouble makers; although I did not know this at the time either. I helped them both explaining my interviews and the processes I had gone through at McDermid's. Lucky me; I had made a new acquaintance.

I felt my two interviews at McDermid's went really well and was shocked at receiving a letter that I was unsuccessful and had failed to meet their criteria. I phoned McDermid's and asked why? They said I was too overqualified and intelligent and would have got bored very easily. It makes you ask: What was their criteria?

I explained that at Abbotts repetition is the name of the game and life at McDermid's could not be any worse.

So bad news part 1; I was now acquainted with Richard and Linda. Bad news part 2; I did not get the job at McDermid's. They say bad news comes in threes. So here is the bit of bad news part 3. I was then offered a full time job at Abbotts and Richard got a job at MacDermid's.

How can that be bad news? I hear you ask. Well on hearing that I was to be offered a full time position; my first reaction was not well done me; but to reiterate that I was a team player and to ask about two of my colleagues.

One had started a couple of weeks before me and had recently learned two new skills which meant he had one more skill than me i.e. printing and he seemed a really good and confident worker. The other had been there a while longer than both of us and had the same skill sets as me but more experience due to his longevity. I know I had a perfect attendance and punctuality record; but the others were really reliable too.

Much as the latter was a right grumpy, hard to please old sod, he had been there the longest and I have no doubt that the other two of us would have assumed that he would have been the first to be offered the next full-time post; and neither of us would have batted an eyelid had that been the case.

However, I was offered a job and could not refuse it. When I asked about the other two, I was told that the fate of others would be told to them individually. Having four mouths to feed I could not refuse. I believe this was just before Christmas or a week's holiday I was due. Two of us had our joy somewhat extinguished hearing the third was still a temp, much as we really appreciated our appointments. It was only natural to think, 'Why not this chap first?' We both probably assumed that it may have been because we had let it be known we were looking for permanent work elsewhere.

It could have been something else; personalities, politics or age. We did not know. But this chap took it really badly and we sympathised with him and felt guilt through no fault of our own. I did not use the smoke shed or the canteen anyway, but was very much sent to Coventry by many of the 'Deliverance' crowd. They hated the new management team and the new arrivals from Abingdon and now the longest standing temp who was most pally with them had been snubbed by the new management. This was a whole new reason to hate me.

Then it got even better. I was told that I was being put forward for Siebler training. That was like being shipped off away from civilisation into the southern outback where I was the only non-family member. I had just offended the whole Deliverance family by becoming full-time too.

Then I really hit the jackpot; being put with the worst crew possible who were never going to help. The three stooges; a smartarse; a mumbler and one of the nastiest, most horrible gits you could ever hope to meet. About 3 or 4 weeks passed and I had got nowhere. I was frustrated at the constant intentional lack of help and excess criticism and let Grumpy know I had had enough of him.

Some people are just nasty as a natural default position. It was not just me. Another female employee, who worked with him, had to go to the manager's office in tears; such was his nastiness.

Normally Siebler training lasts about a month, and these guys said to the management that I would never be able to cut the mustard.

So I was called into the office regarding my lack of progress, which surprised my managers. I said I have an OND in Electrical Engineering; Mechanical Engineering and Mathematics. Give me a week with an Abingdon crew who will actually share their knowledge and I will pass. I duly did and, what is more, became a trusted Siebler operator that even the Deliverance crews were pleased to have on board. Well, at least most times. Even a certain grumpy git, who couldn't be pleased if his life depended on it, didn't mind me working with him.

Now he accepted me, he let on that his other two cronies often covered for him as his eyes were so bad he could not see what he was doing, yet he still insisted on being at the inspection stage of the process. *Yes, Mr Magoo was doing final crucial product inspection of sensitive diabetic testing strips playing Russian roulette with all Abbott's customers' lives, and had been doing so for years.*

If Abbotts doubt this fact then they need only look at their medical records as his sight was eventually operated on, under the company's own medical insurance scheme.

Also Mr Grumpy was exempt from inspecting reworks due to his eyes. This was because he would not be able to spot the product issue like holes in the foil or numbers missing.

Yet, believe it or not, this same man spent virtually his whole time at final product inspection, bluffing and hoping to be lucky.

Then, when machines often stopped and had downtime, he was exempt from rework inspection due to poor eyesight – the eyesight that was good enough to do nothing but inspection in the first place. Confused?

Look at your company medical operations record, Abbott. I'm telling the truth, as always.

The 'cry wolf' culture

At around this time all staff had a harassment, diversity etc. presentation by a member of HR.

I raised a question at the end of her presentation as one member of staff had recently tried to get another sacked by lying about a physical confrontation, then manipulating a witness who later changed her mind and told the truth.

So I asked, in the wake of this incident,

'Is your presentation incomplete? It does not address the fact that there are those amongst us who simply wish to be offended and cause trouble; a bit like all those players we know who go down in the penalty box too easily.'

Her reply was, 'Do you think such people actually exist?' My reply, 'I know they do.' She said she would have a private word with me afterwards. It shows the totally blinkered vision and brainwashing that is required to be a success in HR.

It also suggests clairvoyance on my part.

Chapter 5

Meeting my Nemesis

Obviously as time passed I befriended many of the Abingdon mob. I heard many tales regarding mainly sexual exploits, extramarital affairs, those who swung the lead, those you should not trust, and those who were trouble makers etc., and what some staff got away with in other areas. much of which I will address later in the book.

One member of staff who naturally got talked about was Linda.

Linda's husband Richard was now employed at McDermid Autotype, possibly thanks to my help.

Having befriended me to get her husband a job, Linda sat and talked with me on a number of occasions at work.

She spoke of her Irish alcoholic father to me, made it clear that they did not have the best of relationships, but did not mention any abuse. I was to hear that from others but guessed there may be some darker secrets. She mentioned that he was a soldier in the British army, and her upbringing. She was born in Gibraltar, calling herself a 'monkey off the rock'.

She told me she was estranged from her father's side of the family but some positive contact was being made. I guessed that the estrangement may be as a result of his career choice or might have perhaps related to sending money home for the upkeep of the family, as was common in Irish family politics back in the day.

Was I to her the embodiment of her father with my Irish roots, causing her spite towards me? I was also saving up for a wedding to a girl who had a British army upbringing, just like she did. Did my wife, with her upbringing, represent all that Linda thought she should have?

Did I feel guilt for being Irish like her father? I think I probably did. I'm stupid enough like that.

She told me she had been on long-term antidepressants and had recently had the dosage upped quite considerably. Clearly there was an addiction issue here.

Was I storing trouble for myself, saying I did not have a mobile phone or credit card and had saved a long time for a wedding, hence I'm working nights and driving a crappy little car. I said, I would never buy anything on credit. If I can't pay for it; I would go without.

This was in fact the mirror opposite to the person I was speaking to, who I believe had already been bankrupt yet still wanted the two holidays a year and the new big car and recent wedding etc. all on credit.

But on face value she seemed pretty normal to me, had done me no wrong and, being the soft-hearted caring twat then that I so often am, she had a huge sympathy vote from me. I did not know anyone who had been abused and there was her depression and anti-depressant taking and her husband's gambling debts also. They had not been married that long either.

Some time later, after her wedding, she arrived for work for a few days running looking all dishevelled and unkempt; basically intentionally looking a complete dog's dinner. No make-up, her hair not bothered with, and dressed really shabbily.

This naturally set a few tongues wagging among the Witney mob, and many Abingdon folk explained.

Richard had a history of major gambling problems and had apparently been hiding red letter bills from Linda whilst running up absurd gambling debts in the thousands.

Linda had been off for months on end before with depression. Apparently, said another, she was the nastiest piece of work going, the way she had treated her previous husband; it was good enough for her. This person was going to go into details about her nastiness to her ex, but, being an idiot, I said that I did not want to hear about it. I wish I had listened now.

Another said about her and Richard; that they were the two biggest trouble-stirring grasses going; especially Richard.

Another, who would go on to be interviewed about me, pointed down the corridor at Linda, saying loudly to a new temp so we all could hear, 'Be careful of that one, she has always got to have a story and if she hasn't got one, she will just make it up!'

Another who told me that she was abused as a child by her father, said she was seriously dangerous and seriously fucked up, with a number of screws loose.

With hindsight I should have given her a really wide berth at this stage; instead I felt deeply sorry for her and cared about how she was. Yes, a wise person would probably run a mile, which means I probably wasn't wise and was just too soft. And yes, I did have a sort of sympathetic soft spot for her after hearing of her issues. That is how I am; but this does not translate to loving and caring for my wife-to-be and family any less.

Anyone who knows me will know that I will stand up for the underdog, and I felt sorry for her plight.

Of course, another way to put this would be to call me a half-wit, doormat and fool, which is fair.

During this time I got the first visible indication that all was not right with her. It was a kind of tradition on B nights that, as we often shared a country road home with our colleagues and it was usually dark when we finished, we flashed lights to say goodbye at our turnings off the main road home. Many of us did this regularly and if Linda and I finished at the same time, which would usually be A nights as she bunked off early on her shift, we would both do the same, whether I was in front of her or she was in front of me.

Then one night just before her town, Bampton, I was behind her and she suddenly sped off like a rally driver. I thought, 'Odd, very odd,' but passed no remarks. I could see by the lights that she also sped into a turning that was not hers.

Sometime later my then fiancée and I set an approximate time for the wedding. The subject of the wedding had cropped up before, and I had told Linda she would definitely be invited. I mentioned we had decided to get married the following year. She immediately then told me she was leaving to work in a care home.

Work was slackening and I said, 'Are you sure? I don't normally use the canteen but I'll come up and chat with you about it if you like.' She said, 'Fine.' I duly went up at tea time. Another Abbott extra-marital couple were at the table also. The atmosphere felt odd, uncomfortable and unnatural. I felt estranged as if something was up. Linda was far less communicative than normal, almost cold. Linda mentioned that I was getting married and that these two were getting married but she did not mention leaving at all. I did not like the canteen atmosphere at the best of times and nearly always avoided it since my early days there. This atmosphere felt extra odd, somewhat false. When the male partner from this couple got up to go I left too and went to my car, my usual break place.

I said to Linda later in the week with regard her plan to quit, 'This is not a chat-up line; I'm getting married, as you know, and I'm totally monogamous,' etc. I was intending to say, 'I care about you or am concerned about you leaving,' or something of that ilk, then she was already into a rant. 'I'm a happily married woman, blah de blah.' I said, 'I'm not disputing that and I'm sorry if you got the wrong end of the stick,' and she went ranting again. I then said, 'No, actually, I'm not sorry at all,' and just went.

I never once suggested there should be anything between us, either then or at any other time, and always talked of looking forward to my wedding, and indeed stressed how happy I was with my partner and was certainly not chatting her up in any way at this time. Her misunderstanding seemed hell-bent, totally over the top, and intentional.

There were just the two of us there and I could have easily denied any conversation took place at all. Most in my situation probably would have done. This was, after all, a known loon and fantasist. But much as she went off the handle, intentionally overreacting rather than listening, clearly hearing what she wanted to hear, I must tell the whole truth. I clearly played with fire and got burned here. I was always taught that honesty is the best policy; believe me – it is not. I can now see that, with certainty, from first-hand experience.

Perhaps Linda had reacted through a sense of anticipation or perhaps, more than likely, she was just evil and manipulative as a default position.

Perhaps I was severely handicapped here by having a conscience, or was just out of my depth being as soft as shit and dealing with a seasoned troublemaker. If you instinctively tell the truth and are up against a compulsive liar it's a real handicap, especially because your default position is to expect the other person to be truthful as you aim to be. Gullible is a word you could throw at me.

Within 24 hours I'm the joke of the factory; I'm trying to shag Linda, etc. and she is milking it for all it is worth. With her later lies that I saw in print, God only knows what she was saying at this time. I did not react to any of the leg pulling and did not rise to the bait at all or try to defend myself in any way. I thought this best. Perhaps I was wrong. But what doesn't kill you makes you stronger. No, I don't believe that one either. When a nasty fantasist shafts you and you don't fight back, you lose. You play with fire you get burned, especially when you are naïve, unaware and don't expect a fire to be there, and assume the best in people, like the half-wit I so obviously am at times.

The serious car stunts

Then a few days later, one morning, I am driving home and she is waiting for me, facing me on the other side of the roundabout in Bampton. I turn left to go home as usual and she speeds up behind me, flashing frantically. I just flash back once to show no hard feelings, but I'm on my way home and I'm not stopping to ask if anything is wrong and why such over the top frantic flashing. I assume this is just her feeling guilty about her rumourmongering; and perhaps she is now in a part of a mental cycle where she has a conscience. Who knows what her high-dose medication does to her?

Then, not too long later, one evening I'm on my way to work as usual driving through Bampton when suddenly a car pulls out from the kerb on the oncoming side of the road with full beam on and drives straight at me, on my side of the road, pedal to the metal. I had to move diagonally between two parked cars and brake sharply, somehow not crashing, in order to avoid this car which then mounts the kerb violently on the other side of the road in such a fashion to suggest the driver is on drugs or extremely drunk. In my rear view mirror I can clearly see this incident and the vehicle registration number and read it backwards. The number of the car is M888LAS. This is Linda A Shaw's attempt at a personalised number plate.

Should I have proceeded and turned around at the mini roundabout ahead, parked by her car and confronted the driver? Should I have got out where I was and confronted the driver? This driver was clearly not in a good place mentally. I went on my way to work and did not mention to Linda about this incident or certainly that I knew whose car it was. I did not mention the incident at all to anyone at the time, except my future wife, until after the wedding. Captain Twatface protected the one trying to destroy him with her rumours and who now wanted to kill him.

It probably illustrates how soft or downright stupid I am, but at the time I was not angry; after all, the incident was over. I was unhurt, had no prior anticipation and the incident was over very quickly.

Brief adrenaline that thankfully led me to do the right thing, swerving in and stopping on a sixpence, then normality. Was I not so alert I could have driven into a pedestrian, a wall, or a building or simply crashed head-on into her.

My first reaction was that I actually felt sorry for her. Was I soft or was I stupid, or just soft in the head, which is a kind of stupid? After the event, thinking of when she drove at me it added to my sympathy. I thought of her debt, her upbringing and her dependence on antidepressants.

I did not know if this incident was provoked by irrational hate, as I had never done her a bad turn, or jealousy as I was financially in the black and had saved up years of overtime earnings to get married and give my wife a large wedding to remember. But this was just weeks before my wedding date. She was about to lose her house, too.

Linda had got married in a pub to a grumpy old git who had gambled them into serious debt whereby they soon had to sell their house, and I was marrying someone much younger, having responsibly saved up for years.

I felt pretty sure by the kerb mounting that this driver was more than a little tipsy, or perhaps on drugs, but certainly off the scale emotionally so probably best not approached. She was certainly guaranteed to be irrational, based on her performance.

She could have had a knife or some other weapon. It was pure Fatal Attraction bunny boiling stuff.

Was her first time lying in wait and frantically flashing on the way home a sort of honey trap in her mind, or violent plot, or God knows what else? It was definitely the prequel for the sequel.

The wedding invite and her letter

You may logically argue, 'Then why invite such a loon to your wedding?' Well, chiefly because I had promised over a year earlier that I would. The other option is that if I hadn't invited her, having said I would… The most likely explanation is that I'm just plain soft in the head: perhaps a few sandwiches short of a picnic.

I suppose there was the inevitability that she was going to get me one way or another and by any foul means. Perhaps some people are just evil. Such evil will prey on weakness, softness or kindness, whatever it may be. The worst was still to come.

But it must be said that normally when you give someone a wedding invite you expect by return either an acceptance or a declination.

You do not expect an attempt on your life followed by a letter with threats to report you to HR if you do not stop making comments designed to make her feel uncomfortable or expressing feelings for her, or parking near her, written in someone else's hand.

Only then, weeks after the invite, and the poisonous untrue response she got someone else to write, she then rediscovers her ability to write and posts a declination in her own handwriting.

Now I would think it logical to assume that if someone is getting married to someone else whom they have been with many years, and who is also the mother of their children, that they might just prefer that person.

Now this might just be a letter from a nasty person with previous. Indeed, poor Linda seemed to have had an identical problem at Abingdon, as one of those she brainwashed was to go on to say in his interview notes. Another said she conspired to get her manager sacked; and outside the leaving do at the cricket club, the following year, virtually everyone had a tale of how Linda had tried to get them into trouble. So I was not alone.

Linda's letter was hand-delivered to me at the end of a four-day, 48 hour shift. I was on a high, what with all the wedding preparations ,and immediately showed the letter to my wife. I then stayed up composing a four-page reply, still with the emphasis on clearing things up and sparing Linda's feelings at the same time and showing no hard feelings by leaving the door open for her to attend my wedding should she so wish. A bit stupid, you may think. I can do stupid.

But worse still I was prepared to be even more stupid. As I had told her off a fair bit in the letter, I did not want to destroy her completely, and one bit of her letter said, 'Although you said you have feelings for me, I don't have feelings for you or feel the same way,' or words to that effect. So, remembering her rant before I had the chance to say anything, I did not disagree with what she said in my reply, but will happily take a lie detector to prove I never uttered those words.

This was just one of the many whoppers she was to tell along the way.

Yes, with hindsight I was stupid or perhaps just gullible and concerned. Perhaps worse, I was incredibly stupid. Replying immediately after a 12-hour night shift, still trying not to upset her and not taking into account all her previous nasty deeds towards me shows extreme stupidity and something missing on my part.

Also, in my reply to her nasty letter I mention the driving incidents where she speeds off and frantic flashes after lying in wait, but not the really serious incident, in order to spare her feelings.

Was I, in the moment, mindful that this was not just the woman who had written this letter in response to a wedding invite (or got a friend to do so for her for attention's sake) but this was the loon who had driven at me and had all the depressant, debt and childhood issues regarding her Irish father in the British army, and a woman who people had warned me was totally wired to the moon?

At much later mental health interviews I talk of arrested development pre-programming I suffer, where the default position is to pacify and not offend the aggressor. Perhaps throughout all the time I knew Linda she could sense a potential victim with weaknesses. I do believe that the stuff with her father got her a big sympathy vote from me.

Was it for me, in some respects, like dealing with a spoilt child with a short temper that has the upper hand? If Johnny says he has a rocket and is going into space on Sunday then you just agree with him, avoiding the consequences of not doing so. Did she have control and know it, as I always tried to be as understanding as possible?

I delivered my reply via one of her process coordinators that night after about two hours sleep and having my wife proofreading it. Was it written under pressure/duress? For sure: but how much blame goes to my naivety? And what would the consequences be of doing nothing? I would have had to watch every step, including where I parked, and be in the palm of the hand of a woman who had shown she was prepared to lie in wait and drive at me with malicious intent. I had to be kind yet firm, and almost certainly got it wrong. Spending six hours writing a reply at the end of a 12-hour nightshift whilst still in shock at a poisonous response to a wedding invite with no cooling off time is just not clever.

Perhaps going to HR to complain would have been logical. I had never gone to HR in my life. I always sorted my own problems so don't believe this even occurred to me. Also, just weeks before my wedding, I did not need a war on top of everything else.

I was pressured by her letter; after all, I was preparing a wedding with just weeks to go; and that morning when I got home my neighbour had pointed out that there was a major crack in my chimney after the high winds we had just had. I had so many guests – most from overseas – the outfits, the car, the wedding video, the cake, etc. etc. to sort out. All things considered, most would have lost their rag, not sent an over-understanding reply. As I said, I did not even mention the fact I knew she had driven at me at that time. Mind you, I suppose this was not the time to enter a full- scale conflict, and I knew I was dealing with someone unstable. I could have gone all guns blazing and called her the nasty, lying, evil person that she was, but I rose above, and thought better of it.

I came in that night and parked where I always park. That was a statement in itself. I always parked at the top of the second aisle in the car park. It was nearest the door so the shortest walk when it rained. Aisle 1 was by the entrance and had all the shift change traffic so you could never get out. Aisle 3, although almost as near the door, had this chap with BMW engine on with all the fumes and his loud cough / throat clearance every 30 seconds, and aisle 4 was where all the druggies were that Abbott management ignored. So it was always aisle 2 for me, since long before Linda arrived.

Anyway, moving on to the day of my wedding: It was a great and successful day. A massive event for my family. It is just not that massive in the context of this book.

If I had a complaint, it was that another girl I was great friends with on B shift had come all the way from Cornwall to my wedding. I felt a bit guilty there. I invited a handful from her shift that did not show. With hindsight, although excuses were made and it may have been coincidence, I assume it was Linda's full-blown poisonous rumours that were to be the main factor. Interestingly, when I apologised to this girl at the wedding for the lack of B night attendees I said I had had a bit of trouble with a trouble-stirring female on B nights. Without me saying who, this girl, who had worked with Linda at Abingdon, told me the name of the person it would be and called Linda a fantasist who likes to play the victim. I did not have to mention Linda's name.

To me it was our wedding day, but to self-centred, wired to the moon Linda Shaw it was another episode in the Linda Shaw show. I was marrying the woman I love and the mother of my children, and someone I had been with for 15 years. We are now as many years again together.

Now Linda being the manipulative so and so she is; nearly always did two shifts overtime on our shift every week but she never once did a Saturday Night. She would surely not do all this overtime if she was in any way concerned about me, as she later stated. She also usually saw me 24 hours a week on her shift; when I did overtime; as I was saving for my wedding.

Linda was always given first choice of shifts each week; by her friend who would always publicly greet me on shift with 'Hello Michael Collins and how's the IRA.'

Much as Linda would always do 24 hours overtime; she would absolutely never under any circumstances do a Saturday night as she proudly boasted.

Guess what; that all changed on May 17 2008; purely by coincidence; the day of my wedding. She had a point to make; well in her head anyway.

On my return; I showed a number of staff a collage A4 photo of my wedding; as you would. Linda was on a nearby machine and I thought; I won't leave you out either. When we spoke; she knew the changes in the weather as I entered church; left the church; at reception and indeed throughout the whole day; for events not in these particular photos. Was she watching?

I then; only later found out; that she had worked my wedding night too. If I was working a 7pm-7am night shift; I would have slept during the day before. Had someone from work invited me to their wedding and had I made an excuse not to attend; I would not have ensured I did overtime that night, when I was off shift. Let alone is that just bad taste and nasty; it does rather suggest that this wedding is very important to that individual; especially when this is your first Saturday night on overtime ever, after so many years in the job.

A certain dishonest manipulative director was to later suggest at tribunal that this was the only time poor Linda would ever get the chance to do overtime in safety; trying to make out this blatant nastiness on her part was my fault.

Another person who has known her a long time from Abingdon, suggested that her jealousy may extend to the fact that I saved up and paid for a big wedding with all the trimmings: Much more glamourous than her recent one. She has a massive debt, and a sham marriage. She wouldn't like me being in a happy place and content with life either. Most were amazed that Linda & Richard even got married, as their relationship was openly fragile and his gambling had pushed her to the brink before, and she had, had long time off work with stress over that.

Also on the personal note I heard she absolutely took her first husband to the cleaners in the divorce hearing only to lose all her ill- gotten gains to the gambler she left him for, plus an inheritance also. Could my financial prudence and happiness have made her green with envy?

Relations improving after another incident with her friend
So I continued parking where I always parked since long before Linda moved to Abingdon.

Often on the Siebler machines; I would work with one of Linda Shaw's best mates whom I always got along well with. Linda was even her daughter's godmother. She had been a mate of Linda's for years. One night we spoke of how according to Linda one minute I was a great bloke; her friend; the next I was evil incarnate etc.

I said; I've never done her a bad deed and don't really understand what she is up to and certainly don't get all this nonsense with her playing the victim.

I mention that recently, Linda had now changed from using the canteen to using the car park and following me out for breaks. This was hardly the actions of someone who is afraid of me to be putting herself in a position where she is effectively alone in the dark with me in a car park.

Due to operational circumstances and us having to finish a certain process we are both late out for last break due to issues with the machines.

I had parked where I had always parked. Linda has moved her car during the night, from bay 1 near her friend to two places away from me, effectively next to me in an empty car park.

We then go out for our break at a time when there are no other breaks because we are so late. I go out to my car as always. Linda's friend by this time is already in her car. Next thing, out comes Linda Shaw and gets into her car and stays there for about 5 minutes. She then drives off to bay 1, parking directly behind me. No doubt another attention stunt, as yet again I didn't speak to her when she came out.

She then notices that opposite her best mate is in her car and will have seen all this. Linda returns inside after talking to her friend. She should not have been out at that time anyway. She should certainly not have followed that chap she is so scared of, then stayed next to him.

I have a great 'I told you so' moment when we get back to Sieblers. Her friend knew for years I took breaks alone in my car, as she did likewise and would see me. She could now see that Linda was following me to my car, deliberately outside her break time. A person with absolutely any fear of me, let alone all her made-up lies, would simply not do this, especially alone in the dark.

Predicting this would happen and letting her friend see the reality meant she would have some explaining to do there to wriggle out of that one. Especially after her friend had said to me that Linda was saying I hadn't been very nice to her. I said, 'I don't know what she has said, but I've never once done her a bad deed in my life.' I should, with hindsight, have asked what she had said.

Anyway, after this episode and probably after her friend spoke to her, the animosity seemed to disappear and there was a period where we seemed on good terms and she was friendly back. Her friend noticed the improvement too. I was utterly mistrusting but friendly back. I knew I was right to be mistrusting. There had been frosty periods before.

I later said, in a conversation to Linda, we could be more grown-up and civil and did not have to like one another, but could co-work amicably, or words to that effect. But I seem to remember that had failed pretty quickly initially, before an improvement eventually ensued.

There was then a period of no outward resentment and she was being friendly, except once when she was walking along the corridor chatting away then, on seeing one of her cronies, totally shunned me mid-sentence and looked at a notice board. I could see the double life she was leading.

Just like when she followed me to the car park: There had to be pre-planning on a subsequent night I came in, also from a very late break. She was sitting with her blouse unbuttoned ridiculously low, pretending to do something that meant she had to bend down into the box before her. I passed no remarks and got back into work as quickly as possible.

A short while later, and her being my friend again, she then came out with the highly original line that she had got a new job and was leaving work to go and work in a care home. I immediately wished her well in her new career and said I was pleased for her. Once bitten…

Redundancies
Then within a week it is announced at a meeting that Abbotts are looking for a good many redundancies to take place by June or sooner if you found another job. All staff can go to HR to find out their potential redundancy amount. I had only been a few years in full-time, after a while as a temp, so did not bother, but those who had been at Abingdon for years could get colossal amounts, in the tens of thousands in many cases. However, all staff were clearly told their redundancy package was confidential and the offer would be invalid and withdrawn if disclosed to other colleagues.

Linda then astonishingly confides in me the amount of redundancy she has been offered. She would not do this with someone she feared, disliked or did not trust.

The amount she quoted to me was twenty-nine thousand nine hundred-odd, if those of you at Abbott wish to check this out. (Could she have told me a wrong amount to get me into trouble?)

So I tell her, 'Great! Your new job and all that redundancy money; it could not have fallen better for you.'

Then there is the strangest U-turn ever. She says, 'If you think about it, that money will be gone in no time. It is not really worth it, is it?' She seems to have totally forgotten that just before this she has this new job and she was going to leave the company with nothing, as I reminded her.

Now, bear in mind that this is possibly the second last shift we ever work together and that as well as the redundancies it has been announced that both nightshifts are to merge. Linda is at this stage willing to give up £30k in round figures and her new job in order to work full-time on a new merged night shift with the man she was accusing of all sorts in a letter the year before, and false rumours before and since. Yet this is the one man in the company she confides her redundancy figure to. After this, unknown to her, I am probably only going to work one more shift with her.

Only the week before she was going to take this new job without the redundancy bonus – allegedly. A full redundancy package was to be awarded to those who found work in the interim. Surely she would be gone in days, you would logically think.

The overtime stops altogether while this redundancy process runs its course. The plan was to merge nights into just one night shift as well as the redundancies, it is requested that a number from the night shift should switch to days.

So Linda is now prepared to give up £30K and this alleged new job in order to work with me full-time, a job which may or may not be pure fantasy, but I suspect probably was, giving her propensity for truthfulness and the fact she had lied about the exact same issue before.

I later heard from the son of a patient that she did eventually end up working in a care home.

I, on the other hand was fed up with her lying rumours, playing the victim, split personality and driving intentionally at me, etc. and had paid off my wedding and in various jobs had done 15 years of night shifts. I wanted to re-join the human race so volunteered to join dayshift. Of course, I did not relay this to Linda. I was making my getaway and was glad to be doing so at a time when things were cordial.

The hug which should be a non-event

On my final week of night shift some time later there were many goodbye hugs, in fact hundreds, probably thousands, and many kisses too between staff as so many were leaving altogether or leaving to join days and the rest were saying adios to them.

But, however, B nights were given one final overtime shift on A nights on a certain night in June 2009. I remember the date as it was my birthday.

In the gown lock where we all got ready (just basically put on a heavy blue overall over our clothes) I had not seen Linda for at least a couple of months and as, unknown to her, it was our last ever shift together, I hugged her very briefly for about 2 seconds on seeing her, after walking in, and in a totally non-sexual way in front of about 30 people who saw absolutely nothing untoward as there was nothing untoward to see. (Important in the context of later events). One witness from our shift who also joined days believed he saw her kiss me during this. If this is true, then I have no recollection of it.

Meeting Linda in the corridor later in the shift I joked that from now on, as I was joining days after this shift, we could both celebrate my birthday in future as it would be the anniversary of our last shift together and we would finally be rid of each other.

Being the twat I am I felt a little bad about this as she may well have had the notion of working with me to the extent that she had given up £30k to do so, in spite of what she might say to others. So I had decided if I saw her again that day I would say, 'I'm glad that after all the water under the bridge we had parted as good friends.'

I would say this was quite magnanimous after all her spite from before.

I did not see her again that shift and was certainly not going to look for her. On the way home, well actually slightly off the way home, I went to the local Esso garage for fuel and groceries. As I was pulling out I saw Linda's car pulling in on the other side of the forecourt. So I went back in, wished her good luck and said, 'I'm glad we parted as friends,' and kissed her harmlessly and in a totally non-sexual fashion on the hair on the top of her head, as she is shorter than me, and said goodbye. I went on my way thinking, 'I'm glad I went in and said that; that is a better parting note.'

What a clever person I am ... Not!

For her part, that morning at the petrol station she was very insistent that we would still stay as friends.

From that morning on we were ex-work colleagues.

Chapter 6

The Leaving Do and Last Contact with Linda

A month later is B nights leaving do, which I attend along with my wife, another colleague, a neighbour, and her daughter, now sadly departed, who had also worked on A shift. This was at Cumnor Cricket Club. Linda, her husband Richard and a good few from B nights are also there.

There were few enough for us all to mingle and talk to everyone during the course of the evening. Naturally I spoke to Richard and asked him how it was going at McDermid's. He seemed more preoccupied with the fact that they didn't like him at Abbotts. I spoke to Linda too. Of course, I absolutely loved introducing her to my much younger, much prettier wife. It really was a pleasure.

Did Richard really believe, metaphorically speaking, I wanted to trade in a Rolls Royce, he could see for himself, for an old second-hand clapped out temperamental Austin Allegro, nearly two decades older, in total disrepair with a long history of malfunctions? I don't think so. Any idiot could see that Linda was no competition for what I had. Well it would appear, almost any idiot.

My wife noticed that Linda, with her body language she was leaning into me only to adjust very rapidly on her husband's return. That was a bit like her antics, suddenly ignoring me mid-sentence to pretend to look at a notice board when we worked together and a friend appeared.

Then on the dancefloor Linda, whilst dancing with me and three others, publicly kissed me as I later proved unequivocally by polygraph. She kissed me in full view of her husband and my wife and all else who were there.

This was a non-event at the time, but crucial in terms of later events.

There was one other incident as Linda and Richard left soon after she kissed me. Big tough Richard says as he is leaving, 'This has got to stop.' I said, 'There has never been anything to stop,' and dismissively as much as said to him, 'On your bike, pal.'

In hindsight what I should have said was, 'I agree. Tell Linda to stop the rumourmongering, fantasies and driving stunts. I've had enough.'

Well, that should have been that as they rode off into the sunset with their tails between their legs.

But talking of tales, the night came to a more abrupt end than everyone thought with the bar closing earlier than expected, so most had a good half an hour wait for a cab. Once the subject got on to Linda's lies and trying to get people into trouble constantly. Everyone had a story or two. Was there anyone she had not tried to get into trouble?

I wish I had taken notes. I was delighted my wife was hearing all this too.

About a week later, in the morning, I'm coming into work as I'm now on dayshift. I noticed there was a policeman with a speed/ Gatso gun in Curbridge waiting around the bend catching speeding motorists. On coming into the car park Linda is driving out. I wave out the window to attract her attention and tell her this. She is in a stinking mood and blanks me.

Seeing her at the next shift change-over, I explain that I was only trying to alert her to the copper with the speed gun on her way home. She storms off while I'm in mid-sentence, saying something like, 'I don't care what you say any more.' I thought, 'Fair enough; I'm now on days. I need not ever talk to you again,' and never did.

Well, actually I might have spoken to her unwittingly after that, when answering the phone.

From that day onwards until she went on holiday my family endured a string of silent, number- withheld nuisance phone calls for weeks, that miraculously stopped when Linda went on holiday.

On days, I now mentioned these calls and her driving at me to another member of staff as I had had quite enough of Linda and her antics and being falsely portrayed as the bad guy, and was now well rid as far as I was concerned.

Then months later on coming back from holiday, maybe it was because I did not pay notice to her sitting sun-tanned in the gown lock when I finished my shift, as her friend said…

Perhaps it was because Linda could now be aware that had I complained about the nuisance phone calls my family were getting, and mentioned her driving stunts to others if they talked about her. Did she perhaps decide to act in the interests of self-preservation if she did indeed know she had been rumbled? I had had enough of her lies and would now rightfully put the record straight if asked.

The next incident, thanks to this trouble-stirring nuisance, is that I get called up to the HR offices at the end of a day shift.

This was also at the time just days after my overtime Health and Safety whistleblowing complaint on day shift.

One event could easily be used by HR to justify the witch-hunt triggered by the other.

To explain the timeline: the next chapter focuses on day shift leading up to the same event, with the two timelines dovetailing together with my call up to HR, five months after the leaving do .

Chapter 7

Dayshift and Events Leading up Until the Disciplinary Hearing

This chapter is a bit technical but does raise some key points with later relevance and dovetails with the previous chapter as it also leads to the time I'm invited up to speak with HR.

When I first moved on to day shift I had no doubt that I had done the right thing. I'm more relaxed with new people that don't appear on the set of Deliverance and I even sometimes use the canteen.

Frying pans and fires

Much as on days I felt that I had evaded one problem, i.e. Linda, I now had the often daily reminder that there was still another one who had it in for me, i.e. Pat Cole.

As Pat didn't like me and feared my input at meetings, she would happily pretend I was a lesser life form that didn't exist. Unless, of course, she would see an opportunity to undermine me.

The tape layer machine over-reaction

I then had a new issue to deal with. Working on the new tape layer machine we had to check for a new issue under a microscope. A new feature, a capillary thread that was now part of the new product we were making, had broken on one of the six rows of product my machine was making.

I missed this for a number of cards as this white thread normally passes between two darker squares on a white background. When it starts to drift from position, it stands out against darker background marker squares on inspection under the microscope.

Of course when the thread breaks, under microscope inspection this does not show, as the white thread is on a white background. Only thread drifting out of position on to a darker background will clearly show under the microscope.

As soon as this is realised, the defective rows are struck out with blue permanent pen marking a box by the defective row, and the process is resumed. These marked rows with missing thread will then be removed automatically at a later process when the rows are cut into strips.

This was not technically an 'Exception Report' (or ER) error as the mistake is noticed and rectified by me within the same process.

Being a perfectionist with a conscience I do a report on the error, criticising myself, and present a report on the error to my manager to help avoid future repetitions, with obvious recommendations like 'Do a visual on each card' and 'Don't over-rely on the microscope'.

Another reason I did the report was that another colleague on the shift had fallen into the same trap shortly before me and committed the same error. Someone had to do something to avoid this becoming a regular occurrence; nipping a problem in the bud, rather than ignoring it.

The following week whilst we are off shift, against all company name and shame policy, my name appears boldly on the ER notice board for this total non-ER event. It was a non-ER event as it was identified and corrected at the time of happening and within the process.

Management, who had obviously heard I made a mistake, had gone through my manager's files in his absence, dug up the error and presented it as something it wasn't, with naming and shaming thrown in.

Of course I was targeted. I was the only person to be publicly named and shamed on the ER notice board ever, and for an event that was not even an ER (exception report) error. The details were dug up on someone's orders, undermining my managers, who knew it wasn't an ER. It was also kept on display on a weekly notice board for over 3 weeks until it came down at my insistence.

- It is against the no blame policy of the company to name and shame.
- To do this for three weeks on a weekly notice board is an inexcusable act of bullying.
- I was clearly individually targeted.
- The event was not even an ER, but was made into one because it involved me.

- Another on B days who made an identical error did not get on to the notice board.
- Another on nights who did not correct errors on two rows, probably over at least two batches, and passed the faulty material on to subsequent processes, had his errors totally ignored.

Ironically I was probably one of very few who had never caused an ER event in the five years I worked there, but had the unique honour of being the only person ever to be named and shamed.

One rule for one

A far more serious multiple ER, by a chap who will feature later, led to 33% of at least two batches being destroyed. This actually was an ER as it was discovered two processes later, at row converting, by me. It was covered up against procedure when I reported it to the manager, Mark Davidson. The batch before and after were not investigated either. Clearly not one card on these entire batches had been looked at, and this was a very serious ER.

This also highlights again how corrupt, racist and vendetta-driven the company is.

Two whole rows for the whole batch had missing welds for nearly 10cm throughout the batch. This was the old-style, tape layer machine. The cards have no threads, but welds which are supposed to be 100% visually inspected. This wasn't a missing thread under a microscope.

As I pick this up on the row convertor a whole 2 processes later, this should become an ER with the previous and next batches 100% checked for the same error.

As the errors are not marked out by pen, by the time they get to this process these defective rows are not dumped by a camera on the previous process either.

I am duty bound to report it. I am told by the manager, Mark Davison, to 'just bloody get on with it'. I wasn't reporting it to be nasty or to tell tales on someone. I reported it as we had to, in the interests of customer safety, isolate the previous and next batch and potentially more; until we get back to the start of the issue. Those were their rules!

This, of course, also slows down inspection as 33% of the batch is being lined out. Not as much as a word said to this chap for a far more serious error, nor does he get a mention on the ER board.

There is also the problem that next time he is just going to do the same again.

To make matters worse, after he had finished the following batch which should also have been subject to ER and quarantine he has not even looked at a single card there either. The offending off-cuts that are blocking the welds were still stuck in the same place on the welding machine. So if he had been given the next job on that machine after that – away we go again. More crap product.

He clearly did not do a single visual check over 2 batches when there should have been hundreds. He clearly did not check the machine at the end of each batch as he should too.

Of course, Abbott only ever target certain conscientious people with certain characteristics for naming and shaming. Only one person was ever to receive such special treatment.

The next issue: overtime.
Our wonderful new management team have a fantastic new idea.

Night shift are now to do overtime on day shift, for a full shift, with total priority over day shift.

This was absolutely ridiculous and needless, too, as there were plenty alert day shift workers who did not have to change sleep patterns, who wanted this overtime.

I raised numerous concerns, particularly regarding Health and Safety, during the last two weeks of October 2009. This was in the form of bullet points and a table showing how the new hours worked by those on night shift were in breach of the Company's own Health and Safety policy, which states that workers on day and night shift had to have two days off in every eight.

I clearly illustrated that night shift workers were now working 12-hour shifts over thirteen consecutive days with four changes of sleep pattern in that time. I also commented at the time that I did not think it was right to have a particular night worker (whose name I did not specify at the time) operating machines under these circumstances as he could never stay awake for a full night shift.

He would be up all day spending time between watching porn and being in the bookies. He would then sleep most of the night shift. His wife and family were in South East London.

The entire day shift could see the lunacy in this idea.

I presented a written report with illustrated points and a table to my manager, Darren Stephens, who said he was going to present it to Shaun Smith, his boss, at a forthcoming meeting.

After the meeting Darren explained to me that Shaun Smith had rejected my ideas as Pat Cole 'would not wear it' and was determined that the new overtime pattern should go ahead. So that was the end of that.

Two more ladies from day shift also raised issues with Darren Stephens. He spoke to them also separately from me. One of these ladies accompanied me as we raised our concerns at a meeting with Shaun Smith.

This idea was completely crazy, with no merits or logic at all.

Nights were clearly told when I was on night shift that if you want overtime you had better move to days; but now they were unhappy. They could, logically, have still done some overtime on nights but would have needed a manager and, I assume, a trained first aider present.

I stressed that from a Health and Safety, productivity and accuracy of inspection point of view, this made no sense at all and would compromise product. This was even before pointing out, again in table format, that the hours to be worked were illegal, dangerous to those involved and those around them, and against company Health and Safety policy.

Shaun Smith again confirmed that his boss, Pat Cole, wanted this to go ahead so that was that.

Being a mere minion, who am I to argue? I raised my concerns and was over-ruled.

Was she just looking for confrontation? Was this an 'I'm the new boss and I can do what I like?' mentality on show to put us in our place. If it was, how sad is that?

However, if you want respect that's a commodity you can only earn. Common sense should always be applied before the Jackboots go on.

Kicking for kicking's sake just destroys morale and achieves nothing.

My 'I told you so' moment

On the first day of this crazy overtime the car carrying all the night shift workers fails to arrive.

It eventually does arrive a whole three hours late, and minus one potential passenger.

These staff spent a whole three hours trying to wake the chap who I had said, without naming, would sleep the whole night shift whilst allegedly on final inspection.

The ones that did come in were fit for nothing.

Did I get an apology? Of course not! Even though I was proved right and had acted in the customer's interest, I had poked the bear and seriously dented the Fuhrer's ego. So what about the customer? So what about Health and Safety? this was personal and I was going to get it.

I was to have another 'I told you so' moment within weeks that I didn't know about until a decade later, when virtually all of the year's product made from the month after my exit onwards had to be recalled and destroyed at a cost of tens of millions. Well done, Pat!

Within a week I was on a disciplinary hearing, allegedly due to a six-month-old hug.

- Of course this six-month-old non-event, identical to hundreds that occurred at the same time, is suddenly a serious emergency that may require the ultimate sanction.
- Of course it was bad luck that somebody dug through the files and dug out a non-ER event for naming and shaming just me.
- Of course it was bad luck that someone dug a six-month-old issue to seemingly target me again.
- Of course the disciplinary procedure starting at the same time that I made management look foolish and exposed Health and Safety Rules being broken is coincidence.
- Of course there was no vendetta, and they were not going to hang me under false pretences, breaking employment law several times, for what should have been a total non- event; perish the thought...

Chapter 8

Nicky Albert: The First Disciplinary Interview

Nicky Albert was the HR person who first 'interviewed' me, accompanied by Pete Moran.

I was given no forewarning of this meeting, had already worked 10 hours and, when asked about accompaniment, as I had never been at a disciplinary hearing before and did not know or expect that this was any more than an informal chat that could have been about anything, I did not ask to have a witness present, but was offered.

Nicky then started. 'Linda Shaw has filed a complaint of harassment against you.' I said, 'What? I haven't worked with her for nearly six months, spoken to her in five and joined day shift to get away from her and all her antics.'

I was immediately asked, 'Did you hug her in the gown lock at any time?' I said, 'Yes I did' and even gave them the date as the event happened on my birthday. I told them also that I kissed her on the top of the head in Tesco's/Esso and immediately said also that she publicly kissed me at the leaving function a month later. I then said that the entire night shift staff hugged and kissed each other at that time. All this I said within seconds of the start of a meeting for which I had no forewarning or a witness.

My kiss on top of Linda's head in Tesco's was unwitnessed but Linda's public kiss on me at the leaving event at Cumnor had numerous witnesses. If I was to lie about any kiss and self-protect, it would be the one at Tesco's. As always, I told the whole truth.

To underline this: In my first sentence in response to Nicky Albert's questions when I said, 'Yes I did hug Linda Shaw,' gave her the date and said, 'Linda Shaw publicly kissed me a month later also', and gave the venue. I also stated there were plenty of potential witnesses from Abbott in attendance, at both events. None present, bar Linda, were ever questioned about either incident. Ironically her neighbour, who was present when Linda kissed me publicly, falsely claimed to be present at the gown lock hug, judging by his statement, which was utterly untrue.

Nicky Albert did not ask the date or any details of when Linda kissed me in front of many witnesses at the leaving function, as an impartial person would do. She wasn't interested in fairness or being professional.

I dodged not a single question, although I was unaccompanied. I mentioned Linda's debt and potential house loss and increased, high dosage anti-depressant use and suggested their efforts might be best channelled getting Linda help at this time as I no longer had anything to do with her, or indeed, wanted anything to do with her, hence I moved to days.

My attitude was to try and be helpful towards Linda and get her the help she needed.

I went back downstairs and there was my manageress Jenny who, ironically, gave me a far bigger, much more long-lasting hug in the gown lock than I had ever given Linda. I said to her, 'You don't want to do that. Believe me, that's the last thing you want to do.'

You must ask from this whether my manager had been told the outcome before I was interviewed. Was my fate common knowledge among management before I was even interviewed? From my manager's reaction, it would seem to be the case.

I was soon recalled upstairs and suspended until further notice.

Related issues

I had other issues where I was clearly bullied and targeted by management running concurrently at the time and HR would have known all about this, I'm sure. HR's duty should be to protect me from this bullying and treat all staff as equal rather than to side with this nasty, vindictive management.

Nicky would have certainly known about Linda's propensity for troublemaking as she was a regular at HR. Coupled with this, Nicky now had the knowledge that Linda had publicly kissed me subsequently and that, as we had not talked for five months and I had swapped shifts to avoid her, how on earth could I really be harassing her? My case was like a far more extreme, more ridiculous version of the Belgrano torpedoed in the Falkland's War whilst clearly sailing away from the situation. The difference being I was never a threat to anyone at Abbotts and had sailed away nearly six months ago.

Six months after a goodbye hug that took place, in a week during which hundreds or thousands of goodbye hugs and kisses occurred, all without prior permission, surely just one, in isolation, should not suddenly command the ultimate penalty, especially as the accuser publicly kissed the accused a whole month later in front of his wife and a great many witnesses? Our shift manager on nights, Craig Venner, had also brought us all together at the end of that week to say our goodbyes and invited the hugs and kisses that started all over again, publicly and by the hundred.

To single out one isolated hug among thousands at a point of convenience, nearly six months later, for disciplinary action; let alone recommending dismissal, is not a professional investigation. It is quite simply a vendetta, a witch-hunt and opportunism.

The simple fact is Nicky Albert had her superiors to impress and must have known others had a vendetta against me. She was going to get me, no matter what. This is not the purpose of HR.

She simply was not honest, fair-minded; or even open-minded and was certainly not professional.

This was nothing more than a totally unnecessary, vindictive witch-hunt.

I should not be interviewed 10 hours into a shift without a minute's notice, and it was also illegal to investigate a complaint that is over 3 months less one day old, as I was to find out years later.

Linda should also have been suspended during this disciplinary process as it would prove clear that she was influencing others during this process which was, again, entirely wrong and illegal.

Unprofessional

The obvious question is why my evidence is ignored despite my 5 years of excellence and never having complained about anyone? Also, why is the complaint of a high-dose, mind-altering drug-using, known serial fantasist treated with the ultimate seriousness? None of her other copious complaints ever were!

Nicky Albert is so unprofessional and slapdash that she does not interview a single person from the shift where the hug took place, where none of the 25-30 potential witnesses saw anything untoward at all. No, Nicky Albert gets Linda Shaw's friend and neighbour to say he saw a 'neck grab' and then immediately lost attention after that. He obviously wasn't there at all, and was simply lying, as this never happened.

What the A shift staff and myself would have reacted to is if someone, a male, was having a fist fight with a very heavily pregnant woman, which did happen, but due to woke racial immunity Abbott decided not to bother with that one. Some people had feelings and I don't. Also the fact that I told the truth counted for nothing either.

There were 20-25 or so potential witnesses from Abbott to Linda Shaw publicly kissing me on a dance floor. Why didn't Nicky Albert ask a single question to anyone about this either? This again underlines the vendetta and that my fate was determined beforehand.

She just had evil intent towards me. Yes, this woman recommended I should be sacked for a harmless hug, yet refused to find out if the public kiss a month later occurred.

She obviously had a desired target and a vendetta and was made fully aware of all the hundreds of other public hugs and kisses that week when I hugged Linda.

Condescending
I am told in bleeding heart fashion that HR need to act according to perception. Talking to me as if I was stupid: it's all about perception.

'You see, Michael, if Pete Moran and I hugged and were good friends the perception would be that would be fine, but in Linda's case she perceived the hug to be threatening or unwelcome.'

This clearly begs the questions: so why did Linda publicly kiss me a month later and why didn't Nicky investigate this if we are all treated fairly? Again, I say, I immediately informed Nicky of this incident within seconds of the meeting starting, that I was totally unprepared for and not expecting.

Therefore I spontaneously told the truth.

What part of fist fighting a heavily pregnant woman that happened between staff, that is reported immediately after the event, is deemed non-threatening and welcome?

Why did it take Linda half a year to suddenly find this hug unwelcome, and just at the exact time I whistle-blow about management breaking Health and Safety rules?

Biased and corrupt premeditated racist evil
Nicky Albert and her HR colleagues think the one who fights a heavily pregnant woman deserves the ultimate in understanding, doubtless due to wokery and skin

colour. The two pugilists can continue on the same shift, although the female colleague was involved in another alleged fist confrontation with a female, and other wrestling matches with males before. But then again, they are Nigerian and I'm a white male, so I am a clearly desirable target according to the unwritten law of positive discrimination.

The hug, identical to hundreds or thousands that week and nearly six months old, however, in Nicky Albert's eyes is sackable, but only if you are Irish, white and called Michael Collins. In this case, too, you deserve all the daily IRA comments you get from another of Nicky Albert's selected so-called 'witnesses'. My subsequent complaints about this were to fall on racist, deaf ears too.

I seem to be frightfully unlucky.

Ms Albert's inability to report and investigate accurately

Regarding Linda publicly kissing me: Why did Nicky Albert and then Shaun Smith refuse to ask a single question or investigate this vital evidence? There were plenty of people there! Why take the word of a known fantasist and troublemaker over someone with a perfect disciplinary record? Why indeed? Sounds like there might just be an ulterior motive.

If you refuse to investigate whether this incident happened should I, at least, not get the benefit of the doubt?

Clearly this kiss meant Linda was at least as guilty as me. So why was this not investigated?

Why was Linda not charged with harassment?

Linda trying to kill me in her car, as I pointed out, makes her a million times more guilty too. Why was this not investigated? Why the hell was this not harassment either?

Nikki quotes herself in her report of our meeting using literate, logical, flowing English and misquotes me in her notes as a simpleton with lines like, 'No one remembered it was my birthday,' as if I was annoyed.

What I actually said in literate, flowing English was that 'I remember the date of the hug as it was my birthday', and told them the date.

I am then later accused by a bent HR Director of hugging and kissing Linda simply because it was my birthday to an outside investigator, totally ignoring and deliberately misreporting the fact that the hug was a goodbye gesture only, identical to hundreds which occurred that week.

So Nicky Albert's amateurish intentional misreporting is later to be further misreported as factual at a further great cost to myself.

She should be ashamed of herself.

What an utterly corrupt company.

Chapter 9

The DHL Document Debacle

After the Nicky Albert interview and with virtually no notice I am then to have a disciplinary interview with production manager, soon to be director, Shaun Smith.

03 Dec 2009 at 5pm (Thurs) I am sent a DHL document bundle to my home, in my absence, and without me being pre-informed, which informs me of 07 Dec 2009 hearing.

The documents are then in a DHL depot in Swindon as I wasn't there to sign for them. I eventually manage to get these documents e-mailed to me late afternoon Friday 4th of December by one helpful HR employee.

Some 'interview notes' that appear later at tribunal are intentionally withheld from this package.

I am then informed late on Friday that my hearing is now 10 am Monday not 12 noon as first advised.

What I then read is the most jaw-dropping set of lies and fabrications beyond anything I could have imagined or feared.

Many of the most damaging fabrications I detail in the 'Linda's rumours and lies' chapter that is next.

I did not read all this shocking evil nonsense until the Saturday and now had to attend a disciplinary hearing rescheduled for first thing on the Monday, so naturally brought along my pre-prepared documents from before this bombshell arriving.

Were they hoping I would just fold and go quietly at this time of redundancies when they were desperate to get rid of staff?

A slight diversion over the next few chapters

I'm going to divert from the lineal process now to cite some events, many shocking, both at the workplace in Abbotts and in my life outside work that I see as relevant.

These are, I feel, essential to paint a whole picture of events at Abbotts; events involving Abbott staff and events in my life, too, relating to the title of the book.

I then return to events lineally in Chapter 18, 'The Shaun Smith Hearings.'

Chapter 10

Linda's Rumours and Lies

As part of the DHL bundle and then in other illegally withheld documents; I was to read the most distressing untruths. These were deliberately and cynically withheld until just before my so-called disciplinary hearing or illegally withheld completely until later at tribunal or, illegally again; actually after the Shaun Smith 'verdict.'

To have to go to a meeting having read this untruthful rubbish was clearly an underhanded attempt aimed at my total surrender.

All that is contained in this chapter is what is reported to be said, although later, having seen Abbott's manipulation of what I said at meetings, it must be treated with the utmost suspicion.

I naturally read it at the time as genuine reporting, and you can just imagine the psychological effect this had on me going into the meeting.

Second-hand lies

My problem was not just with Linda's testimonies but reading the alleged testimonies of others who have heard Linda's malicious gossip and then stated this as fact, or at least have had this attributed to them. Those I encounter later and challenge, completely deny what they are alleged to have said.

Witness 1: '*She has mentioned he has been harassing at breaks. Linda mentioned it to me that she has been harassed; Sexual harassment over the last 18 months.*'

This is from the guy who publicly greeted me most days with, 'Hello Michael Collins and how is the IRA?' I later met up with him again in Sainsbury's, Wantage, as I was talking to another former colleague of ours. He came over to say hello. I reminded him of his alleged comments regarding Linda and his frequent IRA comments. He denied speaking in derogatory terms about me with regards Linda. He said Linda had tried to get him into trouble (A seemingly universal theme); and said before this witness that he had never even seen me talk to Linda. He says he is not happy about this and will talk to Pete Moran. Perhaps he just says the right thing by whoever he is with.

The key words above may be, 'Linda mentioned it to me.' This is not evidence.

Everyone, this chap included, knew I always took my breaks alone in my car and was almost never in the canteen. The two of us usually passed each other in the car park at breaks. Using the term 'sexual harassment' he is surely just quoting his latest conversation with Linda – if he indeed even said this. Why as a manager did he never speak to me if there was an ongoing problem for at least 18 months? Why did he give her 24 hours overtime each week on my shift? Did he not think also, 'I regularly passed Mick as he went to take breaks in the car park as I was returning from my break?'

Witness 2: *'They are as bad as each other,'* then, *'He is obsessed about her.' I wasn't there when he grabbed her in the gownlock: that's assault. It's weird how much he likes her. The police should be involved if there are silent calls. Whether it would take that to stop him. She had a similar problem in Abingdon.'* (Quite an unfortunate coincidence that; it should have raised HR suspicions.)

I once said to this chap, 'I know Linda's your friend, but if you hear any rumour about me following her to her house, it's just not true.' He said, *'What would you follow that home with, a guide dog and a white stick? I wouldn't take any notice of a word she says. No one else does.'*

Apart from him, obviously!

I witnessed when this guy publicly pointed to Linda, whilst next to me in the corridor, to a new starter, saying, *'Watch out for her; she has to have a story, and if she hasn't got it, she'll make it up.'* Against procedure he was interviewed twice, clearly listening to Linda, whilst I was suspended and his 'second interview notes' were illegally only handed to me after dismissal, along with Linda's second interview notes.

He is clearly in a mood on the second interview as Linda has been illegally feeding him assault and nuisance call lies during the disciplinary procedure, whilst I'm suspended. Linda only decided she, too, was receiving nuisance calls, only after I complained about her harassing my children by phone. This then becomes a fact against me to the thick HR department.

He also says he would like to punch me in the face. If we ever meet, he will certainly be offered that opportunity. I'm very confident he will very meekly and apologetically refuse to take it.

It must be asked why HR don't dismiss or sanction him for such a threat; or Linda for such lies? Silly me – punching is OK; well, depending on who you are. If you are a director in a gang fight in the car park, for example, which actually happened. Or if your opponent is pregnant, no problem!

The sad fact, ironically, was that actually Linda was beyond all reasonable doubt harassing my family, including minors, with nuisance calls. I even went on to prove with a polygraph test that I had never phoned her in my life.

Witness 3: Her neighbour: *He grabbed her from behind; I didn't see anything else; he grabbed her by the neck from behind.'*

So why did you not help her then? No one who was actually there saw anything untoward and there were 25-30 of them, yet not a single one was interviewed. So you saw your friend grabbed by the neck from behind publicly and just turned away and lost interest?

Witness 4: Linda *No overtime for a while as I walked in he grabbed me on the head and *****

*Kept kissing me on the head and ******* (even I don't know what the stars indicate. 10 June 2010 I asked HR Director Amanda White for the umpteenth time for clarification, but the original documents were conveniently lost.)

Linda says to another that I am always offering her a lift,(she has her own car, FFS) stating she would never tell me where she lived or give me her phone number. Maybe that is because she was never asked? About 18 months before this, I had followed her to her house, according to another lie.

He tried to snog me.
I did not hear what he was saying. I wanted to see if he was gone. I went to Tesco, he grabbed me and kissed me. Been at the freezers. He kissed me.
Pat Cole: What did you say ?
Linda: Nothing. I was frightened
Not on the lips

He can be very angry
He was very cross and this frightened me
He stood there and said, 'I did not get to say what I wanted to say, I have feelings
for you.' He became aggressive
Pat Cole: He declared his feelings, you sent a letter
Yes. I tried to go a different way. He was following me
He frightened me and that's when I decided to write my letter. (You mean 15 months earlier just before his wedding you told lies and got someone else to write this letter).

Linda Shaw explained about the phone calls. *Heavy breathing. It is funny about phone calls and Mick Collins. I am frightened and upset*
I tried to avoid him to be polite
He started coming on again
He can get in a rage
I confronted him when he came out of the lay-by and it's referenced in his letter by flat denial. He can come over as shy and timid but when he speaks to me he frightened me

And there's more, re the twice-alleged boob comment on the stairs I never used.

My boobs were bouncing up and down and he mumbled something and I ignored his comments. Later he crept up on me at the mesher and apologised and I said I did not hear it. And previously.

One night when coming down the stairs he made a comment about my boobs. He came into the meshers where I was working and he was panicking, saying sorry and that he did not mean to say what he had.
(See my polygraph results about this alleged boob comment). This is from the woman who wants everyone's sympathy as she is telling everyone she does not want to get me into trouble.

There is the 'Me too' again, with the lay-by reference. Like the nuisance phone calls my family were getting; she was the one referenced in my letter lying in wait for me before she did this a second time, driving intentionally at me. Then there is all the 'Not on the lips', 'He can get in a rage', 'I was frightened.' Outside of her twisted imagination, when and where did all this bullshit occur?

Then, she either did not hear anything one day then heard a boob comment the next and still to this day nobody knows what this boob comment was. That is because, as proved by my polygraph test, it never happened.

I'm also alleged to be waiting in three different locations for her every morning, even though she would finish half an hour before me most days as she bunked off; yet, whatever way she went home she would find me waiting there. Abbotts never questioned this.

How can I be in three different places at once when I'm actually in a fourth? i.e. still at work.

She also allegedly went home numerous different ways to avoid me, but I was miraculously there waiting. Really?

How come I was invisible to all the other potential witnesses on the way home, especially at the locations just outside work and on these alleged different routes where some must have travelled?

What did I do once her car arrived where I would be waiting? What could I do in a Fiesta that struggled with hills and took 15 minutes to defrost on cold mornings, especially as my breaks were in my car? The frost was inside and out. She had a two litre speedster.

A bit like the nondescript boob comment . 'He made a boob comment,' or, 'He was waiting.'

What was the boob comment? What was his purpose in waiting? Who else witnessed him waiting? These would have been obvious questions if HR were impartial.

I wonder how many lies she has told about me that I have not heard.

Also my letter of 2008 addresses her latest false rumour at the time, that I followed her to her house (part of the ongoing harassment I suffered).

Then a year and a half later, she says I'm pestering her for her address. Liars always trip themselves up. She then goes on to rant about heavy breathing phone calls and Pat Cole later says at tribunal she believed Linda was genuine. What films do you two both watch?

There is also the small fact that I haven't worked with her for six months or spoken to her in five.

Yes, then later in the 'You couldn't make it up' section, Abbott and then Abbott's solicitor both send me Linda's subsequent address after she lost her house to hubby's gambling, and I tell them off for doing so.

The real harassment and bullying came from Linda's false rumours bandied around as fact.

I was the victim, not her. Professional questioning would have tied her in knots.

Again, this could have been avoided and the truth been documented had Nicky Albert been professional and questioned anyone from the shift where the harmless hug took place.

Questioning anyone who saw the initial hug or was present when Linda publicly kissed me would have sufficed.

The whole company knew she was a serial fantasist. I would suggest Nicky knew too.

Timing

Imagine suddenly getting some of this shocking nonsense (some was initially withheld), by email Friday night, not reading it fully until the weekend then having to go to a hearing rearranged to be first thing Monday morning.

But for my actions and the one helpful HR colleague e-mailing me the details, all this would have still been in a DHL depot that Monday morning.

We can guess their motive:

Chapter 11

Linda's Witness

I often felt sorry for Linda hearing her debt, depression, and difficulties with her father and her husband's gambling.

But Linda wasn't the only one I was kind to and helped.

I also helped the woman who was Linda's witness/companion whilst she spouted her lies.

Previously, on my way home from work, I spotted Linda's chosen witness had a flat tyre and then found she had a punctured spare and helped. Being kind-hearted I even offered her my spare or to drive to get both tyres fixed.

Like with Linda driving at me, I told no one of the spare tyre incident to spare her blushes. Nice to see how you get repaid: this was the woman who egged Linda on through all her lies about me.

Did she even think at all? She knows that the first thing I did when helping her was get her to call my wife to say I would be late home, which showed I would never hang around on the way home.

Also if I had regularly hung around on the way home, this woman would have been statistically more likely to see me than Linda would, as we both finished our shift at the correct time and were from the same shift.

It also showed I didn't have a mobile phone from which to make the alleged nuisance calls to Linda.

But she just consoled Linda as she lied about going three different routes home and always finding me there, even though Linda finished half an hour before me most days. As a printing supervisor, although not from Linda's shift, she would know this too.

It beggars belief that this woman just sat there whilst Linda claimed I was so psychic as to know her plans for different journeys, and how I could be so invisible to everyone else, including herself, who would have passed the locations where Linda said I waited for her. The other alleged routes Linda took home to avoid me she did not clarify. Who knows what they were? Whatever they were (we know they didn't exist) would have added so many country miles to her journey as there was just one logical route to travel. Again she did not specify these crazy routes, or get questioned about them by HR or her witness.

She found me psychically lying in wait each time she allegedly took these routes, although she bunked off half an hour early on her shift. No one questioned a thing.

No one questioned what the purpose was of me waiting in all these places that somehow I miraculously knew she would arrive at.

Surely HR would ask, 'What happened when you saw him?' 'What did he do?' To this day we still don't know. That's because it never happened and HR desired a specific result.

The most obvious question would be, 'Well, Linda, how do you think he knew these new routes you would be travelling?'

If we assume that I'm not psychic then Linda must have told people; 'Don't tell Mick but I'm travelling home via Timbuktu today.' Then I must have asked everyone, 'has Linda said she is travelling home a different way today.' FFS

I would then, have to be able to time travel to be waiting in this location. HR Abbott can't see anything illogical in this.

Also whilst Linda was talking of alleged boob comments with differing tales each time: Why did no one ever ask what the boob comment was; that I either said clearly or mumbled about but then apologised for making? We still don't know. Neither does Linda; as they never happened.

This woman; Linda's witness had sex on site with her boss and her f**k buddies in the company toilet.

Linda's witness also got genuinely assaulted with a metal ruler whilst she was incapacitated by having her head and torso under a machine.

She would have known that her assailant would regularly fantasise about her too.

He used to fantasise openly about her rear.

Yet I'm the one accused of assault; a boob comment and harassment. You couldn't make it up. But Linda could and did.

The only harassment was the lies told to destroy me.

What a shithouse company.

Chapter 12

Racism at Abbotts

In this chapter for brevity's sake I will again just cite a few highlights of the most evil and ridiculous racist discrimination that Abbott HR clearly saw as justifiable positive discrimination.

It is incredible that a heavily pregnant Nigerian woman reports being involved in a fist fight with a Nigerian man. She reports this well within 24 hours of the event happening and both parties are allowed to continue on the same shift at a later date.

This happened in the car of an elderly lady who gave this couple a lift and was absolutely petrified by loud screaming in Nigerian dialect and the trading of fists.

It is incredible also that another regular passenger of this car used to intimidate this woman by standing in her driveway and preventing her going to work unless she took him, too. She had previously stopped giving him a lift.

The woman in question confirmed all this to me at a wedding we attended.

This was the chap also who had a wandering hand inside Linda's top. Amazingly, Linda never reported this; or did she?

Another chap of Asian origin, with so many warnings and final written warnings and last chances, with a deplorable attendance and work record, can then leave a girl in floods of tears who had to run away from him to our room in tears to feel safe.

He could then after the shift, send the most vile, poisonous text relating to work matters and an alleged affair, which this girl reported the very next morning, and these two are also allowed by Abbotts to continue on the same shift together.

I was on day shift and Linda was on nights, but I deserved the ultimate sanction. Really!!

The girl in question shows the text, sent from this man's phone, to Abbott HR within 24 hours and he says it was obviously from his wife who didn't even work for the company, and Abbott believe this in its entirety too. Why wasn't I and the other chap she came crying to interviewed as witnesses?

Pat Cole even then states this phone bullshit as fact to a judge at tribunal who later then calls her a credible witness. Obvious questions might be: Why would his wife get involved? If she could text, would she not have a phone of her own? Why would she use her husband's phone anonymously as this would get her husband into trouble at work and affect the family income?

Pat also misleads the tribunal as she demonstrated the fist fight as playful wrist- waving with two open hands waving with arms still, having said the pugilists could only use one hand. The judge swallowed this bullshit hook, line & sinker, too.

What would be the point of that and why would this lead to a complaint? Pure lies, Pat. Under oath too!

Pat also claimed that the texter's wife was a good friend of the victim from church at tribunal. It is quite normal, and a Christian thing to do, to suddenly send another member of your congregation (who you, in all probability, don't really know anyway) poisonous texts on your husband's phone immediately after your husband has a heated tirade at her, at their workplace. I doubt that this is the sort of thing he would mention coming home. Being on nights, he probably would not have seen his wife before the immediate complaint, too. Food for thought.

A more logical conclusion

Anyone reading the last two chapters can see how every bit of clearly fake evidence against me from a serial fantasist is unscrutinised and taken as fact, and how happy Abbott are with this ridiculous text explanation from a serial offender that the playing field is not exactly level. In fact it is a complete cliff face in my case – one Abbott so cynically pushed me off.

The same texter can also hit another, he openly fantasises about, violently with a steel ruler whilst her upper body is under a machine, risking head injury too. He also had a string of final warnings, but knew he was Teflon.

In fact the above, in reality, faced no sanction at all bar paid suspension that some see as a bonus.

The texter never seemed to return to work on time from any holiday, as he invariably caught some bug whilst away. The whole factory would correctly predict this would happen on each occasion.

He caught the lateness bug too, on a near daily basis being delayed by traffic that never seemed to afflict his neighbours.

There is one of Linda's witnesses who always greeted me with, 'Hello Michael Collins, and how is the IRA?' quite publicly.

Imagine if he made 'Twin Towers' comments to others due to their religion or ethnicity. Would Abbott HR ignore that?

Michael Collins can suffer regular IRA comments at work due to his name and ethnicity and that is absolutely fine, too.

I am named and shamed, as I explain later, on the weekly ER notice board for 3 weeks for a non-ER event whilst the Nigerian who was also involved in the fist fight, through pure neglect and not checking a single item, destroys 33% of at least two whole batches and leaves the problems still stuck to the machine, and does not even get his error pointed out to him by management.

Another gets caught red-handed with his feet up on a product table, eating in the controlled area. Then after numerous complaints by other staff, management, who are too scared and too useless to act, issue a stern letter that there will be severe consequences for the next person caught doing this.

But to Abbott, in what is a far more serious incident, according to Les Muggeridge's explanation to employment investigators in Southampton, I'm sacked for hugging someone because it was my birthday, which is total bollocks anyway.

I was sacked six months after the event for a goodbye hug and subsequent asexual kiss on the top of the head, identical to hundreds, if not thousands of hugs, kisses and goodbyes that week due to so many redundancies amongst staff.

My hug of Linda was reciprocated with interest a month later in view of many witnesses.

Yet all the above escape any real punishment and I receive the ultimate sanction.

All the above were involved in plenty hugs and kisses the week of my hug, too. Everyone was!

I will just say for the record: I have no issue with Nigerians or Asians. I do have an issue with HR staff (all white in this case) who positively discriminate and judge differently according to skin colour.

The simple obvious question

Apologies for the above repetition, but:

If you ask yourself the simple question: Had I punched a pregnant woman and a Nigerian given an innocent goodbye hug, as everyone in fact did anyway:

Would I just be casually warned for punching a heavily pregnant woman and put back on her shift?

Would the Nigerian be sacked for a hug? (They did and they weren't.)

If the answer to the above is 100% no, then Abbott are 100% racist.

Similarly: if I left a Kenyan girl in floods of tears (who ironically came to me after the event to feel safe) and I then sent a poisonous tirade to her by text on my phone: Would Abbott believe my wife must have in fact sent the text?

If the answer to the above is 100% no, then Abbott are 100% racist.

Just to give you a little clue as to how racist Abbott are: my wife submitted a four page signed, dated and handwritten letter detailing Linda kissing me in public, etc. to Shaun Smith at my disciplinary hearing.

Filthy racist Abbott

Abbott HR were willing, in an act of excessive over-wokery, to believe that the text nastiness, that was reported immediately, and which came from a serial offender member of staff's own phone, was sent by a complete stranger with no motive who has never claimed to have sent the text that she, in all probability, knew nothing about.

Yet My wife, who was clearly at the leaving do and saw Linda kiss me publicly, and writes a handwritten letter that she signs and dates; cannot have her evidence believed.

All they had on me was the hug; and here we had a hand written statement; which was also submitted at tribunal stating unequivocally that Linda publicly kissed me a month after the hug; rendering their one crumb of comfort for dismissing me, totally invalid.

I'm struggling to think; what conclusive proof they have linking this outsider to the phone text.

Yet! My dismissal was the only option; in spite of my wife's hand written letter; later to be proven by polygraph to be a true statement.

Yet! These are the same people who fall over themselves to clutch at any straw Indian boy offers; no matter how ridiculous; despite his previous final written warnings and shocking disciplinary record.

Looking at the above. Clearly: My only crime was to have the wrong skin colour.

Abbotts: Has your wokery and positive discrimination perhaps gone a tad too far?

My wife's letter proves me innocent. I'm sacked. Nothing at all happens to the one who had to be sacked. What racist filth!

Even when someone drives intentionally at me in a premeditated act. It is not as important as this hug.

From what I hear from a good source, Abbott had also recently at that time covered for this chap whilst he spent time at HMP Bullingdon in Bicester.

I sincerely trust that, after this book is published, no one could possibly believe that Abbott is a non-racist, equal opportunities employer, ever again.

Chapter 13

Good Management and the Not so Good

If technical and work-related explanations are not your thing, you may wish to bypass this chapter.

Good management

At Bookham, a previous employer that I worked for, there was a lot of development and experimentation involved in making what were, at the time, cutting-edge photonic transceivers that were to use light via fibre-optic cables to increase speed and storage of data and increase digital communication to whole new levels.

The manufacture of such photonic chips involved the deposition and etching of layers of materials including gold and sometimes even platinum. The work involved working to nanometres.

Bookham's aim was to develop a consistent reliable process at every stage to mass produce these chips from silicon 'wafers'.

Every batch of 'wafers' was accompanied by a batch record.

There were generally written descriptions of what was required process-wise in one section, other criteria and information elsewhere and the results section at the back without a specific format.

Another issue regarding these wafers with layers deposited and etched, one above another, was that one tester/engineer might measure the deposition/etching in one place and someone else in another. Some graphs had a dip, a horizontal then another dip, depending on previous depositions.

With everyone switching from process page to results page, etc. by the end of the process the batch records were always dishevelled and curled up.

Having in the past designed and built a working wave power system at college that was innovative and produced a perfect AC sine wave on an oscilloscope on first test, and having designed three more that were outside budget to also make,

I could do design and improvement; in fact this was a natural way of thinking to me.

Over one weekend the cogs started turning and I designed a new batch record.

I designed it so process one was on page one and you went from top left page one to bottom right page x at the end of the process in a page by page order.

Also the 'how to' description and desired results were now on the same page as the results table, and a picture of where to and what to measure, what the graph should look like and what part of the graph gave the required measurement, were now all on the same page.

With this came a consistency of measurement from the same measuring place by all employees in a batch record that was as tidy at the end as it was at the start, and nothing missed along the way.

I didn't ask for any praise or bonus. I was just part of the team and glad to help.

My manager welcomed my ideas and spoke to his managers and they implemented them.

I also tended to be one of those who asked questions at meetings. This might involve suggestions and ideas of requests for clarity on issues, etc.

It was always in a mature, positive environment.

Unfortunately, company spend eventually led to the need for redundancies. Due to my communication skills, the staff on my area all asked if I would be their representative at the redundancy negotiations which involved joining those in the boardroom for talks.

This seemed quite daunting and responsible. This was a brand new pressure and responsibility that could be overwhelming but I was determined to be positive and give it my best.

The vast majority of staff and management were positive, too. I had to sell the staff ideas to management and management ideas to staff, and back again, also raising concerns.

It went really well and I got a standing ovation for my efforts that I really appreciated, along with the whole team's efforts.

Insecurity; spite and the not so good management

At Abbotts I often had the confidence to input positively and seek clarifications at meetings.

There were others who would moan all day every day but who never said a word at meetings. I was the reverse, doing a great job and raising my issues at meetings, i.e. at the correct time.

Previously I had manufactured compact discs and often covered for sickness and holidays on the printing department.

The printing process making CDs involved up to six different colour silk screen prints applied consecutively to produce a photo-like image.

The stencils to produce these silk screens were aligned using cross hairs like a rifle sight.

At Abbotts the diabetic testing strips were made from one initial rectangle of card-like material that had a number of depositions upon it that was to be, in subsequent processes, cut into six rows, then eventually into individual testing strips just before packaging.

There was only one ink to print and cure. This print formed the insulation layer on the manufactured product. It did, however, have a very crude method of alignment on the area of card outside of the actual print itself.

During printing and curing the screen, squeegee, etc. the print could and often would become mis-aligned with the product card, causing a good many rejects i.e. those initially spotted and a good many before and those still curing afterwards.

The method of alignment was a dot inside a circle and the product deemed failed should the dot make its way outside the circle.

The problem being, if this dot exited the circle at the bottom right you could not tell if this is a movement down and to the right or a clockwise movement. This had to be assumed and the product cured again wasting production time with a loss of product, should the assumption be wrong.

So although not officially a printer I had worked in an environment that did six prints on top of each other with an accuracy that looked like a photograph.

I had a Eureka moment. In my own time I drew up documents with diagrams showing my idea.

I thought that, much as cross hairs are too fine to print, a cross within a cross like the centre of the Norwegian flag would be so much better than a blob within a circle.

Any slight clockwise or anticlockwise movements would be exaggerated by the arms of the cross and if there were no clockwise movement issues the centre of the cross could be quickly re-aligned with up or down movements. The product could be corrected proactively, not randomly reactively. Production could improve and waste could decrease. It was an all-round win situation for profits, efficiency and the environment.

A previous or subsequent process could even align outside this cross, too. The process managers, some very hard to please, thought my four-page presentation with diagrams was ingenious.

My idea was passed on. A couple of months later I still had no feedback.

I then made a criminal error with new, insecure director Ms Pat Cole. I suggested, at a staff meeting, that it would be good practice, when someone puts forward an idea, to give feedback.

I got a few spiteful comments from her away from the meeting, belittling my efforts, and saw a change in her from then on.

My next helpful error

As time moved on, at another meeting the point was raised that our shift had no CCF rep ('Colleague Circle of Friends', or something like that) as the previous rep had been long-term sick with cancer for years.

Like at Bookham, colleagues asked me to stand, probably because I would ask a sensible question. I didn't want to as I had the inclination of moving to days when the shifts merged, to avoid working with a certain someone, but agreed to stand as dayshift was by no means a certainty, depending on applications.

A neighbour of mine, a manager at Abbotts, who is now also a director said to me, 'If you ever have an issue you can always talk to Pat Cole.' That was not the greatest advice I ever received. Many others, I later learned, would rightly see her as extremely vindictive.

I phoned Pat Cole and put forward my ideas for overtime when the night shifts were due to merge and she said she would talk to me. I also said I was standing for CCF that night. She said she would definitely be in and would talk to me.

She spent a long time talking to the shift manager, then a long time talking to the other three in my section, deliberately excluding me. Then she went around and spoke to everyone else on the shift.

I spoke to a good friend of mine, a Caribbean chap with psychology qualifications, and said I felt an undercurrent of ill-will from that one, and felt very singled out, like there was a targeted vendetta against me; especially the look I got as she left my section, and her deliberately not talking to me.

He replied that no one should be made to feel like that.

I told him and others of my night shift rota idea, which also allowed for night shift overtime. A couple of weeks later this became management's idea for the new night shift.

The CCF election followed that night with the others being told the result, but not me. The first I hear about the results is someone screaming to me, 'It's a f*****g fix.' Then I ask about the results to a manager who won't even raise his head to look at me but insists it was all above board. That was a point I hadn't questioned.

I was also not called in to hear the result, like the other three candidates had been. I asked how close I came, in case I might ever wish to stand again – like on a future day shift, for example. He then told me that I didn't even come close. So there were four candidates, and seemingly over half the workforce thinking it was a fix as they had voted for me, and I didn't even come close.

Other examples

Then, some time after this on dayshift, as I said before, I'm singled out and named and shamed on a notice board for an Exception Report error that wasn't. No one is allowed to be named and shamed in this way under company policy.

In writing a report to prevent a recurrence of this error, did I cost myself dearly by being helpful? Was it now perceived as undesirable, an underling actually thinking?

My six or so ideas for radically improving the row convertor process, that I detail later, were not even looked at.

Warning of the pitfalls, unworkability and health and safety and product risks in Abbott's new overtime initiative beyond all reasonable doubt led to my dismissal, especially as what I predicted would happen, did happen, and happened on the first night of this initiative.

My fears and warnings of what might happen, coming to fruition, were clearly ego damaging for a new insecure management. Were they now out for revenge?

The difference in attitude

At both companies my input was similar: remarkably constructive and always had the end product and therefore the customer at heart.

Was asking for feedback on a presented idea deemed by a new, insecure, possibly out-of-her-depth Abbott director as an affront to her authority?

In both companies I never asked for praise or anything. I just wanted to help the team.

There was a lot of positive input, listening and teamwork in the first example. There was insecurity, spite, bullying and division in the latter.

Concluding

I didn't really want to stand as a CCF rep but was asked to stand by my colleagues as I could provide clear, positive communication. Management resented this.

I did not put myself forward but was asked by my colleagues to represent them at the redundancy talks at Bookham, too, for much the same reason. Management embraced this and all was positive.

I was also, many years later, just doing the best I could at a time of the Covid national emergency and was singled out by my colleagues for an award due to my efforts and communication, which I totally did not expect

I shouldn't really expect to receive the ultimate sanction for my positivity and helpfulness from Abbott.

Chapter 14

Linda's Exploits

This chapter details a lot of stuff involving Linda that did not result in disciplinary proceedings, possibly because with most of it, she would be too ashamed to mention it.

I have witnessed other members of staff repeatedly slap Linda on the backside, multiple times and on numerous occasions. One, whilst doing the repeated slapping on multiple occasions, on one occasion repeatedly shouted loudly, 'Yeah baby yeah, sexual harassment, go report me baby.' Who knows, perhaps this was for my benefit if she had been lying about me yet again. Mind you, she had a history of reporting everyone.

Linda doesn't mind touching other people from behind either. She frequently played the game where she sticks her fingers into other people's sides from behind whilst they are seated to make them jump. Not the worst crime in the world until one day when an older temp, who did not expect this, falls off a quite high chair, injuring her back.

Most disturbingly, also in the gown lock, on another occasion a Nigerian chap who intimidated another elderly lady by blocking her driveway each morning said of Linda, whilst many were waiting for the shift change in the gown lock, 'This is my new girlfriend long legs, sexy legs, sexy face.' The chap who regularly slapped her arse replied, saying, 'More like sit on your face.' Our friend with the new girlfriend was rubbing his fingers over the exposed part of her back, before proceeding to rub further down inside her clothing, looking at her chest with his head over her shoulder, presumably to see if his rubbing brought a reaction.

He also had his arm around her with his hand suspiciously low inside her clothing whilst walking down the corridor on another occasion. Some married woman, or does she sometimes forget? This puts my hug into perspective and again underlines her pure nastiness and vindictiveness.

Perhaps she is just a selectively married woman when the occasion suits.

I would never have considered acting in such a trouble stirring way towards her, and she even ran me off my side of the road in an act that could have had fatalities .

This, wandering hands chap, was also boasting to one of his friends in Nigerian about 'Lindaah' and you could clearly get the gist of the conversation amongst the high fives. The other chap in this conversation, the one who watches porn all day and sleeps on nightshift, was later openly boasting on that same shift that he would like to give Linda one up the ass, complete with actions. What did he hear earlier?

This chap would regularly make contact with Linda's backside and smile. Linda has even brushed my backside whilst I was logging on in the product visual inspection area. Didn't pass much remarks at the time, assuming it to be accidental, but bearing in mind all her evil lies about and actions towards me since, should I now take offence? No, I'll just be grown-up.

One night, after having to take a later than scheduled break, on return I have walked in to the gown lock to be met with the sight of Linda with blouse unbuttoned ridiculously too low, bending down reaching into a box for no apparent reason, for the whole time I was there. Even this failed to register a boob comment, as I proved by polygraph. I just gowned up and returned to work.

There was also Linda following me to the car park alone, as witnessed by her friend. This happened once again, after I had to take a late break. This would suggest she watched my movements before acting to engage with me on both occasions. Her evidence also suggested before that she was watching me on my wedding day.

Another chap from our shift can confirm Linda Shaw was a sexual predator. On a company night out, even though his wife was there and he told Linda in no uncertain terms where to go, she would just not take no for an answer. Linda subsequently, at work, threatened to tell his wife all sorts of lies if he did not comply with her wishes.

This shows dishonesty and spite, and that she gets very bitter seeing others in a happy relationship. Sound familiar?

If she has reported none of the above, and has decided to report me, the only reason can surely be a personal vendetta, or jealousy, with the time lapse casting considerable doubt with regard to any genuine offence being taken.

Her antics the night of my wedding, turning up for overtime, although invited, raise questions about possible jealousy.

Her sense of proportion and honesty needed serious questioning. Such questioning was unfortunately never forthcoming from a very amateur HR department who, beyond all reasonable doubt, had a vendetta against me too, especially comparing my treatment to others.

It would be fair to question if Linda felt 'perceived betrayal' as I had long since moved to day shift at the time of her complaint.

She had also requested a last minute redundancy on hearing that I was not going to be working with her on the newly merged night shift. (Again, apologies for repeating myself in this chapter).

A question of conscience

Some might say that with the mental health issues you have been caused should you not be conscious that Linda, although she has done you wrong, has been on antidepressants for years and this book may not be good for her in that respect. (I don't even know if she is still alive.)

I would reply to that, stating that I didn't declare war, am just rightfully defending myself in putting the record straight and I certainly don't owe her any consideration.

Anyone who does think like that may wish to point out to Linda that she might indeed wish to consider others after the damage all her lies and stunts have done.

Chapter 15

Sexual Exploits on Site at Abbotts

Detailed below are happenings I reliably believe or know to be true. Many involve management as they had the keys to the upstairs rooms.

This list features only selected highlights for the sake of brevity.

This is before we mention drugs and violence on site, which even involved a director.

I was sacked on false hearsay, so believe I have the right to utter that which I believe beyond all reasonable doubt is true. Obviously, I was rarely present for any of these events.

I didn't want to write or even mention any of this but, after the ridiculous overreactions to a non- event I have suffered, this became absolutely necessary in terms of context.

It has now become essential to show a real wolf to those who so enthusiastically cried wolf.

Here we go:

One chap had long-term history of sex on site on many nights over a number of years in the product storerooms in Abingdon then upstairs in the store rooms at Witney with a supervisor on our shift who also worked in both places. They had graduated on to anal at Witney. If you were an Abbott customer and found anything a bit suspicious smeared on your product, it might be because of these two.

I heard another character from our shift had a go with this woman as well. I'm sceptical that one happened at Witney as this guy was busy enough with another employee's daughter, much to her father's displeasure. This father was involved in a gang fight in the car park that included a company director, and was later jailed for other offences.

The storeroom 'sex on site' boy was an incessant letch and sexaholic renowned for his inappropriate hands, even grabbing the crotch of strangers on the high street. I certainly saw him have a handful of another's breast at work, a temp he later made pregnant, costing him his marriage, and not doing this girl a lot of good either.

I was present in the gown lock with others when he just publicly pointed at another girl, and twice loudly said, 'Nice piece of pussy, like to fuck it, innit.' He was obsessed with and constantly harassed a member of the canteen staff as well, so I hear.

One that I have heard both parties confirm involved a girl who definitely gave this chap a blow job in the car park whilst he fingered her.

This girl was vulnerable, had a few issues and had not let go of Mum's apron strings. She got into ridiculous debt to lend money to another who used her credit to buy himself a new motorcycle. Some people just want to be loved at any cost.

This same girl was also lured away by another couple at Abbotts to the coast and had some really depraved acts performed on her over a weekend which I believe, from what I'm reliably told, also included her being restrained on a bed.

Then there is the one who helped me get sacked by egging on Linda during her 'evidence'. She too was one of the night shift manager's conquests upstairs. She also shagged a Siebler worker in the on-site toilet. Apparently she likes her fuck buddies, as I heard she calls them.

The poisonous text harasser, who left a girl shaking and in floods of tears, whose exploits I detail elsewhere, took great delight in whacking this girl's ass with considerable force, with a metal ruler. He did this whilst her whole upper torso was under a machine. He openly fantasised regularly and obsessively about this girl's rear.

The shift manager I have just mentioned only seemed to come out of his office to talk filth, mostly with the female staff. What I saw and heard was really vile 'give me a bucket' stuff.

The super letch shift manager also had trips upstairs with another girl. He boasted of rear-ending her although he did not rate her.

He preferred his trips upstairs with another on our shift, whose marriage he subsequently wrecked. They were still an item a number of years back.

This chap also sacked a third girl on the evidence of the two he was shagging. This girl also used to suffer really loud, regular intimidation from another on the other night shift on overtime, that the whole factory could not avoid hearing loudly.

A temp who mistakenly signed with his real name one day, before crossing it out, used to make regular breast gestures to a Polish girl with an ample frontage seemingly each time he would see her. Another who engaged in this type of behaviour was the one who wrote Linda's letter, who mimicked Linda with the same frontage gesture, saying to others, 'Who's this? Long legs!'

But it is me that gets falsely accused of a breast comment without any relevant detail given, whilst being possibly the only one not to mock Linda's physique.

This temp' two names' also lured a Czech girl on Sieblers to give him a blow job that she described to her colleagues. At about this time, too, he got a South African employee pregnant. She had to leave the first week in May 2008 because of this. I remember this because it was my last shift before my wedding. Grooming was standard everyday practice for some staff.

Another manager from upstairs who worked with equipment supply used to partake in a bit of sex on site at Abingdon with some bit of stuff he had over there, before he became a company man.

My supervisor on Sieblers was legendary for her conquests. On one occasion, three engineers come in to the room together to work on a Siebler we were working on at the time. The other staff joked all of them knew her intimately.

Her Abbott notches on her bedpost ran into double figures and she was simply too much of an over-reactive prima donna to be a supervisor, but got promoted.

Anyway, her son worked there for a while. A member of management walked into the canteen. Her son says, 'I know him from somewhere,' and then pauses. 'Oh yeah, coming down our stairs from Mum's room in the morning.'

Another serial incessant letch on our shift who was like a dog on heat most of the time ended up with her daughter, who was half his age, when she became a temp.

Another Siebler worker would leave his place of work virtually every half hour to chat up the victim of the poisonous texter, mentioned previously. She did not welcome his attention. He also bought her presents she did not want, such as perfume. The only time this girl got a break was when another from B nights worked overtime. He had a skinny women fetish. He even had a thing for Pat Cole. It takes all sorts, as they say.

She was also the victim of the company flasher, at close quarters too, but unlike the poison texter bully, of whom she was also the victim, he was disciplined.

There are plenty of other relationships I could mention, but I think there is enough there for you to get the gist. There are probably at least as many again that I have not heard of.

As they said on B nights in Abingdon, you had your wife and your Medisense wife. (Medisense were taken over by Abbott).

But I'll save the most outrageously jaw-dropping one for the next chapter, as it is quite something.

Chapter 16

The Most Disturbing Case of All

I have saved this one for a chapter on its own as it is truly shocking.

We had one 'lady' who worked with us, and I use the term in the loosest possible context, who had a bit of a reputation for notches on the bedpost and loose behaviour, to put it mildly. In short, she was known as a bit of a nympho whose Abbott conquests even outnumbered our friend, the supervisor on Sieblers. She would have had a few friends with benefits in the right places.

As we know, the management at Abbott are a kind, caring lot who never misjudge staff at all and treat everyone equally, and on merit.

The woman I refer to is, after all, a pillar of the community – a special constable. She is very special alright. This nympho cannot resist telling colleagues that during the course of her duties she could not resist undressing a corpse to see if he was well hung.

I assume she may not have been alone at the time. A decent copper, if there were any, would have said to her, or she might even realise, that her plaything was someone's son, and in all probability someone's husband, dad and brother, too. She was inexplicably unashamed of her actions.

Yet another example of Thames Valley Police displaying the ultimate in professionalism. There will be many more examples to come.

Then one night all the staff are called together so an announcement can be made.

We hear a tale that we would normally only expect to hear on the news.

Our good friend nympho's husband has just been sent down for a while for having sexual relations with their daughter.

She wants you all to hear about it together to avoid all rumours and questions that will inevitably follow, but is not barring you from talking to her.

That sounds fair enough, I thought, and probably the right thing to do in the circumstances.

I did not know about her corpse episode at the time but when she then told me that she was off to South Africa to get away from it all for a bit I thought, 'Yes that will be good for you both. The daughter could especially do with a change of scenery.'

A few weeks later she is back. Not just back, she has a nice new car and an engagement ring. Guess what: she is getting married.

I wouldn't have thought she had had the time to divorce the husband in the clink and also thought that this was a holiday with her daughter.

Then when listening to workmates my jaw near hits the floor. She didn't take the daughter who had been abused by Daddy. She was off on her own.

Next thing we know, our poor friend the nympho corpse fiddler has been moved to a dayshift office job to help her cope with the strain and the stress.

Then we hear a bit later…

While our friend was away with lover boy on holiday, it was now the son's turn with the daughter.

Then some truly great news: our corpse fiddling friend has a new job in a funeral parlour, FFS.

Later I read of the son's exploits as it is all over the county press and online.

The headline reads. 'Two women whose lives have been devastated by sex offenders have vowed to fight the unusually lenient sentence of a paedophile in Oxford.'

Those two women are Shy Keenan and Sara Payne, whose 8-year-old daughter Sarah was killed by paedophile Roy Whiting. They insisted that this paedophile should get at least 6 years.

I don't know, but doubt, if the daughter was the victim in question that the son was on trial for. And I only have second-hand evidence about the son abusing the daughter, but at trial the son asked for four other similar offences to be taken into consideration.

Judge Julian Hall ordered that he attend a sex offenders' treatment programme and gave him a three-year community order, i.e. no real punishment at all, which Judge Julian later strongly defended. It was best for the son long term. What about the victims!

I must be really evil. There is nothing Abbott wouldn't do to help this wonderful member of staff, yet saw fit to attack and ruin the lives of my family and even ignored nuisance calls beyond all reasonable doubt from a member of Abbott staff to minors in my family.

Dare I question Abbott's judgement?

Especially where the welfare of children is involved?

Chapter 17

Gone Overboard

People will hate you because others have lied about you. Tell me about it
This chapter relates to another episode from earlier in my life.

The title of this book is, after all, *The Damage Lies Can Do*.

I tend to stand alone and stand up for that which is right and get hated for it.

Referring back to an incident in the late 80s involving an old friend of mine now sadly departed.

A key part of his lovable rogue's charm was where he would never let the truth get in the way of a good story. There were a number of occasions when I was left holding the baby after his bullshit.

Another friend was once doing nicely on the chat-up front when all went pear-shaped. This chap had told the girl he had Aids.

On another night out a large fight broke out and another injured him, stamping on his nose. The culprit was not local and was long gone. This chap then called a war committee of his friends.

Unlike myself, he wouldn't stand up for himself alone and needed backing.

Our friend with a passion for BS decided to blame two others for holding him down whilst the act took place. I was thereabouts the night of the incident and saw one alleged perpetrator elsewhere, although I didn't see the incident. I knew when the two accused spoke with me, alerting me to this event, I could tell that they were innocent.

I stood up at the war committee, aka a meeting at the pub in another town, and said, 'I don't believe you, and will have nothing to do with this,' and left, alienating myself from all those remaining.

Then on returning to my usual haunt a much larger crowd than the last one I faced, who were friends of the accused, were equally angry and turned on me for being friends of the accuser.

I should have been called 'lucky.'

I'm left holding the baby and offering to mediate. Then there is the rumour that the initial crowd have turned up at a pub down the road looking for the accused. I'm then left standing in a doorway, getting jostled, trying to get this mob not to go.

Then a few minutes later, after this mob had gone, I'm standing between the dads of the victim and the accused, both of whom want to knock the hell out of each other. These were my friends too, up until that night.

Then later the original war committee crowd turned up. Someone said that the other mob had gone off looking for them and I was in the same doorway keeping the peace again. How did they avoid each other?

Within a few hours everyone I knew seemed to hate me because I was trying to hold everyone else's baby whilst a lie that had nothing to do with me had caused WWIII.

Then the following week all parties are set to meet up again as there was a coach trip to a riverboat disco on the Thames by Tower Bridge.

I was really looking forward to that – NOT! To my amazement, when everyone got together, nobody seemed to have the courage to utter a word to anyone else about the previous week.

Later, whilst going onto the top deck through a narrow opening at the stern of this large boat, I see someone jump off the bow. I run forward shouting, 'Man Overboard.' I see his head bobbing. I then see there is an external ladder at the stern. I descend the ladder, going down past the floor where the disco is taking place and into the darkness towards the river below. Keeping my eye on this bobbing head, using what little reflection there was on the river, and shouting, 'I'm coming to help!' I descend the ladder. I'm then a deck below the disco in darkness with just the cold Thames beneath me.

By this time the chap has drifted to the middle of the Thames but is now making an effort to swim and save himself.

This chap was to become the only person ever, including myself, to benefit from my Fire Brigade ladder skills and my Engineering and Maths skills.

I had seen the arc with which he swept away and had to guide him back in by a similar but more upstream arc, taking tiredness and river flow into account so I could catch him as I leaned out from the ladder as he passed. Once he went downstream of the boat he was going to be washed up in Kent or Essex, depending on the tidal effect which I later assume must have helped us.

When he was in the middle of the Thames there was not a one in a hundred chance of saving him, but through his swimming and listening and my vociferous encouragement as I aimed him at the bow to catch him at the stern, we did it. Another then joined me at the top of the ladder, too.

Like with Linda driving at me it was sudden, there was adrenaline, then it was done.

I never made a meal of the event afterwards either.

It wasn't until decades later that I thought of the consequences had we not succeeded, as was, by far, the overwhelming probability.

I had just become public enemy no 1 and was despised by everyone I was friends with the week before.

Just how hated and how blamed would I have been, had I not saved him, as was likely?

Then years later at the accuser's funeral, the lovable rogue's parting gift to me was a rumour that I had given a well-known and idolised Irish footballer a hard time on a night out in Lancashire.

We had met this footballer on a previous night and I just said hello to him from a distance whilst he played darts with his mate and spoke with some of his family.

The following morning I met them all again as he lived across the road from the village pub / hotel and was putting a high-powered car through its paces, along with friends and family members. There were no crossed words with me at any time. Surely if there had been some aggro at the pub the night before and I was now so outnumbered, then there would have been at least some words said.

At the funeral, I did not know the exact details of the rumour but joked along that this chap's playing form had dipped since he met me.

An event that day, and the spite aimed towards me, led me to realise how dangerous appeasing rumours and not reacting can be.

As Les Muggeridge, HR Director, in a rare nice mode moment said to me at my hearing with regard to Linda, 'You know how to deal with rumours; just ignore them.' The obvious question is why didn't he take his own advice?

As I said before, I can no more stop rumours than I can hold an ocean. I nearly had practice of holding a river.

This funeral happened at the depths of my depression around the time of my hearings. Another destructive lie had now further led to my sense of injustice and my world falling apart, and was the last thing I needed.

Just as I never made a fuss about the riverboat rescue, I was also self-effacing after this lie.

Once more your good deeds counted for nothing, but one lie, everyone will jump on this and destroy you.

Again I say, 'What if, as in all probability, that rescue had gone wrong?'

I would have been despised and blamed and was already on a sticky wicket for standing up and helping those wronged. It would obviously have been catastrophic for the chap I helped rescue. The long-term mental health issues for me would be too much to contemplate. Even though the rescue was a one in 100 chance, would I ever have forgiven myself had the right outcome not occurred? It was adrenaline then over before there was time to think and assess; but that might have killed two of us.

The common factor is me always putting my head above the parapet and volunteering. It wasn't my fight but I stood up for the innocent victims: I did not have to go over the side of the boat, but that's just me. I always stood up and asked questions in the meetings at Abbott too.

Keeping your head down is sensible and what I would advise, although I never take my advice. No matter how good it is, the thing you do, you will always be resented in the end by those less brave and more spiteful and insecure.

All my good work at Abbotts counted for nothing and the lies of a known stirrer prevailed.

All the good I did those two weeks culminating in the rescue counted for nothing in comparison to the lies of a known bullshitter which were embraced.

I've kept my counsel for years.

I don't like writing this. It sounds a bit like 'poor me', but it's fact. The damage lies can do.

I could mention a few more incidents where I risked my life or well-being to protect others. But that's what us Twats do. That could be another book.

All risk and no reward. Perhaps this book is the latest example of my foolhardiness. But that's me.

I do hope there is a good and just God.

Chapter 18

The Shaun Smith Hearing

Anyway, back to Abbott and the 'Disciplinary Process.'

So after the totally biased debacle of the hearing with Nicky Albert, for which I was given no notice and had no witness present ...

Next is the meeting with Assistant Director, or whatever he was at the time, Shaun Smith.

This meeting is rearranged for first thing on Monday morning and I'm asked who my witness is at a factory I have been excluded from. I said, 'I'll choose Jenny my manageress.' Jill from HR, who e-mailed me the documents over the weekend, was also present.

I'm still in shock at the nasty lies I have read over the weekend.

At my hearing on 7th December 2009 after Shaun's deliberations we came to the point where I started to read my evidence. I began by listing some sexually inappropriate behaviour involving Linda Shaw. I was interrupted by Shaun Smith saying, 'Are you alleging that sexually inappropriate behaviour in the workplace is commonplace?' I tried to continue, stating that what I was saying was relevant.

If you have read recent chapters you would know that sexually inappropriate behaviour at Abbott was commonplace and almost compulsory for career advancement in some cases. He would have known about much of this too.

I was also interrupted again, asking how long my evidence was, and could I stick to the relevant points as we had little time left.

My submissions were obviously written before the e-mails so rightly focused on my amazement at the vindictive targeting I was suffering lately from management, and that my treatment was so different to others.

HR policy suggests that everyone should be treated equally.

From what I recall, I expressed my shock at the bullying aimed at me, an obvious example being named and on the ER board when I had never committed an ER in 5 years, yet real ERs are ignored.

I was amazed at the reaction, too, to a simple hug identical to all staff that week, half a year ago, and the incomprehensible singularity of the sudden extreme reaction to me so many months later when I no longer work with or talk to Linda.

I tried to point out through the interruptions that I saw it as racist that Nigerian staff, including a pregnant woman, can have a fist fight and an Asian chap with a history of vile deeds can make a Kenyan girl cry with his nastiness, then send her a poisonous text after work, etc. and that all these staff still worked together on the same shift without sanction.

I also stated, without naming names, that regular sex on site in the store rooms for years, which no doubt he knew about from his days in Abingdon, that was still continuing in Witney, did not raise an eyebrow.

My brief continually interrupted evidence all focused on genuinely serious incidents that Abbott ignored.

This was crucial as all are to be treated equally regardless of their differences, not differently because of them.

I could not see any logic in the mother of all overreactions to a total non-event unless, of course, there was a genuine vendetta against me from the person I had shown to be breaking company Health & Safety rules, who was now acting as judge over me. This was the point I tried to make.

I felt hurried and under considerable pressure at this stage.

I was told again that he was pushed for time, I would have to condense my notes only to that relevant to my case and get my evidence in quickly as he wanted it 'done and dusted by the end of the week'.

If I'm being treated thousands of times more harshly than others, then that is relevant. It is just very inconvenient and unsuitable to his twisted agenda.

I was yet to really properly engage and I could cite company misdemeanours that he did not want to hear or want the two others in the room to hear either.

He wanted me out before the end of the week and, more importantly, before I had the chance to speak. My knowledge was dangerous because it would show how unprofessional and vindictive Abbott management were.

It would also show their arrogance and contempt for company rules.

What was about to come would underline this vindictiveness still further.

With hindsight I was too meek and submissive and should have asserted my points more strongly, but had never been at a disciplinary hearing before.

I believe that my fate was predetermined anyway and, however I would have approached this, he would have run for cover and been pushed for time, constantly looking at his watch only to run off down his cowardly little rabbit hole in 'Alice in Wonderland' fashion.

I submitted my evidence on Wednesday 9th December 2009. Upon submitting another piece of evidence by email on Thursday 10th December 2009 I was told to come in for the verdict the next day.

Interviewing inconsistencies

At her interviews Linda is never interrupted, and often empathised with, and regardless of the level of her fantasies and how impossible they seem, she is never properly questioned.

I was hurried, constantly interrupted and the meeting was cut short.

Chapter 19

The Verdict Hearing

Friday 11th and I'm coming in for the verdict hearing; not any sort of reconvened hearing that Shaun Smith was to later intentionally lie about occurring in his false evidence under oath at tribunal. Gill and Jenny were again present.

There was to be a brief summary and I was to be on my way.

The previous meeting was suspended on the Monday after I had been constantly interrupted as soon as I was getting started, as Shaun was so pushed for time. (Or, in reality, afraid of the truth I could utter.)

Surely as he hadn't realistically heard hardly any of my evidence or properly questioned me on any of it, a logical person would assume he had come to his senses and he has realised that the vindictive, trumped-up charge against me was just ridiculous.

So he starts his brief summary. 'There was a hug and you kissed her on the head, as you have admitted.' 'Well, yes,' I said; that's because I'm totally honest.

Now there is all the stuff we can't prove. Linda allegedly kissing you at Cumnor Cricket Club, which she denies. The driving incident and who phoned who, etc. Attempted murder; trivial stuff compared to a hug, I'm sure you will all agree.

I should have said, 'You would have evidence of the kiss at Cumnor Cricket Club, but elected not to interview a single person among the 20 or more who would have seen it, and the incident is described in detail in my wife's handwritten letter too.' Anyway, back to the verdict hearing.

But what I did do is say to Shaun, 'I'm looking you right in the eyes,' as I described in detail every event as Linda intentionally ran me off the road in her car. I then insisted we both brought in our phone statements.

So apart from describing Linda trying to kill me in detail and insisting we both brought in our phone records and saying that my efforts to get these checked were **ongoing** with the police… That was it. I was sacked for a hug.

During the interim Linda Shaw and the other staff member would have been interviewed on the evening of 8th December. My statement was submitted on 9th December. One would surely expect Linda to be officially questioned after the reconvened meeting date in relation to the points I was to raise at this hearing: A hearing which was, in fact, the verdict hearing of 11th December that, later at tribunal, was falsely alleged to be a two-hour or so reconvened hearing. It could and should be argued that she, too, should have been suspended at this time.

After being informed of my dismissal, I was illegally presented with an envelope by Shaun Smith containing my **pre-written signed letter of dismissal** at this alleged reconvened hearing, as he was later to refer to it.

Also presented was an open envelope containing two further statements, one from Linda Shaw and one from another, both dated 8th December, presumably to read at my leisure after the verdict. This 'evidence' was **illegally withheld** from me until after my dismissal.

The envelope also contained the minutes from my interview on 7th December. Shaun Smith told me, when presenting me with the envelope, what the contents of the envelope were when I received it at the very end of the meeting, so was fully aware.

Presenting unseen statements to me after dismissal makes that dismissal illegal.

There were then more documents in the subsequent bundle at tribunal that I had never seen at all during the 'disciplinary process.' This was also illegal.

I was then informed of a mild pre-Christmas financial sweetener.

Shaun sacks me for 'harassment' then informs me that I will receive the rest of the month paid and my annual bonus. This shows his guilty conscience.

If he genuinely thought I was guilty of harassment…

I said to Shaun that he may feel technically correct but he was morally bankrupt. I also said I always gave 100% to this company and have not done a bad deed to anyone, at which point Gill Matthews, a decent person, in my opinion, visibly welled up.

She could see what was going on.

I said, 'I wish to leave the building with the dignity I deserve.' Security would usually be summoned at this point.

In a magnanimous gesture of goodwill I shook all their hands and wished them all well before making my exit.

What's more, in these unseen statements I will be falsely accused of assault and even heavy breathing phone calls just for good measure in Linda's latest, more extreme and desperate testimony and by the guy she was illegally colluding with during the disciplinary process, who wasn't even on shift when the hug occurred but had mentioned he heard of us dancing together at the leaving do. I wonder if he said a bit more about this that was perhaps conveniently not noted.

He turned out to be livid about my alleged assault and constant phone calls because **Linda was influencing a witness with her lies during the disciplinary process.**

There was also a new boob comment story that totally contradicted the first story.

Both stories were, of course, lies but I had already been sacked before being given a chance to read this.

My future lie detector test confirmed and, but for their shameless cover-ups, the police could have confirmed that Shaun had been all too willingly hoodwinked. Beyond all reasonable doubt Linda had been harassing my family. I even get TalkTalk to confirm they know who the harasser is but the police cover this up too.

The sweetener: I was to waste on a solicitor who misinformed me about tribunal representation, only to then find I had now relinquished the rights to a solicitor on my home insurance as I had dealt with the initial solicitor who said I was covered for them to represent me by said home insurance. All this solicitor did was change the word 'I' to 'my client', using my notes.

All I wanted at the time was the correct 'not guilty' verdict and all relevant apologies for what I had been through. I had more than earned double the bonus of most others with my output anyway.

In spite of the fact I have moved to day shift and haven't spoken to Linda in five months, and I have been on days for nearly six months, and have the best work record imaginable, there is no alternative to my dismissal.

PS Coincidence: here is a beauty. I have written/checked this chapter on the day Dominic Raab, deputy PM, has resigned following allegations of bullying/harassment due to various claims.

I find out today, because of this, that all claims relating to harassment must be submitted within 3 months less 1 day of the event by law.

That's four examples above, outside of this time and complete untruths anyway, that HR legal expert Les Muggeridge on appeal and then the judge at tribunal conveniently missed.

Most extraordinary of all is how Linda trying to kill me and frightening minors in my home is regarded as a comparative non- event to the reciprocated event I'm sacked for.

How bent Abbotts are.

If they wish to complain about my disclosures involving company practices during the book...

Had Shaun Smith listened and acted accordingly...

The truth must be told in fairness to my mental health and you didn't want to hear...

Had you done your jobs properly...

Chapter 20

Thames Valley Police

The first time I visit Wantage Police Station is during the Shaun Smith hearings to report 'Linda's driving incident' and nuisance phone calls to Annabel Sheppard, insisting the calls were traced.

Had the police done their job it could have saved me 15 years of hell and, after all, the information had been traced by TalkTalk at my insistence and was waiting for them.

The bent coppers at Wantage Police Station simply wanted to suppress this.

Eventually there was a so-called 'inquiry'. Many, many letters to the IPCC etc. followed thereafter.

Below are some highlights of the internal short investigation or 'fudge', as I call it.

Detective Chief Superintendent Nikki Ross; Head of Professional Standards dept., 'God help us', allegedly conducted an enquiry into my complaint via Inspector 1853 Ian Money.

Officers involved
27/11109 – C8768 Annabel Sheppard (SDO)
7112109 – PS 4354 Karen Hanks (Response Sgt, Now Response Inspector at Witney)
4/10111 – PC 5751 Kristy Ellison (Response PC, Now Response Sergeant at Newbury)

Having discussed the non-recording of your complaint with all officers involved, I can only conclude that there has been a very unfortunate miscommunication. It would appear that the officers involved, who are all fully aware of the correct process, would not deliberately or maliciously fail to record your complaint, and have no clear recollection of the conversations. All officers state that had they understood your wishes, then they would certainly have acted accordingly.

You wish the nuisance calls between July and October 2009 to be investigated now, and to be provided with details of the caller.

It is therefore unfortunate that as this 6 month time limit has expired, an investigation can no longer be undertaken.
Having spoken with you at great length this evening, I appreciate how upset you are, and having spoken to all parties, I feel there has been genuine misunderstanding as to your wishes. I am truly sorry that you feel a deliberate decision to fail to assist you has been made, and I would like to reassure you that this is certainly not the case. It is extremely unfortunate that so much time has passed since your initial complaint, which makes any subsequent investigation extremely difficult, and I am sorry that I could not resolve it to your satisfaction.

PS Taitt 2866 Wantage neighbourhood team.

I visited Wantage Police Station a few times with the objective of getting these calls traced.

This lot, although seeming attentive and helpful initially, were never going to help me. On one of my first visits, one officer, I believe, Kirsty Ellison phoned Les Muggeridge (HR Director) in my presence. I don't know what he said; perhaps he might be a friend of their commander down the lodge. Her attitude switched there and then. Thames Valley Police go on to do all his bidding as if he was their boss. Suddenly there is a 'can't do' attitude: Thames Valley Police always obeyed Les. Later, for example, with harassment warnings to me for posting my polygraph results: 'Absolutely no problem Sir; happy to help.'

The main reason I was displeased when PS Taitt spoke to me was that I was originally told by police that in order for my calls to be traced I had to contact my provider to confirm they had the details and then the police could proceed.

I contacted TalkTalk and they indeed confirmed they had the details of the person conducting the nuisance number withheld calls to my family, including minors, between July and October 2009 and my complaint was in November

2009. (Five months inside the six month limit) I remember saying 'The surname wouldn't be Shaw, would it?' They said I needed to go to the police to get an authorisation number or code, and they could then divulge the identity of the caller. There was only one suspect.

This was my first Eureka moment like doing the lie detector test later, as the facts were there to prove my innocence and someone else's guilt beyond all doubt.

I go to the police station again and Annabel Sheppard and another officer are not very helpful. I cannot even get my complaint logged to show it has happened, although I insist upon it. I stay put, say I'm not satisfied. 'I have done what you asked me to do and I want these calls traced,' I said.

Eventually I'm seen by Sgt Hanks, full of herself, condescending and thoroughly unhelpful.

She insists **that under procedure she is not allowed to trace the calls for fear I may indulge in reprisals** should I find the identity of the caller. She added that she would not be allowed to reveal the caller's identity, even if she traced the calls and dealt with the offender.

If the above were true then surely the police would never solve any crime. Many nowadays think they no longer do.

So basically, as Sgt Hanks has later confirmed to Chief Super intendant Nikki Ross, she knew procedure, she blatantly and intentionally lied to me.

I go home very unhappy and determined to complain.

That evening I watch a 'neighbours from hell' programme on TV and a woman with a nasty aggressive neighbour has her nuisance calls traced and is told that the culprit is the next door neighbour she suspected. Then that neighbour is charged.

In short, this programme verifies that Sgt Hanks is either totally unaware of the correct procedure she claims knowing about, and contrary to what Ian Money and PS Taitt say in the report, or she is a complete and utter liar. Either way she has lied to someone.

I've dealt with Wantage and Maidenhead police stations and the IPCC just so many times, as well as Dame Sara Thornton DBE QPM, on whose watch the culture of non- reporting i.e. fiddling the statistics and getting promoted became institutionalised more than ever.

Even during the grooming scandal a crying child with a bleeding crotch was sent packing by TVP.

From my experience there was a cover-up culture; they are all intentionally evasive. The whole of Thames Valley Police are institutionally corrupt and I volunteer to take as many polygraph tests as any police officer likes to prove what I'm saying is true. They are utterly unfit for purpose.

I've had 15 years of my life wasted because Sgt Hanks would not do her job when the evidence was waiting for her. I had done the groundwork. My life is wrecked while she gets continually promoted.

The conclusions detailed by PS Taitt are all lies and cover-up without exception. The evidence was there and Sgt Hanks corruptly refused to act.

I don't take pleasure in saying all this either and it should really hurt the police when the likes of myself lose all faith in them.

To say I was as sad as anyone when PC Andrew Harper was killed after being dragged for more than a mile is an understatement. I can relate to this tragedy personally.

When I was just a pup, as many who have known me a long time can testify, I was dragged along the road on my knees over a long distance by an ice cream van.

It's there with all my other psychological scars that sadly the police, Abbotts and the judiciary have added to.

I'm always on the side of justice and just wish the police and judiciary were also.

The boss of these useless coppers. It comes from the top
There are numerous articles on Sara Thornton, always idolised by David Cameron and Theresa May, the two MPs at the Abbott sites.

Here's one more from the 'you couldn't make it up' section: Here goes…

You could not, or would not dare make it up.
Many were horrified at hearing Sara Thornton of all people, the 'Grooming Scandal Police Chief', was appointed as the Anti-Slavery Tsar.

The crassness of the appointment simply beggars belief and underlines the uncaring, arrogant, out of touch nature of the establishment.

Yes, Sarah Thornton, who had to apologise for looking the other way whilst 373 children that we know of, mostly female, were groomed, often drugged and plied with alcohol before being sexually abused in Oxfordshire, was now Anti-Slavery Tsar.

She was Chief Constable of Thames Valley Police between 2007 and 2015 and in 2013, seven members of a grooming gang were convicted of rape, trafficking and prostitution involving girls as young as 11 between 2004 & 2012.

Thames Valley Police totally abandoned these victims, leaving them nowhere to go for help.

Sara Thornton later apologised and accepted responsibility, but her conscience did not feel the need to resign.

One might ask why she ever had the option to resign and the decision was not taken for her.

By the time the damning report then arrived in 2015, Sara was already head of the National Police Chief's Council (or NPCC).

With regard her appointment as Anti-Slavery Tsar, the mother of one of the victims said, 'It's unbelievable. Her force didn't protect my daughter. Now she has to protect hundreds of girls.'

Some critics believed that as Sara was very close to and admired by David Cameron and Theresa May her appointment may have been an old pal's act by the government, whose priority was simply to not 'rock the boat.'

This woman would basically get a new gig on £140,000 a year for continuing to be Sara Thornton and probably changing nothing.

She never experienced any consequences previously for dereliction of duty when all her officers, seemingly without exception, ignored the plight of so many, or when she suited and booted her sub-ordinate married officer lover at taxpayer expense, stealing from the taxpayer and abandoning her duty of perceived impartiality to all other subordinate officers in the process.

Speaking from experience: When I went to report what the police themselves, describe as attempted murder and my children being harassed, that after initial politeness Thames Valley Police were 100% supportive of the criminal in each case through wilful inaction. I'm very saddened but not at all surprised at TVP intentionally sweeping all the grooming events under the carpet. There was a deliberate culture of not reporting crime that came from the top. I did write to Sara on numerous occasions. What a waste of ink that was.

Meanwhile, of course, the likes of David Cameron are hoodwinked as the crime figures are coming down. Of course they are when TVP have a policy of not logging serious crime.

Then, four months after the Grooming Scandal Report:

Order of the British Empire
Civil Division

Central Chancery of the Orders of Knighthood
St. James's Palace, London SW1
8 June 2019

THE QUEEN has been graciously pleased, on the occasion of the Celebration of Her Majesty's birthday, to give orders for the following promotions in, and appointments to, the Most Excellent Order of the British Empire:

D.B.E.

To be Ordinary Dame Commander of the Civil Division of the said Most Excellent Order:

Sara Joanne THORNTON CBE QPM.

FFS.

She had also been awarded the Queen's Police Medal.

Many believe she would have been made head of the Metropolitan Police had Cameron had his way.

But she has now retired in 2022 after three years as the independent Anti-Slavery Commissioner. She was appointed to this post by Theresa May's Home Secretary, Sajid Javid.

I wonder how many pensions she now enjoys and how many jollies at taxpayer expense were involved in praising and saying goodbye to this Great Briton; an outstanding example to us all.

The next independent Anti-Slavery Commissioner after Sara left in April 2022 is appointed in December 2023, over a year and a half later. Sounds like a bit of a non-job with a massive salary if no one was needed for so long. What did Sara achieve in her 3 years there?

Her final establishment medal – well, final one of five so far – is ... wait for it The Police Long Service and Good Conduct Medal; that no doubt required another taxpayer-funded jolly to present.

So home-wrecking with a married immediate underling whom you no doubt favoured over others of the same rank, whom you suited and booted for a jolly at taxpayer expense, and of course being an invaluable asset to the Oxfordshire grooming gangs through sheer negligence in nearly 400 cases that we know of, merits a presentation for a lifetime of good conduct at taxpayer expense.

As far as I'm concerned, every day that she was employed after stealing from the taxpayer to take her married underling bit of stuff on a jolly at Windsor Castle was an act of theft from the taxpayer. She should have been sacked there and then.

Dame Sara in her article in *The Guardian* calling for more radical positive discrimination said, 'Unconscious bias still exists in policing and there were problems in promotion.' Would this be like having a married lover as an immediate underling, Sara, of the same rank as other underlings?

I can say from personal experience, she was useless.

It must be a real bonus in bent Britain not to have a conscience, like Dame Sara. It is incomprehensible to all fair-minded people that she would think, 'Yes, I'm the ideal person to be the Anti-Slavery Commissioner with my years of actively enabling the perpetrators.

Regardless of what scandal the likes of these are involved in, or how shit they have been, these people are impervious to it all and just want to climb the next rung of the ladder, and invariably do.

On a national level
Mind you, one of Jimmy Savile's best mates is our new monarch, and all kowtow to him, present company excluded.

There was a time when the whole nation was rightly disgusted at Sir Jimmy. Wind the clock forward and everyone is then gladly subservient to Jimmy Savile's subservient Brolly Wally, and all shouting, 'God Save the King.' What a nation of numpties. Just goes to show how easy to manipulate most people are.

Why, also, do this bunch think they can tell a deity what to do?

With regard to deities and things ecclesiastical, I'm on the side of Neil Todd who eventually took his own life after the likes of the current monarch and the then Archbishop of Canterbury clearly sided with his paedophile abuser, Bishop Peter Ball.

Building Jerusalem in England's green and pleasant land: that has to be one of the worst ideas ever.

Also – in which part of the national anthem does the nation feature?

Back to the police: home-wrecking with a married man can clearly get you some pretty exclusive titles.

Dame Sara's awards and the fact her morals let her accept them surely puts her in a very macabre, notorious, exclusive club alongside the likes of Sir Cyril Smith and Sir Jimmy Savile. You have to ask, which of these three was the greatest danger to children? It's all so shocking, repulsive and sickening.

The MPs for the Abbott constituencies that I wrote to during my issues with the police at Witney & Maidenhead were Prime Ministers David Cameron and Teresa May. The head of Thames Valley Police at this time was Sara Thornton. What hope did I have?

If there ever was an honest copper in Thames Valley Police I can say that, during all the time I engaged with them and referring to all those I encountered, I have never met one.

Perhaps justice could be served by putting me on Sara Thornton's pension and putting her on 10p a week that I ended up on after the calls were not traced.

As I was growing up a few of the lads, the real rough 'uns, used to shout 'Pigs' and 'Filth' as a police car went past. Much as I said nothing to them, I used to find this wrong and quite embarrassing.

Perhaps it was me who was wrong and needed educating.

Chapter 21

I Appeal to Les Muggeridge at the Abbott Gatehouse

Procedure, protocol, legality and illegal dismissal

Naturally after the debacle of Shaun Smith's clearly unfair dismissal verdict I obviously decide to appeal against my dismissal, so write a letter of appeal to Les Muggeridge, Head of Human Resources, as instructed on dismissal.

As there is an appeal time limit, to avoid any postal or courier issues following the DHL debacle I decide to take my letter of appeal to Abbotts in person and get a receipt for it.

This ought to be a straightforward transaction, one would logically think.

So, I arrive at the Abbott gatehouse with my letter and explain to the chap in security that I want to give my letter requesting an appeal to the HR department and I wish to get a receipt or 'with compliments' slip to confirm that I have requested an appeal hearing within the required time as per Abbott company/legal protocol.

I'm offered a seat in the gatehouse while the security chap phones HR.

I speak to one of the ladies in HR who says she will be down to collect my letter and give me a receipt.

She is interrupted and over-ruled by Les Muggeridge who is going to come down in person to collect my letter.

I'm not greeted by him with any politeness of formalities.

His only plan was to intimidate me. He was as obnoxious and intentionally as menacing as he possibly could be. Abbott's HR Director was a complete ogre performing far more menacingly in those few minutes than anything I had been falsely accused of.

I still insisted on a receipt for my letter; he continuously refused me this courtesy.

Eventually he said, 'Don't you worry, you'll get your hearing, but it will be with me and Pat Cole.'

This was clearly designed to intimidate me and let me know that my hearing would have a foregone conclusion as he knew Pat Cole hated me and knew I knew it, too.

He then stormed off in a deliberately nasty huff with my letter of appeal that he had not opened.

Had this legally astute HR Director focused on doing his job properly as he should have done…

He would have been polite, then after opening and reading my letter would have seen that Pat Cole was unsuitable to sit in judgement at my appeal as she was 'the accused' in my reasons for appeal.

A professional HR Director would not instantly decide who would sit at this hearing.

Les Muggeridge's intimidating tactics, and a clear showing of bias in a pre-planned appointment of someone with an agenda and motive to get rid of me, showed a lack of professionalism and ethics.

It also displayed an arrogant 'I can get away with anything' attitude 'due to my position and influence'. I was later to find out just how far this arrogance and influence stretched.

Pat Cole's involvement in any position, let alone in judgement, would clearly make my dismissal illegal.

He could have changed his mind in the interim between receipt of my letter and the appeal hearing, had he been a professional who cared about or even followed protocol or procedure.

It is also fair to say that at the subsequent hearing, when Les Muggeridge heard me accuse Pat Cole by name, he should have stopped and reconvened the hearing or declared my dismissal illegal there and then, as he and Abbott had clearly not followed procedure, just as they failed to do on my initial dismissal by Shaun Smith.

In truth he should have declared my dismissal illegal on the grounds he had clearly not followed procedure, just like Shaun Smith before him, and this was a serious breach.

There were so many other blatantly obvious facts to deem my dismissal illegal anyway.

It does seem odd that such a vile, nasty, intimidating former dot-knuckled, tattoo-handed thug can go on to be a director for a large multi-billion dollar pharmaceutical firm. It is also odd that one who clearly thought all coppers are bastards so much that he had it tattooed on his hands would go on to have the influence that he so clearly did in more than one Thames Valley Police Station.

Chapter 22

My Appeal Hearing with Pat and Les

I start this chapter by repeating a paragraph from the previous chapter.

It is also fair to say that at the subsequent hearing, when Les Muggeridge heard me accuse Pat Cole by name, he should have stopped and reconvened the hearing or declared my dismissal illegal there and then, as he and Abbott had clearly not followed procedure, just as they failed to do on my initial dismissal by Shaun Smith.

At my appeal hearing I did, of course, have the right to a witness present but was not allowed to speak to any member of staff to arrange this.

I only had options from the day shift on duty that day. I asked was a certain someone present on that shift as he always seemed a fair-minded, reasonable chap with a good sense of honesty.

A new cordiality

I was shocked somewhat that at this meeting the total 'rabid Rottweiler' I had seen such a short time before at the gatehouse was now a polite, and on the face of it quite an amenable and rational chap.

There was plenty of water on hand and the room was not boiling hot and the four of us – Pat Cole, Les Muggeridge, the witness & myself – entered into a meeting with an outwardly friendly atmosphere for the two- or three-hour duration.

I think even Rottweiler Les would have been embarrassed in front of Ms Cole and my witness if he was to let his animal instincts go on show again.

Bravado

At one stage in the meeting Les produced a couple of bulging folders, probably invoices, saying, 'There are 30 or so of these folders; we investigate everything and no stone is left unturned.'

A more honest gesture would have been to show us nothing on the table and to say,' You see that? Exactly. There is nothing there and, whatever your input, when we document this meeting there will be none of your evidence in it.'

Smoke mirrors and the velvet glove
At the very start of the meeting I insisted that we could do two recordings of the interview and keep one each, exactly as they do at police stations. I had brought with me two recorders. We could both then have an exact record of the meeting with no room for confusion or error about what was said.

This was very robustly refused by Les. In the fullness of time I could see why he would not want the meeting recorded. His cordiality was just for show and he was going to produce completely inaccurate minutes that were to totally exclude my input altogether.

Only Pat Cole's introductory statement was to eventually appear in the official minutes.

In less than a fortnight Les Muggeridge had turned from an uncontrolled savage to a polite, understanding, gentlemanly type but there was the avoidance of the fact that Linda Shaw was a known liar and fantasist and her letter was not factual. Just selected lines from Linda Shaw's and my letters were read at the meeting. My witness commented to me as we left that Linda Shaw was a known troublemaker with plenty history. Yep; that's another one.

Crucial points from the appeal meeting with Pat & Les
The problem with liars – the great own goal and smoking gun left by Les Muggeridge.
Most of the meeting involved the pre-prepared pages I took in to read out and twice as much again, apart from this, that I explained in my lengthy evidence.

I was happy for Pat, Les & my witness to all have a copy of what I was to read. Les, of course, had the pen and timed and dated that which I presented at the meeting in his own handwriting.

Les's timed, dated and much annotated copy was what Abbott's solicitor produced in the bundle proving Abbott's minutes of the meeting were deliberately false, one-sided, heavily edited, weighted and intentionally incomplete, eradicating virtually all that I said.

This verbal and written evidence would have amounted to at least 20 or so pages of input by myself alone. The meeting took a few hours.

One-trick ponies

One question Pat Cole was to ask me at the meeting was, 'Why after the letter Linda Shaw sent you would you even touch her with a barge pole?'

The fact that I had joined days and hadn't spoken to her in five months does suggest evasive action on my part, most logical people would have thought.

The main theme for her was trying to link the hug to the letter.

But there is the fact, as I pointed out, that much as I don't accept what is written in 'her letter' that arrived, the letter was just before my wedding, not just before the hug, as I made clear by my 'whole' reply. There was a time lapse of well over a year between the letter and my hug.

Was she saying that when people had a disagreement of any sort that they should remain sworn enemies forever?

Living in that actual moment, it was our last shift working together and Linda had recently confided in me her redundancy amount; an act of misconduct in Abbott's eyes. So it was fair for me to assume that in the moment we were on good friend terms. Throw in the fact that she publicly kissed me a month after the hug and someone thought he saw her kiss me in the gown lock, and she did not complain at the time, and 'her' letter was over a year earlier, and Pat & Les's argument is totally dead in the water.

I remember saying that the letter and the hug were over a year apart, and that things change, and quoted the example of Gerry Adams and Ian Paisley now sitting together, mentioning my witness and myself both had Northern Ireland connections. This was, of course, one of many things I said that were conveniently not in the minutes.

I guess a few of my values have cost me dear. Turning the other cheek and not reacting to rumours, for one, as I said. That is exactly what Les Muggeridge said you should do to rumours – ignore them. Ironically, they both reacted to Linda's rumours by approving my dismissal.

The hug and the letter were their agendas but I did address all the nastiness, vindictiveness and targeting that no doubt led to my desired dismissal, contrary to what the fudged, woefully incomplete minutes suggest.

Pat's concluding letter

Naturally my dismissal is upheld by Pat Cole, one who is both judge and jury as well as the accused in the case.

Pat Cole's letter does not address my reasons for appeal or provide meeting minutes to me.

Postscript

As well as Pat Cole being the accused and illegally judging herself...

She also acted illegally in not addressing my reasons for appeal in her letter upholding my dismissal.

The judge was to go on to excuse her, saying I did not mention my reasons for appeal.

Oh yes I did. It was just not minuted by Abbotts.

My reasons were submitted and are even timed and dated in Les Muggeridge's own hand, so there can be no legitimate confusion.

Page 146 of the bundle is timed and dated in Les Muggeridge's own handwriting.

Pages 150-151: Pat Cole is mentioned in full by name twice on page 150 and again on page 151 but is referred to many times. Pat and Les were duty bound to stop the interview right there and then.

'No stone is ever left unturned. We are always thorough.' So says Les. Amazing he didn't dismiss himself for his performance in the gatehouse then, or his bent minutes.

So why, then, when I detail in my letter to HR Director Amanda White on 10 June 2010 the most horrific acts of violence, including sexual penetration and intimidation, acts which were ongoing for years, that which Pat Cole calls 'the peripheral stuff,' was there no investigation at all?

Why were Les, Pat and Shaun not sacked for gross misconduct regarding my dismissal? I officially complained more than once.

Pat Cole is also so low in her morals that she refers to my hug as 'inappropriate touching' to Amanda. It was called 'assault' more than once, including by their solicitor, and a 'neck grab from behind' too. Just how low can these people sink?

Yet again, as in the previous chapter regarding racism and how what I do is treated so harshly and magnified, genuine penetrative sex, violence and grooming on site is peripheral stuff,; whilst only my hug among hundreds or thousands similar that week gets exaggerated out of all proportion.

A simple public brief act of kindness becomes a neck grab, inappropriate touching and assault to these vile fantasists or, should I say, blatant liars.

But don't worry, it's only me on the receiving end of all this vile filth.

Chapter 23

The Depression Really Sets In

The attack on everything

It seems so commonplace in every instance of character assassination, especially through lies, that the person's life and family life are ruined totally.

It is a form of post- traumatic stress disorder as far as I'm concerned.

The whole world you knew, you suddenly feel you need to exclude yourself from.

I went from working 72 hours many weeks, or six of every eight nights, to having no desire to get out of bed. Life seemed pointless.

It was not just my job and livelihood, healthcare and future pensions that Abbott targeted. The very accusation of harassment targeted my marriage, my family, my home, my good name, my dignity, my health and my sanity. In short, everything! I had just put in so much over the last few years, working towards our wedding, yet a few nasty pieces of filth are allowed to ruin everything.

There was the added pressure on our marriage financially, too, on top of all this.

We were newly married at the time, and around £8,000 of potential honeymoon savings after the wedding went up in smoke as I was put on 10p a week after the initial weeks of approximately £60 at the DHSS. This was because I was always honest and declared my savings. That would have pleased Linda's vindictive streak. I had a round trip of 35 miles to Witney each fortnight to sign for my 20p.

Let alone was I targeted just after our wedding, we never did get to go on the honeymoon we were saving for either. Thanks, Abbott.

An overnight change

Locally I was often out, either with the pool team, when available, or at weekends. Like with working 48-72 hours a week, I went from having a regular social life locally to suddenly completely disappearing. This was to more or less continue until this day.

Meeting former friends after you suddenly disappear completely is a real issue, too.

Confidence, trust, my outlook on life – everything was gone.

I thought it was best to stay clear of socialising completely if possible. Soon enough I would not be able to afford it anyway.

I didn't like liars and kiss-asses and didn't want to meet any, and knew this was likely.

You are also hit by the untruths you have read and suffer insecurity, wondering how stigmatised you could be by someone you may encounter. This person or that may have heard a false rumour about you. You also wonder what nastiness was unleashed after my dismissal, now that the liar finds herself vindicated. Her lies even grew outrageously during the disciplinary process.

She was now officially a victim, and I'm sure everyone else would think after my dismissal, 'There's no smoke without fire.'

Shaun and Pat have got away with bullying and ruining my character to cover their wrongdoing, thanks to a bent, judge yourself, closed-shop dismissal.

Even though my social life stopped, even going out shopping, you feared what someone you meet might have heard about you. It was all-encompassing.

Mental health

I was soon getting mental health counselling through Talking Space and a number of Oxfordshire NHS mental health departments.

My sessions were due to last an hour. I always went beyond my time slot as always, never avoiding a question, and feeling I had barely got started.

In my younger days I suppose with the horrific ice cream van incident I detail elsewhere and a 'spare the rod spoil the child' upbringing, I used to have the most terrible visible panic attacks that could only be likened to Dan Biggar's pre-spot kick routine in Rugby, only 20 times worse. Rolling eyes, the lot – you name it, I had it.

These were mostly gone but came back with interest and a vengeance after my dismissal.

I had now decided to take the case to tribunal even though I was in a really dark place.

Every bit of correspondence from a solicitor or Abbotts can send you right back into the dark. I suppose even worse is waiting for correspondence, and what your mind can put you through. It was like waiting for exam results all over again.

Correspondence may then remain unopened for days while you imagine the worst.

Revisiting paperwork from tribunal and seeing yet another Linda lie sends you right into the depths. You can sometimes forget just how bad these depths are. Then you revisit them.

Getting nowhere and then picking yourself up only to get nowhere again, and so on.

I have no doubt that knowing I have been wronged and wanting to put it right gets me back on the horse time after time, no matter how often I'm knocked off. That 'don't let the bastards win' attitude.

Lots of long walks alone and appreciating nature was my positive therapy. Even then I would return home with ten new issues I had thought of and had to write down.

I was never going to take mind-altering prescribed drugs, although they were often suggested to me.

Media

I was now hit harder by watching the news and stories of corruption and dishonesty.

Stories involving a victim who has been wronged, injustice and bullying attracted my attention most and did me no good at all.

Injustice, bullying and unfairness were definitely my triggers.

They still are.

Chapter 24

Les Lies

Fired up by Nicky Albert's misreporting and still with gusto for putting the boot in:

06 April 2010 – Les Muggeridge writes to Mr O Morton at Jobcentre Plus, Southampton, falsely claiming that Mr Collins hugged and kissed the employee in the gown lock due to it being his birthday, and found this to be acceptable behaviour.

This is simply a cynical misrepresentation of the facts.

Les Muggeridge then states in his letter to Jobcentre Plus in Southampton that I needed to be dismissed to protect other members of staff.

This vile, evil thug clearly has no scruples at all.

After what I experienced at the gatehouse I know who Abbotts staff needed protecting from. I looked pure evil in the eyes that day; it was quite an experience.

Yet the pugilists in the pregnant woman fight and the steel ruler wielding, poison texter and his victim all still worked together.

Abbott will lie to protect these people and lie again to destroy me. They clearly have no sense of shame, proportion or morality.

I had left the night shift six months earlier and not spoken to Linda in five months at the time of this trumped-up complaint. I was absolutely no danger to anyone, and never had been.

It would be evident to any rational person that I had joined day shift to avoid working full-time with Linda.

Ironically if there are people that staff need protecting from it is the likes of ogre Les and Linda Shaw with her driving stunts that Abbott ignore, or from her lies, which Abbott embrace, or from Pat Cole's irrational insecure vindictiveness.

Chapter 25

The Tribunal in Brief

Before the tribunal I suggest to the judge that Linda Shaw needs to attend as a witness. How can you have a trial when it is one person's word against another, if Abbotts reason for dismissal were remotely believable, but the person whose clear self-contradictions and lies caused all this trouble is not going to be cross-examined? This was very convenient for Abbott and a slap in the face for any chance of justice.

This has to be questioned as an abuse of authority and lead to questions regarding influence and the judge's impartiality. Linda is beyond doubt Abbott's key witness.

I was then informed that she no longer works at the company. She gave up a 30K redundancy to remain, so clearly didn't intend leaving so abruptly.

Did she get special redundancy payment for getting me and her manager and whoever else sacked?

Was she told there would be a tribunal and that she may have to testify? She would know her lies were indefensible and that she wrote her husband's letter, etc.

Did she fall on her own sword? Did the company then use her own lies to finally get rid of her, too? Was it getting too hot in the kitchen?

So she has left Abbotts and possibly lost her £30K. Perhaps she got even more. The judge could, and surely would, call her as a witness if the real reason for my dismissal was Linda Shaw's testimony against me.

This was nearly as bent as Pat Cole judging herself at my appeal hearing.

Surely Linda's attendance was an absolute must and I should have been allowed to cross examine her evidence, even via a third party, but certainly at the tribunal.

The judge's two sidekicks should certainly have had to ask her questions about the blatant discrepancies in her evidence and in her submitted documents.

There were clearly documents in Linda's evidence not by the suggested author, and proof that this was the case, too. One was even in someone else's handwriting. Sadly; the judge and his sidekicks are not professional enough to acknowledge all this.

My argument was that I was dismissed for whistleblowing. It was Abbott's argument that I was dismissed for conduct towards Ms Shaw, so Abbotts should have wanted her there as much as me. Or should I say if they were honest in their convictions, they would have wanted her there as much as me, not laid her off with whatever hush money she in all probability received.

Why did she leave so soon and so conveniently from Abbott's point of view? Did she leave empty-handed?

She was one of the two key witnesses. Her absence, after my request for her attendance, underlines what a premeditated sham the tribunal was.

At my so-called 'tribunal' I had to represent myself against a billion-dollar multinational and their legal team also.

I had been virtually bedridden with depression between dismissal and the tribunal and was not allowed to even see a tribunal in action beforehand, although I specifically asked the judge for permission. Not seeing a tribunal beforehand meant that I all but wasted the first day of the two allocated as I did not know how to cross-examine Shaun Smith to the judge's approval.

On day 1 I did not get to cross-examine Shaun Smith at all as my style of delivery did not suit the judge. Perhaps I may have asked questions to his satisfaction had I been allowed by him to attend another tribunal beforehand. I should have been afforded this courtesy.

What was also extremely unfair and belittling was the judge's insistence that I watched the pen he was holding at all times whilst speaking, on the instructions that each time he released it I was to stop speaking. This was a humiliating, unnecessary distraction that made a very difficult job nearly impossible. I'd call it an arrogant abuse of authority. I had no choice but to comply with him.

Or perhaps, as Abbotts had legal representation and we were supposed to have been aiming at justice, I might have been afforded representation, too. Is justice not represented and depicted by scales at the Old Bailey? My tribunal was not exactly balanced. In fact it was about as balanced as my initial disciplinary hearing at Abbotts. Hence justice did not occur as again I was not given free rein to promote my case.

Understandably I did not sleep the night before the first day at tribunal. I had to then write afresh all the questions for Pat Cole after day one in preparation for day two, to be judge compliant, having been awake for nearly 48 hours and having the stress of the tribunal thrown in.

But I did write some good questions, albeit holding my eyelids open that evening. On day 2 two I cross-examined Pat well and delivered my statement well, albeit breaking down when mentioning the effect on my family. This was totally spontaneous and genuine and I carried on reading the last few pages in tears.

Protected characteristic

I was, of course, prevented from mentioning the all too obvious racial discrimination from Abbotts in my treatment compared to others, on legal 'protected characteristic' grounds that prevented me from telling the whole truth I promised to tell under oath.

I addressed the differences in my treatment compared to others without mentioning race. This should have sufficed, were the tribunal fair and impartial.

I showed the judge, however, that I understood what diversity training is supposed to engender in employees. I said the line, 'I believe that everyone should be treated equally regardless of their differences, not differently because of them.'

The judge congratulated me, saying he could not put it better himself and that I clearly fully understood what diversity training entailed. I did not get this from Abbott's 'cry wolf' culture engendering so-called, diversity training. This statement came from my own morals and sense of fair play.

It is a shame that as the judge clearly understood equality and inclusivity he denied me justice when I was clearly targeted by vindictive Abbott directors and treated infinitely more harshly than others.

The judge was also man enough to congratulate my honesty throughout at the end of the tribunal.

I did not duck a single question, and even showed great restraint when being accused of assault by Solicitor Wilcox over a kind hug. The judge reprimanded Wilcox over that.

At the end of the two days I was surprised that there was no verdict. Time was amongst the factors stated for this.

If we hadn't spent most of the two days on ridiculously long and unnecessary breaks, and finished so early, there would have been time for summaries and a verdict.

Did the judge not want to look in my eyes and deliver a clearly corrupt verdict to me, having publicly congratulated me on my honesty and understanding of diversity training? It would, in time, be easier for him to deliver this irrefutable injustice the cowardly way – by post.

So, instead of a verdict there and then, Solicitor Wilcox and myself were instead sent away to write our summaries and then when we had finished I was to send my summary to Mr Wilcox, who was to send both our summaries together to the judge.

At the end of the tribunal Solicitor Wilcox copied a couple of example cases to me to show the sort of thing I might look at.

The idea here, with these summaries, is to quote other cases that I have no access to and to quote the legal ramifications thereof. It seemed unfair that this was expected from a lay person. The scales of justice seemed more than a little lopsided.

Was I expected to trawl through the entire archives of British legal history, that I have no access to anyway?

Was I then expected to deliver the selected highlights in perfect legal speak?

Is justice not supposed to be seen to be done? In reality it is a game weighted against anyone outside the clique.

In my summary I explained this and said that my summary would deal with facts, deal with right and wrong and justice in plain, easy to understand English, as that is how I conduct my life.

I was going to deal with the relevant case, this case.

I will not make this chapter too much longer as the greater detail from the tribunal is quite abundantly detailed in other areas of this book.

What's the point of taking the oath and telling the truth when the judiciary are on the side of those who don't, and lets them do so with impunity?

Abbotts went to the tribunal knowing they would be dishonest. They must have known they could. Their solicitor even taunted me pre-trial, saying I could not win. Was he privy to the result beforehand? I actually went to the tribunal expecting fairness. What an idiot I was. There again, it was a new environment to me. It's tough enough taking on a billion-dollar company and their representatives in an unfamiliar environment. I did not expect to have to take on the judiciary as well. I expected them to want justice.

I believed that British justice was in most cases fair. There are well-known exceptions, especially to those of an Irish background, but then we hear lessons will be learned. I now see British justice for what it is.

Les Muggeridge had already, before tribunal, confirmed beyond all doubt that his meeting minutes were corrupt by timing and dating my representations that he subsequently excluded from the meeting minutes, along with much else in his own handwriting.

I'm not speculating Abbott's meeting minutes were bent. It's an indisputable fact that is in black and white and proven on page 146 in the bundle onwards.

Postscript

I was accompanied at tribunal by my wife, who had handwritten her account of Linda's public kiss and other details to Shaun Smith during the disciplinary process, and this was in the bundle.

I mentioned Shaun ignoring my wife's statement at tribunal.

This vital handwritten testimony, which she could have been asked about, had no bearing in the judge's summary.

This same highly intelligent judge calls Pat Cole a creditable witness; this the woman who ignored this handwritten, signed and dated proof but who also insisted in the poison text issue detailed elsewhere, that the identity of the poison texter was not the person whose phone the text came from, but someone who didn't work at Abbotts.

I insist that this judge was far too intelligent to be so gullible as to get these two issues so wrong.

Postscript 2

A key line in the bundle:

Bundle page 52

Was it ethically correct, I ask, on bundle page 52 for Pat Cole to be the one to decide the outcome of the appeal hearing when her conduct is mentioned in the evidence?

On pages 151 & 152 I mention Pat Cole three times in my evidence

Chapter 26

I Receive the Judge's Summary

There is the clear elephant in the room that Linda's complaint is not less than three months less one day after what was a total non-event, and that a learned judge and his two learned sidekicks all conspired to miss this, along with crucial bundle dates that underline that I did make the necessary references to my reasons for appeal.

(Apologies as this chapter inevitably involves some repetition from before.)
Each and every inexplicable error in the judge's summary completely favours ADC.

After the carefully concluded one-sided nonsense that was Judge Barrowclough's summary I reply, correcting him on so many issues.

At one stage the judge throws in this (3.12):

Clear boundaries of behaviour which Claimant had repeatedly breached.

Where does this repeatedly breached nonsense come from? I hugged her on our last day together and kissed her on top of the head, which was later reciprocated. This was the same as everyone else did at the time. I then left and joined days, and there was nothing before or since.

Grow up and get a life. This is simply victimisation aimed at me, whilst he wilfully ignores the relevant serious issues that were intentionally ignored by Abbott which underline the clear victimisation and targeting I suffered.

Linda did kiss me at the leaving do, in full view of many witnesses. If he is prepared to accept my testimony that I kissed Linda on the head in Tesco's, where there were no witnesses, why will he not accept this? My wife corroborates this. Her testimony is ignored and **ALL** other potential witnesses were not asked. Why?

Anyone reading this drivel would certainly logically suspect that this is the work of a freemason protecting his mates. I'm not saying this is the case as I have no proof. But it certainly looks like a duck, walks like a duck and quacks like a duck, with no impartiality in clear sight.

My polygraph results eventually correct this ridiculous, totally biased inept judgement.

Let's not forget: for some reason not told to me the venue was switched from Bristol to Reading, near Maidenhead, where the police can't act impartially either. Is there perhaps a common influence behind this? This tribunal case also got to be heard alarmingly quickly. Was this to give me as little time to prepare as possible?

Linda's identical issue at Abingdon is also sidestepped and she was not there to answer questions, although she is vital to Abbott's false claim of fair dismissal. Why? I requested that Linda, this vital witness, should be present, and rightly so.

Why did the Health and Safety meeting notes just prior to my dismissal disappear and why didn't the judge question this?

I show in words and tabular form that Pat and Shaun are committing gross misconduct in wilfully disobeying strict company Health and Safety guidelines. That is in the bundle, too.

So I lost my job, my reputation and future hope destroyed, and our wedding memories are wrecked by a liar and unfair management. Well done, Judge Barrowclough! Not !

My dismissal was contrived, desired and opportunistic but was in no way merited.

Pat Cole

I clearly state in my summary appeal to the judge:

Was it ethically correct practice for Pat Cole to be the one to decide the outcome of the appeal hearing, when her conduct is mentioned in the evidence?

The judge forgives Pat Cole for not addressing my reasons for appeal, on account of me allegedly not raising them at appeal. This is a blatant lie.

It's a fact my reasons were presented and are timed and dated in Les Muggeridge's handwriting, and are clearly present in the bundle, just corruptly excluded from Abbotts' minutes.

He even describes Pat as a creditable witness, such is his bias. She was obviously lying and tying herself in knots, especially describing the incident of genuine violence involving the pregnant woman. She said that as they were in the car they could only use one hand, then physically showed them using two but only playfully moving their hands whilst keeping their arms still, like kids playing pat-a-cake. Only in this case it was Pat's-a-fake.

In my statement section 60 which was read out, 'I believe there was never the will to investigate my evidence as I believe they wanted me out the door because I had the courage of my convictions and complained about a Health and Safety issue.' This was clearly the truth.

In section 90 I have no doubt I was removed from my post by the company for my Health and Safety concerns as: (91) The minutes of the Health and Safety meeting conveniently disappeared and (92) when I pointed out the real and ongoing sexual harassment involving Linda Shaw they weren't interested in investigating it and didn't care.

My timed and dated representations bundle page 146 onwards show Abbott making Judge Barrowclough look incompetent.

I did make all relevant representations and Pat Cole's failure to respond to these makes my dismissal illegal, not forgivable.

The fact that Pat Cole is clearly mentioned by name in these representations and is then sitting in judgement on herself definitely renders my dismissal illegal.

Is this why the judge and Abbotts pretend these representations are not there? Even after I point it out to him?

Why did Pat and the HR Director fail to stop the hearing immediately on her mention?

This is the question a decent, honest and competent judge would surely have pondered.

The fact he and his sidekicks did not even address this strongly suggests, at the very least, a lack of professionalism, perhaps even downright incompetence.

There is also the three months less one day rule for a complaint of this type (which I find out years later). Linda's complaint was six months after the event and five months after her publicly kissing me. During the whole 3 months less one day before her complaint I never spoke to her or even worked with her.

I moved shifts to get away from her. She, on the other hand, gave up a £30k redundancy and new job in the knowledge, or so she thought, so that she would work full-time with me.

At the tribunal I also questioned Pat on her describing Linda as 'dramatic' in her interview with previous HR Director Amanda White after I complained about Pat's gross misconduct to her.

Pat's mantra at tribunal and my appeal hearing was to repeat herself. There was a hug and a letter to falsely create the impression at tribunal that the letter and the goodbye hug were related consecutive events, when they were in fact 15 months apart

The letter was brief, made false assertions which I corrected in reply, and Linda didn't even write it.

The letter was simply a spiteful attempt by Linda, using a friend, to cause trouble just before my wedding.

The legal experts, with all documents dated before them, in date order sidestep this 15-month time lapse. What utter bias! I find it hard to believe they could be this incompetent. Missing clear important dates on documents is a recurring theme, with page 146 being an obvious example.

The goodbye hug came on our last shift together, and after she confided her redundancy amount to me against company rules, so she was on good terms with me.

Linda was prepared to forsake this and the job she got in a care home to work on the new merged night shift, actually with me. I was going to join day shift so hugged her on our final day together, just like so many others hugged and kissed that week.

When I told her I was joining days I knew it was too late for her to change. These were the circumstances of the hug at the time. Linda should have been there and questioned as to why she then asked for a last minute redundancy only after learning I was joining days. The letter was 15 months earlier and came at the time she got a wedding invite.

A wise judge might conclude that her complaint about me at a time I no longer had anything to do with her was, at best, perhaps a tad unsound.

A wise judge might also consider that this six month delayed, ridiculous overreaction by Abbott to an event all staff were guilty of at the time certainly coincided with a Health and Safety complaint I had made, the week before, which to management's utter annoyance and embarrassment vindicated me on day 1.

Shaun Smith
There is a lot I need to question the judge on here.

The judge chooses to believe Shaun Smith's blatant lie about a reconvened hearing.

So where are the minutes of this reconvened hearing?

I just turned up to a verdict hearing and was dismissed before the meeting was due to start in the only document Abbott officially timed, signed and dated as the judge himself pointed out at tribunal (excluding Les's handwriting page 146, which the judge refused to ever see).

Why am I handed vital documents I have not seen that underline Linda's self-contradictions only after dismissal?

This is again totally illegal yet the legal experts, who cost the taxpayer a fortune, sidestep this.

Who turns up at a reconvened hearing with a signed, dated letter of dismissal? Shaun Smith does!

Who gives new, unseen, interview notes to an employee to read after dismissal? Shaun Smith does!

Who sacks an employee for gross misconduct then awards them nearly an extra month's pay and end-of-year bonus?

Shaun Smith does.

Other statements I should have been presented with at that time I did not even receive after dismissal.

I don't see them until the tribunal bundle. Again this is totally unsatisfactory, as are the judge's conclusions in their entirety.

Linda Shaw

The judge believing Linda's alleged statements fills me with incredulity also.

For the judge to be correct here, we must significantly not just change the law of the land but laws of physics, too.

Linda clearly states that no matter which way she went home, she would find me waiting in the various places every morning. The gateway outside work, and at lay-bys in Curbridge and Bampton. There is no motive or account of what I was ever supposed to have done when she allegedly arrived either.

Can Judge Barrowclough explain how my car and I can be in three or four places at once and invisible to between 12 and 60 witnesses, depending on location?

Can we also have clarity on Linda's four different routes home, as there was really only one obvious route? Any diversions on these country roads would have been in the tens of miles. How the hell would I guess she would be on such crazy routes home and then be waiting?

It seems strange that, at a time when she has just lost her house through her husband's gambling, the issue at the forefront of her mind is an ex-colleague who now works on days and has not spoken to her for five months and clearly wants nothing more to do with her.

A logical person might argue the complaint was revenge for my perceived betrayal, after the redundancy payment she had given up. Did she have it in her mind that we were destined to be together? Was this, to quote Les Muggeridge, 'A woman scorned?'

Failing to spot Linda's dodgy paperwork

It's inexplicable that the judge believes Linda's letter and the alleged letter from Richard (bundle pages 63 & 66). It's very amateurish for a judge and his two assistants to do this.

These two letters are definitely written by the same person. Why does Richard send a formal letter to 'Nicky', not 'Dear Mrs Albert', and end it with 'Regards, Richard', just like Linda's letter. Both letters also contain 15-line sentences. Both letters contain the same sort of spelling mistakes (e.g. good by and a long) and have identical punctuation mistakes. Neither letter is signed or dated: the list goes on. If Dicky is that familiar with Nicky, this raises ethical questions also.

I also subsequently met Dicky, who knew nothing about any letter he was supposed to have written.

These two letters represent more evidence that the judge and his two learned sidekicks who were expertly pawing through the bundle totally missed. How conveniently amateurish.

All this is still in the bundle to this day!

The judge dismisses my wife's letter to Abbott's which states that Linda kissed me at the leaving function in July 09. This letter is handwritten, signed and dated. My wife was at the tribunal in person also, so could have been questioned, rather than cowardly being as good as called a liar behind her back in a pathetic one-sided summary.

Well, Judge Barrowclough. My wife, my polygraph test and myself are a lot more honest than your summary, and the evil, dishonest ones from Abbott you so incomprehensibly decided to believe and side with.

Shame on you!

Chapter 27

The Alleged Letter from Richard

Apologies to the reader.

I am repeating some information here, too, but will now go into slightly more depth about Linda's fake letters which, along with her lies that I prove by polygraph, underline the false accusations against me and her unreliability as a witness still further.

I had helped Richard when looking for a job at Autotype, then later Linda cost me mine.

Linda used to moan also about Richard hiding final demand letters from her, and her giving him pocket money, so they did not have a trusting relationship.

One night as my wife and I were talking, she had one of those 'Eureka' moments. 'Richard's letter, was it signed?' 'I need to look at this,' she said. So the ball started rolling.

Let's now compare Linda's letter, bundle page 63 with 'Richard's letter', bundle page 66. Let us also bear in mind Linda, as in so many other deceptions, has got form. Remember Linda's letter of March 08 that subsequently became another colleague's letter of March 08. She has form in faking authors.

In the case of Richard and Linda's letter, the similarities include:-

Both letters are not dated.

Both letters are not signed.

Both letters contain 15-line A4 page sentences.

Both letters use capital letters inappropriately.

Both letters make the same standard sort of spelling mistake. 'Richard's letter' spells 'along' as 'a long'. Linda's letter spells 'goodbye' as' good by', and again I stress it's inconceivable that two separate people could both use such long, incredibly out of proportion sentences.

Both letters have the same layout. Both finish with 'Regards' not 'Yours sincerely'.

Both letters are addressed to Nicky. Surely Richard was not on such friendly terms that he would be this familiar, and if he was, that would be a cause for great concern also. You would surely expect Richard, who only worked very briefly at Abbotts in Witney, to write to Ms Albert.

Did Ms Albert previously work in Abingdon? I don't know, but do know that like Linda, Richard was renowned for complaining about his fellow staff a lot.

'Richard's letter' is marked 'Not to be shown to Mr Collins.' Why not? My wife's handwritten letter is not confidential and is signed, too. I don't get to see 'Richard's letter' until the bundle in another act of illegality by Abbotts.

The first I knew of 'Richard's alleged letter', was seeing it just before tribunal.

It should have been shown to me during the disciplinary process with the address blanked. There again, there were so many other documents I should have seen that were either withheld, lost or destroyed.

Abbotts' solicitor then sends me Linda's new address after they lost their house due to extravagance and Richard's gambling debts. I tell him off for this and point it out to the judge.

This letter suggests that if Linda has any faults it is that she is too kind and friendly to those who have no friends. Of course, it states Linda has not seen this letter and does not want to get anyone into trouble.

Who indeed wrote this letter that Richard was subsequently completely unaware of?

Could Ms Albert kindly confirm how familiar she was with Ricky, or should I say Richard?

When questioned face to face by myself, with my son witnessing this, it turned out that even Richard had not seen 'Richard's letter.'

I have absolutely no doubt that if we got an expert to analyse these two letters the conclusion would be that the same person wrote both. What a shame the judge's sidekicks at tribunal were so useless.

The question must be asked, did certain people at Abbott's enthusiasm to get rid of me blind them to logic and common sense? There are just too many paperwork errors. I was always taught at Abbott's that we make paperwork first, then product. If the paperwork is defective so is the product.

How right that proved to be: or at least should have proved to be in this case.

But there was not Linda's only dodgy paperwork that was questionable. Linda clearly has a real problem with being truthful, ever. Linda got somebody else to write her letter to me from 15 months earlier and eventually admitted this.

Then in another 'about turn' in her evidence to get me dismissed she says, 'He frightened me and that's when I decided to write my letter.'

She clearly has two different types of handwriting as proven in her eventual reply to my wedding invite, weeks after her so-called letter.

This is all from the woman who thinks I can be lying in wait in various different locations whilst I'm still at work.

She has to get her friend to write a letter for her that is allegedly from her. Wind the clock forward 18 months and this poor soul who couldn't write her own letter is now writing 'invented' letters on behalf of someone else. She clearly has honesty issues.

Also with regards telling the truth, on overtime I was just about the only member of staff that did not call her 'long legs'. Her friend who wrote her letter mocked her breasts with a gesture and said, 'Who is this?' 'Long legs.' Linda was somewhat short and broad and walked with a waddle, hence the long legs comment.

Linda chooses to invent a 'breast comment' lie about probably the only person that worked with her regularly that never mocked her physique.

Strange, too, that this happily married woman does not report our Nigerian friend who intimidated the driver of the car where the other two had fisticuffs, who in the gownlock had his hand down Linda's back, saying to his audience, 'This is my girlfriend, long legs, sexy legs, sexy face innit.' He also had his hand inside her top walking down the corridor. One must ask how close was the relationship this happily married woman had here to allow this.

To clarify, at a later date my son and I met Richard at the local recycling plant. I told my son, to his face, who he was and that he wasn't worth an introduction. 'People seen you do stuff,' he said. 'Like what?' I said. 'And what about all the crap in your letter?' His reply was, 'What letter?'

'What letter?' indeed!

For all this bloke's tendency for BS and trouble stirring, he was genuinely unaware of any letter. This was not an act.

Me thinks the bundle needs revisiting ... and on so many counts.

A related issue

I used to work bloody hard for Abbotts and would never moan but then, come the meetings when questions were invited, I had the courage to ask. There was another there, one of the fuck buddies, who never stopped moaning all day long.

The only time he shut up was at company meetings. As soon as we got up to leave, the switch was on again on the way out.

Regarding the above, who would not shut up, and in Linda's case, just like getting others to write a letter for her or beyond all reasonable doubt, inventing one from Richard, then with all her fantasies and rumours, there is this constant need for peer approval. Then scrub beneath the surface veneer and they are completely vacuous. Linda's lies don't hold up to scrutiny and the only time this chap stops moaning is when he should speak.

Unlike the cases above I challenge authority on my own and with good evidence, and if you perhaps look, for example, at my actions regarding the riverboat incident (trust me, I could cite many other examples) I act alone and do the right thing.

The thought never occurs to turn around to others and say, 'Are you with me?' If I believe and know it is right I will face my fears and go ahead with it. I won't try and gather a committee for approval. I can't intentionally lie about someone either.

Chapter 28

A Case of Relevance for the Judge's Perusal

I will now detail events involving an actual boob comment at work and much worse besides.

This is relevant to my case as it shows difference in treatment according to influence between my case and another which made it into the papers.

Can I remind Judge Barrowclough that, as a civilian, he expected me to plough through legal cases I would struggle getting access to, in order to produce a summary of past cases that are relevant to mine.

Faced with this impossible scenario, and suffering immense stress at the time, logically, I summarised regarding the case that mattered; the one I was actually involved in.

Below is an event that happened after my case, written in plain English that inexplicably, unlike my case, wasn't even serious enough for dismissal, and hence a subsequent tribunal.

Will this Rebekah Sutcliffe case do as a comparison, Judge Barrowclough?

In this bent world we live in, her actions did not merit the ultimate sanction as she was a female police chief and they must be portrayed as wonderful at all times, just like the likes of the useless Dame Sarah Thornton DBE QPM etc., regardless of their misdemeanours.

Breast Flash Greater Manchester Police Chief Rebekah Sutcliffe keeps her job

Reform of the police misconduct process has now been called for by police chiefs to the Home Secretary, after one of the country's most senior female officers, Rebekah Sutcliffe, kept her job after bullying allegations towards a junior colleague regarding the size of her breasts.

The disciplinary panel concluded that Assistant Chief Constable Rebekah Sutcliffe was guilty of gross misconduct following an **hour-long drunken tirade** against Superintendent Sarah Jackson.

Ms Sutcliffe loudly ridiculed Superintendent Jackson at a conference, insinuating that her 'credibility was zero after her boob job' and called her 'a laughing stock who would be judged professionally on the size of her tits.'

Greater Manchester's highest ranked female officer then allegedly exposed her left breast, saying 'Look at these, look at these,' which suggests she exposed both. 'These are the breasts of someone who has had three children.'

She then went on to say, 'They are ugly but I don't feel the need to pump myself full of silicone to get self-esteem.' I would imagine that in an hour-long, loud tirade she would have said plenty more than that.

The investigating panel concluded that 'Ms Sutcliffe's behaviour had breached professional standards and taken her to the very precipice of dismissal.'

They then went on to praise her, as this was out of character, and recommended that a final written warning was suitable punishment.

Greater Manchester Police Deputy Chief Constable Ian Pilling agreed with the panel and decided that Ms Sutcliffe could keep her job.

My conclusion regarding the Ms Sutcliffe case
So, Judge Barrowclough, police chiefs have called on the Home Secretary to standardise their misconduct process in the wake of this incident for clarity of disciplinary procedures.

I would like that in the wake of this we have country-wide disciplinary procedures in place so that someone who was clearly innocent of, and twice falsely accused of, a boob comment does not face infinitely harsher sanction than a very senior police officer who is clearly guilty of this charge and worse, like indecent exposure, in a drunken state, and witnessed by so many colleagues who alarmingly took no action.

I rest my case, Your Honour.

One rule for one: influence and affluence prevail, with justice as the casualty
This was all done in a room full of police officers and the public celebrating female achievement in policing. What is more, Supt Jackson allegedly had not even had a boob job. Thankfully Rebekah Sutcliffe made matters better by driving in the next day (beyond all probability still intoxicated) to repeatedly apologise.

They took into account her previous excellent work, too. Bet she didn't have a near-perfect output and attendance record like me. Rebekah was described by former Chief Constable Sir Peter Fahy as a powerful and original thinker. Did I not design a superior printing process upgrade and submit CAPAs written in my own time, to prevent a common error recurring? Did I not show directors, with tabulation that they were breaking company overtime rules to help them out, only to be sacked for this? Or could anyone believe I was really sacked for falsely manufactured boob comments and a hug, identical to everyone else's hugs at the time, as Abbotts so falsely pretend?

Why don't we look into police having less drunken jollies at taxpayers' expense to celebrate every time an officer achieves something like, for example, in this case, being female? As for the honours handed out to the likes of Dame Sarah: don't get me started.

No, I'm not anti-female police officers. I'm just mentioning the purpose of this particular over-exuberant shindig.

When I was in the Fire Brigade in the 80s we had to learn a lot of paperwork, including disciplinary procedures. The London Fire Brigade, like the police, was a public service with ranks.

We learned that two charges that constituted gross misconduct were 'insubordination' and the fail- safe to counter this, and to show fairness, 'the abuse of authority.'

I will state also, Judge Barrowclough, that Abbott directors engaged in an 'abuse of authority' in treating me infinitely more harshly than other colleagues for falsely alleged offences, whilst ignoring and covering up actual serious offences.

There are so many obvious examples stated elsewhere that underline these inconsistencies irrefutably, that were referred to by myself at tribunal but were deliberately ignored by the judge in his conclusions, ironically in yet another act entailing 'abuse of authority' in a clear dereliction of duty from which the judge himself seems sadly immune.

Unlike myself, Rebekah Sutcliffe was someone on a six-figure salary, in a responsible position, who knows the law. By all accounts she was nearly half as ferocious in her delivery as Les Muggeridge aka Thuggeridge was to me, and clearly made loads of offensive boob comments whilst performing indecent exposure in a room full of police officers.

Rebekah Sutcliffe was not arrested, nor was the intimidating thug at Abbotts, even though I reported him, but I eventually got a harassment warning after sending in polygraph results to clear my name. Not exactly a level playing field.

In comparison

I repeat! Rebekah Sutcliffe publicly made a boob comment before disgracing herself and breaking the law through indecent exposure and, in all probability, committed a motoring offence the next day by driving in drunk to apologise. She did the former in a room full of police officers and was not arrested and was not breathalysed the following morning in the station either.

I lose my job, and so much more, because I'm falsely accused of a boob comment as proven by polygraph and Linda's self-contradictory made-up stories. To this day we still don't know what the boob comment allegedly entailed, as it never happened. I was also the victim of a serious motoring offence, probably by a drunk or drugged woman, probably both. Both of which the police also refused to investigate.

I lose my job because of Linda's lies. Let alone is drunk driver Rebekah Sutcliffe not arrested for lewd exposure either and intimidating public comments in a room full of police officers, she keeps her job, her position and her salary and is relocated. Linda keeps her job and the book is thrown at me after I'm the victim of a very serious motoring offence and pure lies.

Is my crime perhaps being a white male, as Linda Shaw and Rebekah Sutcliffe have never had their collar felt or faced appropriate proportionate disciplinary action?

The summary at tribunal

We have a **one-hour public tirade with breast flashing thrown in** being deemed acceptable but a two-second hug proven to be reciprocated by a kiss a month later deemed a dismissible offence. Screaming boob comments is acceptable, proven to be fictitious boob comments, where I am in fact the victim of Linda Shaw's lies, that's serious.

Apart from the fact it is not funny, your verdict, Judge Barrowclough, is an utter joke.

Will he now accept that Rebekah Sutcliffe's case renders my dismissal illegal and his conduct immoral? Rebekah's case was, after all, not even serious enough for dismissal and hence a subsequent tribunal. Explain that!

My suspicions regarding the police, the judiciary and the masons beyond all reasonable doubt look even more credible now. Especially when you refer to former dot-knuckled Les Muggeridge's inexplicable sway with the police, and the unjustifiable verdict at tribunal. Years later, referenced in further chapters where Abbott were to act above the law again as it didn't apply to them, Les's friends once again turned a blind eye to clear criminality. Surprise, surprise.

We should get experts to look at the evidence

By getting the experts to look at the evidence, I clearly don't mean Judge Barrowclough and his mates as, although ridiculously intelligent, in terms of delivering justice they are proven beyond all reasonable doubt to be absolutely useless.

As said in the previous chapter with the two letters with the 15-line sentences, etc. where we could clearly prove that Linda and Richard's letters were beyond doubt written by the same person:

It wouldn't really take an expert to ascertain that Abbott and, in particular, Bully Boy Thuggeridge have 'influence beyond that which would be deemed normal or acceptable'.

We see from the above that a blind eye is turned to all the 'in clear and plain sight' acts of law-breaking for which Rebekah Sutcliffe is forgiven, even keeping her job and being praised in the process.

And why? Because she is part of the gang, so to speak.

In the past we all know too well of cases where bent coppers, rather that arresting evil, intimidating, criminal thugs like Kenneth Noye, find it easier to recommend he joins them and their friends in the brotherhood at the lodge.

Evil intimidating thugs still hold full sway with the police to this day.

Thuggeridge is a menacing, intimidating thug who in actions listed so far in this book and even more in later chapters clearly feels and knows he is above the law. They do his will, not just sometimes but on every occasion.

In Judge Barrowclough's judgement a similar blind eye is turned to every illegality and lie performed and an unjust, dishonest verdict is defended regardless of every appeal, clearly underlining that injustices have occurred.

I don't know that Les Muggeridge is a member of the brotherhood. I just know he is a vile, nasty, intimidating, controlling thug who gets away with everything and has unhealthy sway with Thames Valley Police.

I would also suggest this, doing my own personal profiling, knowing he would find the lure of every underhand advantage irresistible.

Comparing the cases

Perhaps my theory is wrong, in which case I would like someone to explain to me how so many allegedly grown-up, responsible adults such as Amanda White, Miles White CEO, Les Muggeridge, Pat Cole, Shaun Smith, Nicky Albert, Judges Barrowclough, Taylor and Latham and Ombudsman, Admiral Sir John

Brigstocke, then latterly Jane Ingram and then Andy Payne can find a reciprocated hug identical to so many at that time, and falsely alleged boob comment, so false that nobody knows what it was, so offensive as to be sackable, yet:

A room full of coppers and latterly the chiefs who investigated the incident see nothing wrong with an hour-long, very loud, public tirade about boobs with indecent exposure thrown in and even end up praising the perpetrator.

The probability of the judgements in the last two paragraphs, and all concurring in judgement, happening by coincidence and without corruption and influence, is in the billions-to-one category.

Then ask yourself how all the above would react if I punched a heavily pregnant Nigerian woman or intentionally drove my car at a female colleague, or lied at tribunal, or hit a female colleague with a metal ruler, etc.?

Then there was another case, Police Sgt Andrews in Wiltshire. He can drag a female around the station by the hair Neanderthal-style, over a minor motoring offence, then leave her unattended on the floor of a cell, possibly unconscious, certainly dripping with blood and in danger of concussion, compression and choking. It takes public outrage at the video for any action to be taken against him. The system is so bent, depending on who you are. I'm living proof. Well, for now anyway.

Again, as with the calls I got traced and they intentionally ignored, in this case, too, the police just won't do their duty. Never mind that minors are affected. They are simply a gang who serve their friends.

Get burgled and call the police and you won't see them.

Mis-gender someone accidentally online and you could see a number of them.

Straight white males and their families can be victims too, and have feelings. In fact, most suicides are straight white males, which suggests perhaps society has got it wrong and alienated one of its largest groups.

I don't want preference, just equality.

There is no such thing as positive discrimination. Discrimination is discrimination.

I say in my defence that I was brought up with the words *blessed are those who hunger and thirst for that which is right'* Words from the book I held when vowing to tell the truth.

I suppose I'm public enemy no 1 for taking a polygraph and exposing all Abbotts' nonsense for what it is. Surprise, surprise. The establishment suddenly have time to issue me with a warning for e-mailing this to Abbott.

Maybe I'm public enemy no 1 for showing the judges and ombudsmen a better way of doing justice.

May I remind them also that I'm the guy who, after a woke, HR PC presentation at Abbott, questioned whether there are some people who simply wish to be offended and act like a player taking a dive in the penalty box in football matches.

May I also remind them how right I was proven to be...

May I remind them that I really didn't do anything wrong in the first place. I just acted with kindness.

May I remind the police and judges in the light of the above that I have a case in thinking I've been treated just a tad unfairly.

Anyone with a sense of proportion would be screaming injustice, corruption and victimisation from the rooftops!

Chapter 29

Meeting Staff After My Time at Abbotts

In early 2010 I met one former colleague in Witney. We had a friendly chat and I told him that I hadn't left but had been sacked, thanks to a load of lies by Linda Shaw.

He said she was nothing but trouble at work and that she had also got a manageress sacked with her lies.

Later that year I met another chap from days in Wantage, and also told him of my fate.

He said they were desperate to get rid of everyone; he was going to retire a good bit later but Les wanted him out pronto as they had either lost a Liberty's contract, or lost a contract to Liberty's.

I said either way, they certainly took some liberties.

Then in Witney I meet another ex-colleague who gave an alleged statement in my case.

He seemed genuinely pleased to see me. We had a friendly chat, and he was absolutely astonished to find I had been sacked for a last day hug with Linda Shaw. I mentioned to him he was interviewed in connection to this, but went into no details. I mentioned that I, one of ADCs best workers, was sacked, whilst others can have a fist fight whilst one is heavily pregnant and that is OK.

He then mentioned that all the Africans were found to be illegal workers and had all suddenly disappeared at once, overnight.

That will be more questionable conduct by ADC then. For years these workers had been using any name on medical documents with their identities totally unchecked.

I mentioned to him that in my time we definitely knew of two workers who used two different names. One even signed with his real name then crossed it out.

I met another later in Sainsbury's Wantage whilst I also spoke to another ex-colleague. The one who used to greet me with the regular IRA comments came over to say hello.

This was the supervisor who allegedly cited 18 months' sexual harassment against me according to the documents I read, as I reminded him, along with the IRA comments I also reminded him about.

He said he has no recollection of me ever talking to Linda.

This shocked him, and he said he would speak to Pete Moran, and that Linda had tried to get him into trouble. That seems to have been the case with virtually the whole factory.

I told him to speak to whoever he liked as long as he didn't speak to me as I, now, just didn't like him.

Perhaps he is one who just says the right thing to the person he is with. Another possibility is that he never said what is attributed to him. Nobody signed their alleged statements and I know the minutes of my meeting with Pat had nearly all my input excluded from the minutes.

Chapter 30

I Appeal to Senior Judges and the Ombudsman

Disgruntled at the judge's unsatisfactory verdict I then take next steps of appealing to the Area Judge; Regional Judge and the Judicial Ombudsman. As time then goes on further I eventually appeal to the next ombudsman, too, after my entire existence is denied by Abbott, especially as I'm now armed with my polygraph results. Sadly they are all cut from the same cloth.

I have read online about many decent people with the courage of their convictions who are all, like me, left destroyed personally and totally disillusioned at the shocking, useless UK judicial /tribunal system.

To quote another chap who, like me, went on to have judge Latham and Sir John Brigstocke KCB as his final hopes of justice:

He says, 'I have made serious allegations and if the judges are not called to account for their acts then I should be called to account for my allegations.'

Sir John in his reply concludes, 'I have considered the additional concerns raised in your letter but they do not relate to the handling of your complaint and are therefore outside my remit.'

He adds, 'I understand your disappointment that your complaint has not been resolved.'

I can't find anyone with a complaint that Sir John actually resolved.

Reiterating, Regional Employment Judge Ms C Taylor replied to me on 1 Sept 2011, *I am writing to you as I have received your complaint concerning the decision of Judge Barrowclough…*

It appears to me that your complaint concerned whose evidence the tribunal preferred…

No fooling you, Sherlock!

Having considered your complaint I have decided that there is insufficient evidence to find any Judicial misconduct and I dismiss your complaint.

No meat on the bones, then, I would like Ms C Taylor to be conscious of the fact that the public who pay for her generous wages and non-contributory pension would see judicial misconduct occurring when a judge gives a one-sided, unjust verdict that ignores key procedural and ethical points, rendering the verdict unsafe and unsatisfactory.

I personally consider there to be judicial misconduct where a clear miscarriage of justice has occurred and justice has not been seen to be done; which is, after all, the judicial function.

If you feel that I have not handled your complaint properly, you can complain to the Judicial Appointments and conduct Ombudsman Sir John Brigstocke KCB. Please note that the Ombudsman can only consider a complaint about my handling of your complaint. He has no power to investigate your original complaint about the judge concerned. She underlines as I have.

So basically Ms C Taylor has not addressed a single complaint of unfairness that I have made and I can only now complain about the handling of a complaint that was never handled. Snookered!

So, when a judge gives a, shall we say, 'unsafe verdict' which is realistically the most likely way a judge can commit judicial misconduct, you then can't complain about this verdict to a senior or area judge. You can then only complain to the ombudsman about having the complaint you are no longer allowed to address being ignored by other judges. Sounds like something from *Yes Minister*.

If my understanding is correct, then unless a judge openly takes a bribe or produces a gun and shoots you, in which case you could not complain anyway, then you have no case with Sir John.

I then complained to Area Judge Latham too, but I was again instructed my area for complaint was to be narrowed so much as to render it pretty useless.

The Ombudsman Sir John Brigstocke KCB is allegedly independent of the judiciary and only has the power to address certain points. Basically, as far as I can see, his seems like a lame duck position, a complete waste of time and space and valuable public resources: jobs for the boys of the old school tie brigade. His position is not just that of a toothless tiger, this tiger has no claws or backbone either.

When judges know there is no deterrent from above, or consequences to fear to stop them doing as they please, then we have a system open to abuse.

Surely, as in my case, there is a company director at appeal, who was the accused, the judge and the jury at my appeal at Abbotts, who illegally does not even address my reasons for appeal, which are also immorally excluded from the minutes, which clearly fools the judge, as proven unequivocally in his summary, and...

There is also a pre-written letter of dismissal brought to an alleged reconvened hearing by another 'director to be' where I haven't yet been given a fair chance to defend myself and have not seen vital interview documents handed to me only after dismissal, along with my prepared letter of dismissal.

Then, surely, both of the above are genuine procedural 'red flags' a judge and his side-kicks should be alert to.

My appeal occurred long before I even knew about the '3 month less one day' rule for such a dubious complaint, a rule which the judge would surely have known fully about but failed to implement. This is a 'larger red flag'!

Then, when it is so obvious also that my treatment is so inexplicably different to others and I can't get redress on this, there is a real problem.

That's before we even mention my accusers' lies and dodgy paperwork.

If, in the face of all this, there is a barrier set so we cannot get an ombudsman to say to a judge, 'We need to look at this case, and there needs to be a procedural change to stop this happening again,' then we have a system that is clearly unfit for purpose.

As far as I can see, if a judge commits misconduct this misconduct will involve the abuse of authority by inexplicably siding with the guilty, as the judge so obviously did in my case.

Power corrupts.

Power without accountability absolutely corrupts.

There is the human sense of right and wrong in this, too; a sense we all have to varying degrees, our conscience, which the judge, area and regional judges and ombudsman may wish to consider.

I could not do a job where knowingly I'm watching decent, honest, courageous people with the courage of their convictions have their lives shattered, and I either can't or won't help them through tied hands or by meekly kowtowing to peer pressure.

The public should be able to expect a minimum level of decency as standard.

The appointment itself

These critical appointments should not be made by someone, many of whose close family are masons, with one being at the time at the very head of freemasonry.

Such appointments will, rightly or wrongly, lead to suspicions of a conflict of interest for the appointee.

I have no direct evidence of masonic involvement but the police and judicial performances from the outset, in my case, inevitably led to so many questions regarding impartiality. Without exception, so many implausible errors have only ever favoured one side.

This book had to be written as the judge's summary was unsafe, unsatisfactory, and exempt from proper accountability and fair scrutiny and this is only my remaining avenue in my quest for justice.

I have again presented my case on the basis of the truth and, as near as is feasible, the whole truth and nothing but the truth.

Justice must be seen to be done.

It should be those, so honoured and trusted to be appointed to what should be such revered positions, who should want that the most.

At the time of writing the innocent has so far suffered a 15-year sentence.

Chapter 31

Your Honour and My Hypocrisy

I said in writing to Admiral Sir John Brigstocke KCB that his ilk should strive wholeheartedly to do the service to the public that Her Majesty appointed him to do and that if the likes of him, who are so highly decorated, do not display the standards we should expect from one so honoured, then Her Majesty's honours are clearly not worth piss.

I also mentioned that the nation he should serve involves everyone, who nearly all pay taxes to pay his wages, not just his clique.

I also wrote, 'I'm not in awe of your titles, Sir John, just in despair at the lack of justice in Britain.'

One should expect a man so decorated, and so entrusted, to lead by example and to care more about judicial corruption than a humble serf clearly does.

We should expect chivalry and integrity from a Knight Commander of the Bath who has represented Her Majesty on occasions.

Two points worth mentioning here:

- This was said at the very zenith of my exasperation and depression, with Sir John representing the last hope of justice.
- Sir John is now sadly no longer around to defend himself.

If I was wrong in such a comment and Sir John wanted to do his best for justice, but his hands were tied, then I apologise unreservedly.

Do I feel guilty about such a comment regarding Her Majesty's honours? Yes and no: Yes, when I think of the likes of Simon Weston CBE and his injuries, for example. No, when I think of the Dame Sara Thorntons of this world.

I gave plenty examples of 'not worth piss' honours such as Sir Cyril Smith, whose crimes were scandalously covered up, and the Sir Jimmy Saviles of this world, one of our current King's former idols and mentors.

Then, watching commemorations of the D-day landings and those who perished just being picked off on the beaches from above when they were only teenagers, and those who died in the trench warfare during the First World War, I feel terrible for having uttered such a comment.

Then I think of those who sent these to war, who generally have a lot higher honours and then think that most of those who perished were the 'average Joe' on the orders of the silver spoon brigade. You were right to expect Sir John to uphold and fight for the highest standards of justice.

One year I didn't advertise it but just made a personal decision not to wear the poppy, before having another chat with myself, then wearing one. I did this because the person laying the first wreath at the Cenotaph is a descendant of Queen Victoria, whose three eldest grandchildren were either leaders of, two of the main opposing combatants or, in one case, the wife of the third major power, Tsar Nicolas II. The ancestors of these families have sent many generations to war over many centuries. Then again, if I didn't wear a poppy I was failing in my duty of gratitude to those responsible for many freedoms I should always be so grateful for.

As you can probably guess, I do care and pause for thought at monuments of remembrance. I might ponder that it was not just those who lost their lives but their future generations, too; and then wonder what they would think of their sacrifice if they could see the country now, and all the conflicts in the world since?

Hearing the stories from a 99-year-old veteran who spoke so clearly of the horrors of war and losing your comrades, I know, too, that to protect those comrades you may have to take the life or lives of sons and fathers on the other side who were obeying orders and had comrades, too. That may be an impossible cross for many to bear, along with the guilt of 'Why my comrades and not me?'

I have said that if I was wrong in Sir John's case, I apologise unreservedly. Feeling shame on myself for uttering such a comment as this perhaps devalues all merited awards including, perhaps, his own.

Perhaps we could look at it from the other way, too. Perhaps I was not wrong. Perhaps I do care about these awards, so much that I want those who have them to be as outstanding an example to the rest of us that they can be. We should expect to revere and look up to such as these.

Perhaps I believe that the receipt of an award should be a privilege, but also a beginning, a responsibility rather than a sense of 'job done' and entitlement.

Perhaps he needed yet another telling off from yet another person with a conscience and sense of right and wrong who had their life ruined, whom he didn't help. He was quite happy to accept reappointment after years of either underachievement or no achievement, defending the clique and ignoring the commoner.

Did I perhaps care more about standards and integrity than he did?

A question you could ask is: what useful, practical function does a judicial ombudsman actually have in reality? Nobody seems to know. Another could be: what are the useful, practical functions and purpose of a Knight Commander of the Bath? Would we notice the difference if neither role existed? Nice work if you can get it.

The key values
The key values to me throughout my fight for justice are pretty much many of the supposed values of the judiciary:

- Innocent until proven guilty
- Justice must be seen to be done
- The truth, the whole truth and nothing but the truth
- Everyone should be equal in eyes of law

Her Majesty's family have standards to uphold, too
Confession number two. I have been an open critic of Charles's choice of friends.

To me King Charles's adoration of Jimmy Savile, this paedophile shit and their inter-house visits is no better and just as vile as his brother Andrew's acquaintance with Jeffrey Epstein.

There is also Charles and Archbishop Carey's support of Bishop Peter Ball before and after his sentence for paedophilia, which should raise questions about his judgement concerning his close friends and mentors.

Charles's closeness to his other mentor, Louis Mountbatten, yet another serial paedophile, can be explained by the family connection.

Charles housed Peter Ball post-sentence so must have been aware of his wrongdoing; so this was not just an ill-advised misjudgement. Bishop Peter Ball had the support of Charles and Archbishop Carey. Would Neil Todd still be alive today if this were not the case?

Archbishop Carey was defrocked for this, but then his woke successor Justin Welby ordains Charles III as King. Jimmy Savile's mate is now at the head of a Christian Church. Surely this must be wrong.

Now Charles has the gig as King, the kowtowing forgetfulness is in overdrive.

The Archbishop of Canterbury, who wants God the Father to be gender neutral, has anointed this new King as the New Head of Henry VIII's church.

Henry VIII had his nasty traits and was someone who would have his wife executed so he could conveniently move on to the next.

Thankfully, nothing like that could ever happen today.

Jimmy Savile was even the first civilian to be awarded the Royal Marines Green Beret and he had Royal Marines Pallbearers at his funeral. This has caused complaint by the families of former Marines not granted such an honour. Reportedly, when Charles sent his mentor, Savile gold cufflinks and cigars for his birthday, the note attached read: 'Nobody will ever know what you have done for this country. This is to go some way in thanking you for that.' I think we know now, Charlie boy!

I can see Savile now having a joke, sitting alongside Satan, about how he fooled them all in his lifetime, was buried with his green beret, gold and cigars and now, after his death, how they have made his best mate King. They also made the infallible bloke who made him a Knight Commander of The Order of St Gregory a saint. This church, as well as shielding many abusers, clearly honoured one too, and refused to remove Jimmy's papal knighthood posthumously.

More recently the Director of Public Prosecutions when Jimmy Savile's case was dropped has been made Prime Minister. Sir Keir (yet another Sir) claimed he was unaware back then, that a prosecutor had closed Savile's case.

Over the last few decades I feel that the institution has clearly been valued above moral values, the vulnerable, and the teachings of Jesus himself.

The circling of the wagons and the protection of the institution, or the gang, over doing the morally right thing is a recurring theme throughout this book. Perhaps I'm just an ideological idiot who should just say, 'It is what it is; don't rock the boat, it's pointless trying.' If everyone says that, things are guaranteed to get worse and worse.

Then again, Christian principle teaches forgiveness and surely Charles will be a better King with the whole nation supporting him, and he does seem to be trying hard in a climate of family rifts and illnesses, including his own. He deserves credit for that.

With that argument, some might say you should forgive Linda Shaw and Abbott. Then again, until someone stands up to them, and gets justice, the culture of bullying is guaranteed to remain. Christian principle also preaches repentance and let alone have I not seen any, they tried to destroy me again, years later, without conscience. War was declared on me and my family, so it is right to fight.

If they have shown no contrition and no conscience, and have no obvious deterrent, they will sin again, for sure.

Christian principle can be so contradictory. I was always on the side of the prodigal son's brother.

Vile ogre and piece of filth, freemason Cyril Smith is caught red-handed brutally buggering a boy within a mile of the Houses of Parliament and, for some reason, the police superiors order all records relating to this case to be confiscated, to the dismay of the good police officers who arrested him.

Go forward a couple of years and the establishment gives Sir Cyril a knighthood. How disgusting.

Was his membership of the Freemasons, and perhaps his knowledge of other people more important than himself, a factor in him getting away with this crime and crimes up north on different occasions? There has to be a reason relating to very strong influence for this to happen.

Sir Jimmy Savile was immune, too. Sir Rolf was Her Majesty's portrait painter, and so on. So many Sirs: so many dubious honours.

I apologise unreservedly to those who have been honoured fairly and justly and with full merit for my derogatory term regarding Her Majesty's honours, but I'm sure you can understand my cynicism and frustration. The bad devalues and taints the good.

I apologise again to a good friend for not attending his MBE award celebrations.

I knew what it meant to him. I was pleased for him and torn by not supporting my friend as I said to him, at the time, but would have been a complete hypocrite, had I attended. Especially, with hindsight, as it was Charles who had presented his honour to him.

I explained to him that I had used the quote about Her Majesty's honours to a very high-ranking officer. I said also that I would need to write a book to detail the events relating to it, that I had taken mental health counselling and that all would then become clear regarding my non-attendance.

I felt terrible guilt for not going but would I have felt more guilt had I gone? The head and the heart were struggling.

There is also the question that could be asked of me, 'If the events detailed in this book had not happened to you, would you have attended?' The answer would surely be, 'Yes, unless of course I had some issue with another Sir or whatever.' So basically I am potentially two completely different people depending on life's events. I'm surely a hypocrite again. But on that logic, who isn't?

I have other friends I was pleased for, too, whose duties involved Her Majesty. I wish them well and am delighted for their achievements.

I'm just saddened by much of what I see elsewhere.

Chapter 32

Reporting Shaun and Pat to Amanda White

After the tribunal debacle I test Abbott's fairness and impartiality and launch complaints for the bullying I received at the hands of their directors. As Les himself said, 'thirty volumes, no problem.' No stone would be left unturned.

I get a copy of the company handbook at tribunal, the one issued in 2009 when I was suspended, so utilise it.

I write to Amanda White on 18 November 2010

I would hereby advise that I am reporting Shaun Smith and Pat Cole for multiple offences of gross misconduct as determined under section 26.4.2 of the company handbook.

It is stated in your main terms and conditions of employment that it is my right to raise a grievance even though I am no longer an employee, and no time limit is mentioned.

Gross misconduct offence 1
Actions which are in breach of a statutory responsibility, for example the company's Health and Safety responsibilities

A serious failure to observe company rules, regulations, policy/procedures

Gross misconduct offence 2
Serious neglect of duty, including failure to follow relevant procedures (i.e. the abuse of authority)

A serious failure to observe company rules, regulations, policy/procedures

<u>Gross misconduct offence 3</u>
Any form of discrimination or harassment

Michael Collins 22 November 2010 (Date of conclusion)

You can imagine the detail supplied with these legitimate charges that Amanda White does not even respond to. I was saving HR Director Les 'Thuggeridge' Muggeridge for dessert.

Harassment

I have been accused of harassment at least four times, once when sacked, by the solicitor at the tribunal and in the tribunal verdict and once when issued a harassment warning.

Clearly I did not harass Linda Shaw, as my lie detector and her self-contradictory evidence shows. I merely distanced myself from her, much to Linda's all-too-evident annoyance.

It is not harassment either to protest your innocence to your ex-colleagues and bosses after blatant wrongdoing towards you, and your good name falsely tarnished. I was reactive, not pro-active, doing what is dutifully right, following the harassment I suffered. All my actions occurred as a direct result of my rightful intent to clear my name following unfair dismissal.

There is no justifiable, non-corrupt reason why I should be censored.

My complaints to any colleagues whilst at Abbotts were to clear my name in self-defence after they raised the issue and in all probability over three months before being summoned to HR.

This book is another example of me clearing my name. It is again a reaction to my being harassed rather than harassing. I didn't start or want any of this.

I am the victim not the perpetrator, as I detail below. My cause is a just one.

What is harassment?

- *Harassment is – lying in wait then deliberately driving head-on at someone who is innocently making their way to work.*
- *Harassment is – making 'number withheld' nuisance phone calls to a family with the intent of causing them distress.*
- *Harassment is – conducting a lengthy campaign of false rumours about someone due to your jealousy of that person and their partner's circumstances.*

- *Harassment is – lying deliberately to get an innocent work colleague dismissed due to your jealousy, and the fact they no longer talk to you.*
- *Harassment is – being over-aggressive, obnoxious and nasty in an attempt to intimidate an employee who rightly wishes to appeal an unfair dismissal verdict.*
- *Harassment is – not letting an employee make his points at a disciplinary hearing through deliberate constant interruption, dismissiveness and references to the time.*
- *Harassment is – naming and shaming an employee against company policy on the weekly ER notice board for a non-ER event for three consecutive weeks.*
- *Harassment is – almost daily IRA comments to an employee with Irish roots and by his superiors in refusing to take action when this is reported.*
- *Harassment is – singling out someone of a certain race for seemingly infinitely harsher treatment at disciplinary level than other favoured races.*

Chapter 33

Abbott Policies

Live life with dignity
Taken from Abbotts own website:-

HEALTH AND HUMAN DIGNITY

When people think about health and human dignity, the focus is often on ageing or severe illness.

To us, it's bigger. It's the freedom to live life liberated from the worry and weight of sickness, to reclaim the precious moments that fill up a healthy life. It's the right to regain your self-reliance, freedom and confidence with your health. To be respected and treated fairly. To be seen as an individual and get the care you require in return. Everyone deserves it. And in the quiet of your mind when you're wrestling with illness, we hear you. We see first-hand how health problems can rob you of the life you want.

It's why we're creating advancements that restore your health. Our technologies help bring back all of those everyday moments that are essential to every human life. Because dignity demands it.

Thuggeridge, who is a shining example and cheerleader for 'living life well', is a supporter of the above. You couldn't make it up.

I would have thought that being honest, fair and decent in preference to being a vile, nasty, intimidating thug would reflect living life well a whole lot better. What do I know?

Taken from Abbott code of business conduct:
It is up to each of us as Abbott employees to build our company and brand by holding ourselves to the highest ethical standards and by operating with honesty, fairness and integrity.

Robert B Ford CEO (post-Miles White $1.6 Billion Abbott Depakote scandal)

<u>Abbott health and safety policy</u>
It is the responsibility of every employee to work safely to report practices or conditions which are inconsistent with this policy or which pose recognised or unacceptable risks to human health or the environment. In addition, every ADC leader shall promote an environment that enables employees to practice these principles, and actively support implementation of this policy.

The real truth is simple. Raise a legitimate H & S complaint and you are out the door, pronto!

As I have said in numerous communications, an honest Abbott mission statement would say:

Abbott's actively promotes and endorses dangerous unsafe work practices, slanderous defamation of character, racism, racial prejudice, violence on site particularly towards pregnant women, sex on site, blatant statements of sexual intent at female staff and wandering hands inside female staff's clothing, perjury, perverting the course of justice, eating in controlled areas and regularly sleeping on the job whilst operating machinery and inspecting product, general lies and false evidence and the altering of documents in any way possible, including editing, embellishing, losing, destroying and backdating and creating previously non-existent documents to wilfully create a false impression to the reader. Lies to get innocent colleagues dismissed are also fully endorsed. Genuine acts of harassment, intimidation, bullying, aggression and targeting innocent loyal workers are fully endorsed also.

Abbott's won't tolerate an innocent last-day hug, but this applies only, of course, if your name is Michael Collins. All others are exempt. This applies even if this hug is reciprocated with a public kiss at a later date and applies regardless of any or many hundreds of similar or identical acts by others.

That's all they had on me.

Not even mentioned above was the subsequent whopper by Abbott management destroying a former colleague's life, career prospects and mental health yet again, years later, by knowingly denying he ever even worked for Abbotts!

This lie underlines that Abbott's credibility is absolute zero.

Also, in an act I won't ever forgive, they backed Linda Shaw in her heavy-breathing phone lies, sacking me and affecting my family with all the consequences of this. The real truth is that my child felt intimidated picking up the phone and receiving the silent treatment and then the phone being put down in the 'number withheld' calls we received. They should be ashamed of themselves.

They backed the wrong horse again when supporting the mother of the child from the family from hell who was abused. Much as they can't be blamed for the events that happened when they gave this known sexaholic extended leave, yet another child suffered as a result of their misjudgement and misplaced favouritism.

How can you ignore so totally this woman's innumerate dalliances and vile boasts, and do all you can to help her, yet react with such overwhelming overzealousness to a simple kind act on my behalf, accusing me of all sorts that, let alone you know to be untrue, but that this woman eclipsed a thousand times over? Shame on you, Abbott!

Oh, the hypocrisy when we read of Rottweiler Muggeridge promoting a 'live life well' drive. I also heard Boris Johnson and co. telling us to self-isolate.

Do as we say, not as we do!

Power corrupts!

Do Abbott stand by their values?

You might think that from a PR point of view, bearing in mind their interests in health and human dignity and reminding employees of their responsibilities to report unsafe practices or conditions, as I indeed did just before a clearly unfair dismissal, that:

It would surely be very bad from a PR perspective for Abbott to go after me again.

It would surely be very good from a PR perspective, and morally correct, to show humility, admit the company's wrongdoing and make amends and punish the guilty directors.

After all, my work ethic was to always put the Abbott customer first even though, strangely enough, this meant risking my job at the hands of corrupt, insecure Abbott directors to do this.

Chapter 34

I Take the Lie Detector Test

So having failed or, should I say, having been failed by the justice system, I elect to employ an honest method of delivering justice – the polygraph test.

It's more expense I can't afford but, in terms of mental well-being, I can't afford not to do it either.

I arrange to do the polygraph test with the very best, Don Cargill APA BEPA, chief examiner of national polygraphs and the NADAC group, Chairman and full member of the British and European Polygraph Association and full member of the American Polygraph Association.

I get all wired up and take the test: three sets of ten questions including the three vital questions with irrefutable 'Yes' or 'No' answers. The three sets of graphs are then superimposed for consistency.

All questions concluded with the outcome that there was not the remotest chance I was lying, in Don's words, looking at the incredible accuracy of the graphs.

He first asked me how I feel after the test. Apart from absolutely elated, my response was that I just want to do more tests to prove my innocence again and again. He said it's rare and almost unheard of for anyone to feel like that, as most are just shattered. I was, too, but in a good way.

He then asked me, due to the accuracy of my results, 'Do you ever lie?' I said, 'I don't think I do; it is not my nature; but there must be the occasional white lie and being sometimes gullible and too trusting, relating what others might say, who I wrongly trusted. I'm extremely truthful, hence I wanted this test so much.'

About an hour later, when it all sank in, I cannot describe the high and the elation I felt. Smiles and tears, I thought, 'Yes', and could not wait to post a copy of my results to Abbott.

I would hardly go through this and not tell Abbotts and the judges and Thames Valley Police.

I sent my results to all at Abbott who were involved in the disciplinary process and their CEO in America, Miles White. I sent a copy to all except control freak,' Bully Boy Thuggeridge.'

Next I hear the bullying control freak has taken over this situation at Abbotts totally. After a nasty, intimidating phone call from Les laying down the law to me...

In steps Les's friends (and probable freemasons) at Maidenhead police station. Apparently sending my lie detector results is harassment. They ignore totally Les's attacks on me, both face-to-face at the gatehouse and the fact that he has just intimidated me by phone.

Maidenhead police can phone me and send me a letter about contacting Abbott. Wantage police will cover up Linda's nuisance calls to my children or her running me off the road. Since that, there is Les's multiple occasion genuine harassment they ignore. Who gets the harassment warning?

Great Freemasons, shit police officers unless, of course, there is another obvious explanation I'm missing.

Chapter 35

Abbott's Reaction to my Polygraph Test Results Being Sent

To recap:

25 September 2011 I take my lie detector test.

I send the results to Abbotts, I believe the 26th, to Fraser Logue and all relevant staff, except bully-boy Muggeridge as he is a nasty piece of work who likes to intimidate and cover up.

Straightaway Les is on the phone to me and the rabid dog is foaming at the mouth again. His nose is out of joint. He is not happy and is as aggressive as can be and wants to intimidate me again, fully justifying my decision to exclude him from those I chose to send my lie detector results to.

I did this as he would threaten the other staff should they open the email I sent them, such is the nature of the beast. Believe me, he is a beast.

I naturally wanted the staff involved in the process of destroying my character to see my lie detector results, to show them the truth.

I wanted them to see beyond all doubt I was telling the truth and they had backed the wrong horse, so to speak.

Intimidation is Les's stock-in-trade. I knew because 'knuckles' Muggeridge had intimidated me already and proved this by doing so again.

Regarding procedure, he knew my dismissal was illegal because Pat Cole had been appointed by him to judge herself. I did not want another closed shop excluding my lie detector results.

I have wished to prove my innocence from the outset and defend the right to do so, bullied or not.

I also then receive a threatening letter from Les dated 27 September 2011, two days after my polygraph.

There are three main paragraphs:

Paragraph 1

Firstly to establish control he quotes that Fraser Logue has passed my correspondence to him and he insists that all communications to Abbotts are sent to him and him alone.

So does he think that I would take a polygraph test so I could only send it to him so he could add it to all the other destroyed documents and bin it?

He does not seem to realise that I neither like nor obey bullies, and my innocence means everything.

Paragraph 2

The tribunal decided your dismissal was fair and you have exhausted all appeals and we won't enter any further debate with you, he adds.

Under normal circumstances this would be a valid point.

But you know, Les, that on procedure alone, Pat Cole judging herself with your approval and Shaun Smith withholding documents until after dismissal, then handing me a pre-written letter of dismissal at an alleged reconvened hearing that never occurred, your bent minutes, Linda's bent letters and so on, that the verdict was bent.

Hence the polygraph test to show the truth.

There was a vendetta against me which all the serious stuff you chose to ignore proves.

You are now faced with the fact, too, that your dodgy untrustworthy witness of convenience has again been proven to be a liar beyond all doubt, this time by polygraph, so you don't want this issue raising its head again for fear of your corruption being exposed.

Les knows his position would be the untenable one if the truth would out.

Paragraph 3

He expresses his concern about the allegations being made against the company and its employees.

Try being honest, then. I didn't start this war or desire it. It has taken a right toll on my life and my family.

'For the avoidance of doubt; we (Abbotts) do not accept the allegations made,' he writes. That's nice and vague.

Really, you don't accept that a polygraph shows your star witness to be a fantasist. Look at letters by fake authors or her self-contradictions then, in your tribunal submissions.

Bully Boy then threatens me with the police and civil proceedings whilst I'm on 10p a week and suffering extreme depression due to the targeting I suffered, and accuses me of harassment.

Yes, this is the same rabid Rottweiler who intimidated me at the gatehouse and by phone twice, bringing his intimidation into my house, accusing me of harassment. He now insists I can't contact Abbotts, having earlier said in his letter that I can, but only through him after he phones me.

The poor bully then says he takes no pleasure writing to me in these terms.

I know, because he is angry, as he is a nasty egotistical control freak, albeit with a lot of influence, and I dare to disobey him.

There is then a line about drawing a line as he assumes I'll go away meekly. Still here, Les!!!

By the way, I know you probably can't comprehend this, but if you were a decent person and HR Director and Abbott were a decent company, then, when someone is so certain of their innocence that they spend money they can't afford on a polygraph because you have impoverished them, then you would welcome the evidence and instigate a new enquiry.

After all, you are the same Les Muggeridge who plonked box files on the desk at my hearing, saying, 'There are 20-30 of those and that is just one case. We never leave any stone unturned.'

Looks like we have something in common at last, or would have if you practised what you preach.

Seems like I'm harder to get rid of than the tattoos you are trying to bleach from your hands.

Having experienced your venom and ruthlessness I would not put it past you using any means you deem necessary to achieve that goal.

Worth writing this, should something untoward and a tad suspect happen to me after the release of this book. He is that nasty and evil, and then some.

The alleged purpose of the HR department

The HR department exists to provide a safe and fair working environment and to treat all equally.

Somehow Abbott appoint a UK HR Director who is simply an evil, nasty, intimidating thug.

I have referred to him as Thuggeridge.

This is simply a case of the Thug vs the Hug.

Good vs evil or, as my polygraph test and the response showed, the truth vs lies, evil and intimidation.

If Maidenhead police had any decency, bearing in mind another doubtless intimidated sidekick of Les, Jane Ingram's shocking illegal actions that I will detail later, they should be knocking on Abbott's door rather than possibly comparing notes at the lodge. If it looks like a duck…

Maidenhead police, when they are not lap dancing and gaining national notoriety in the Sunday papers like Hannah Havers, should they wish to claw back some credibility, would be well served to take action regarding the genuine harassment and intimidation by Les on me and the blatant unequivocal law breaking by Jane Ingram.

If there are any honest officers in Thames Valley Police they might wish to investigate the strange influence over their officers that Les seems to have had in both Wantage & Maidenhead, where they confirmed they were acting on his behalf.

The Maidenhead MP Theresa May proved to be as useless and inept an MP as she was a PM when I pointed out the corruption in her constituency to her. At least David Cameron MP and PM at the time, for the other Abbott site, Witney, had the decency to acknowledge my correspondence.

Chapter 36

Get Up, Get Knocked Down Again, Jane Ingram

To cut a long story short, after going from 72-hour night shifts to being bedridden with depression, the tribunal and subsequent appeals and whilst still fighting the fight, I pick myself up and take the only job available at the time in a Bookmakers, working for the one and only Fred Done. There are a few books' worth of writing there, too.

But there were good points. I met a whole load of new people in my locality, most of whom I liked and was glad to make their acquaintance. I stayed there for five years.

In August 2016 it looks like I'm making another step forward with a company called Forterra. There's a new job, a good job and a well-paid job with lots of overtime and bonus on offer too.

I have breezed through first and second interview, they like me and I like them and I have been offered the job subject to references etc.

Kelly Nolan is the girl from the agency NES Global Talent who introduced me to Forterra.

After second interview and my job offer, Kelly tells me there is a problem. Jane Ingram at Abbott Head Office Maidenhead insists that you never worked for Abbotts and there are no records of you ever having worked for Abbotts.

I said to Kelly, I can send an email to Jane Ingram with a copy of my first and last payslip which I will also copy to you so you can see I worked there.

On 18 August 2016 I duly send this email to both parties.

But no, it's not good enough. In an act of totally breaking the law, Jane Ingram still insists that I did not work there.

I send loads more proof to both, but Jane will not budge.

I then tell Kelly everything about my time at Abbotts and how evil they are. Kelly and Forterra say that as Abbott will not supply a reference and insist you never worked there, then there is nothing we can do.

I tell them the whole story about my time at Abbott and the bullying and vendetta I suffered, and even send them copies of my polygraph test, hoping they can see sense, but no. I lost this job and one at Royal Mail that I had turned down to work for Forterra. It never rains ...

Is Jane Ingram's lie another case of Les Muggeridge calling the shots? The 'I can do anything, no matter how low, and why? Because I can, and my mates in the police and judiciary will cover me' attitude. Guess what? The police certainly did.

Jane Ingram clearly committed a crime. So I contacted the very police in Maidenhead who had sent me the harassment warning. Their response, 'We can't help you, Sir. That is a civil matter and you will have to deal with it through the courts.' No arrest warrant for Jane, then; they only help their own.

Then surely my sending my lie detector results to Abbott was more of a civil matter and did not break the law, unlike Jane Ingram's intentional falsification, which certainly did.

I pictured Les behind her, smugly thinking, 'We can tell any lie and there is nothing you can do about it. I've got friends in the right places in police and judiciary. We can break the law whenever we like without consequences. I've got friends. I'm Teflon.' I believe that if this were the case, this is what he would have thought at that time, based on past experience. I have no proof he was with Jane at this time. This is just my by now, cynical thought process assuming the worst.

One thing for sure – someone at Abbotts was doing the dirty on me.

Power corrupts
Jane Ingram never knew me as we worked in different locations, so it is illogical that she acted as she did without influence. Then you would logically think that, in the unlikely event that there was any misunderstanding, the proof I sent her would have cleared it up.

You wouldn't just incriminate yourself, putting your professional credibility at risk, just in order to not provide a reference for someone you didn't even know.

You would even be putting your job at risk, if the company you worked for had morals.

She is now a criminal too for her actions. It has just not been made official yet.

The lie wouldn't have been her idea. Fear and intimidation goes a long way. When they've got you, they've got you. Jane Ingram certainly can't turn back now. Like it or not, Jane, you are a criminal, just one who has been protected illegally by the police at Maidenhead. Did anyone have something on her from before?

I know that when I went to hand in my letter requesting an appeal at the Abbott gatehouse, someone stepped in with their Jackboots on and took over, just like when I sent my polygraph results.

So there was no proof that I worked at Abbott at all at head office, according to Jane Ingram, even though I even then sent her legal tribunal documents; or was there?

This whole episode understandably pushed my mental health, anxiety and despair right back to square one all over again. But Jane Ingram was OK.

The damage lies can do.

Concluding

Some may ask, 'Why put Abbott on your CV?'

Firstly, I'm always honest. Because I have been honest throughout, I can write this book.

You might hope that after receiving my polygraph test and knowing I was unjustly fired before that, Abbott might just think, 'Haven't we done this guy enough damage?'

Lies have a habit of rebounding.

I did not have to wait too long for the next time Abbotts were to shoot themselves in the foot again.

So the story goes on to the next chapter ...

Chapter 37

Meeting Shaun Smith Again:
Andy Payne

Going back to 2011, just after he sacked me, I met Shaun Smith again in Sainsbury's in Wantage. I was polite and said 'Hello', as he was with his child, even though he approved of wrecking my family's home life and that he had approved of Linda Shaw's phone calls to minors in my family.

I was as polite as could be to both him and Pat at the tribunal, too.

We then crossed paths again in September 2017, a year after I had just lost another two jobs thanks to Jane Ingram at Abbott intentionally wrecking my life again with her lies, bringing the tally now to four jobs lost, if you include my original job at Abbotts and another I lost mentioning my unfair dismissal at interview.

I encountered Shaun Smith as I was walking out from a far checkout at Sainsbury's, Wantage, past a checkout where Shaun was just finishing his shopping. Shaun smiles and says 'Hello' like I'm his mate, and we leave Sainsbury's side by side, so to speak, but certainly not in love.

I question his conscience and ask if he would now like to apologise for all that he has done and the damage he has caused. He is unrepentant.

His car is just outside Sainsbury's in a disabled bay he has no right to be parked in but, of course, Abbott are above the law.

Without raising my voice I let him know what I think of him in a blunt but very unspectacular fashion. He tells me that I need to keep on moving and I do, mentioning that that bay he is parked in is for disabled people, as I went about my way. Part of me was quite pleased because I had been calm and said what I had without any emotional emphasis.

A few days later I get a letter from yet another UK HR Director, (they seem to have a lot of them) this time a chap named Andy Payne.

He is warning me of my conduct and my duty as an ex-Abbott employee to be nice to poor 'Cry baby Smith', who has felt very intimidated and hurt by my behaviour. Try meeting another UK HR Director at the gatehouse during his time of the month which, although 1,000 times more nasty and serious, and actually on-site at Abbott too, is conveniently not a crime at all to them.

So now I'm suddenly an ex-employee again, although I wasn't the year before. My details are clearly still on the records at Abbott because Andy Payne's letter has been sent to my home address, but if I had written one to them then that would be harassment, according to Maidenhead police, even though now according to Abbott Maidenhead's insistence, I never worked for the company.

Work that one out …

Here are a few exact quotes I wrote in my reply to Andy in a letter attached by email then sent by post.

Further to your letter AP /ap dated 4 September 2017 I advise as follows:-

For your information, I have already posted a more correct version of events to Jane Ingram in your HR department on Monday 28 Aug 2017, the following day after I encountered Shaun Smith. (One document in error quotes Sunday as 28th August, but the rest are right).

You, personally, have fallen into the same trap as the corrupt HR department did in 2009: taken the words of a liar and not questioned or researched both sides, then added two and two and got ten.

You have also proven Jane Ingram of your HR Dept. a complete and utter liar as she stated that there were no records of my ever working at Abbotts.

Then questioning his right or relevance in writing to me regarding a meeting outside of Abbotts' grounds and telling me off, when I never worked for Abbotts, according to Jane.

I would first ask you the question as to why I would react unfavourably to Shaun Smith. After all, I'm just a stranger on the street according to Jane Ingram, who should not even know Shaun Smith as I never worked at Abbott. Now that you and Shaun Smith insist I have, at least you are right there.

Your tactics

Eight long years and no lessons have been learned by the most pathetic, corrupt, useless HR department in history.

Once again I'm being blamed, threatened and assumed guilty before both sides of the argument are investigated.

In fact, as before, you blindly with no research or professionalism jump in head first to the totally wrong conclusion, having just heard one side of the evidence. Quite why you're assuming authority over someone Jane swore never existed at your company is incredible.

What has a conversation at Sainsbury's got to do with you?

How have you got the address of someone of whom Jane Ingram said no records existed?

Shaun Smith's credibility

I would suggest that Shaun Smith, being so easily out of his depth in the most basic situation, tends to lie, panic, exaggerate and behave totally irrationally and dishonestly with a view to self-preservation at all costs.

The path to the truth

I would suggest if you want irrefutable proof of what actually happened at Sainsbury's you take any of three paths to your destination.

Firstly you can get the CCTV evidence, which will show this was a chance meeting with a private, non-aggressive conversation that negatively impacted no other customer whatsoever or came close to doing so. You will see this from the lack of reaction elsewhere as there was nothing to react to!

It will also show that this was brief and I never blocked or impeded Shaun Smith, 'the employee you would not name,' at all, contrary to your fictitious claim.

CCTV would also show that your wonderful director was also parked illegally in a disabled bay. I hope that was in his report to the police. Go on, get the footage! I hate lies.

Wantage police aren't even interested in attempted murder or the bullying of my children, so good luck with this pathetic, untrue complaint.

Secondly you could get me to take a lie detector regarding this event. Included in these lie detector questions you could also ask, 'Was I the victim of **attempted murder** by Linda Shaw previously, in a stunt where she lay in wait and drove her car head on at me on my side of the road when I was on my way to work?' I think you should do this.

So I now face further false accusations and more one-sided uninvestigated exaggerations. This time by yourself, albeit quoting an anonymous somebody else.

Isn't attempted murder more serious? In fact isn't it more serious a thousand times over than a hug and Shaun Smith's allegation?

Thirdly you can have better communication between departments. Last week immediately after the event I sent a full truthful account of the incident to Miles White CEO, Jane Ingram, the FDA, The IPCC, Thames Valley Police and Reading employment tribunal, etc. etc. etc. as I vowed to tell the truth, the whole truth and nothing but the truth until justice.

I included the use of profanity on my behalf, and the fact that when I gave him the opportunity to apologise for his dishonesty and he refused I said that he was not fit to be called human.

An evil piece of filth. Of course I hate him

Shaun Smith as a site director ought to be intelligent.

What Shaun Smith needs to realise is that when you behave in such a vile, evil and deplorable manner, and totally without conscience or remorse, such behaviour will naturally generate you enemies. I don't apologise for loathing him, it is a perfectly natural reaction.

He is suddenly so fragile and sensitive, yet does not mind wilfully wrecking the lives and reputations of others including my entire family, through premeditated targeting and dishonesty.

I don't apologise for what I said to him as, in truth, he fully deserves thousands of times worse.

Einstein's theory of relativity: for every action there is an equal and opposite reaction and the equation e=mc2, Shaun Smith's evil being the e and mc being my initials.

If you are going to clearly be dishonest for no good reason and attack someone's livelihood, reputation, marriage and family they are not going to say 'Thank you'.

There are consequences for such vile evil targeting.

What did he expect the other day, a hug? Even that is now offensive in his warped mind.

If Cry baby Smith is so fragile, then explain to him that telling the truth about his evil deeds can release him from his torment. Better still, explain his evil deeds to him and give him the long overdue boot (i.e. dismissal) and see how he likes it. He deserves a whole lot worse than my disgust.

There is a vile cancer that has been left unchecked at Abbotts for years due to weak ineffective and corrupt leadership at Abbotts who play pretend and won't face up to their responsibility.

Shaun Smith, Pat Cole and Les Muggeridge's positions are indisputably untenable and the paperwork is there to prove it. They are racist sexist filth who blatantly attacked me in the most overzealous, evil, racist, targeted way imaginable. This was totally out of proportion with anything before or since.

They must still be removed. The only reason they are still there is that Abbotts HR department is institutionally weak and corrupt.

The irony of better communication between departments

I sent my report to Jane Ingram as she cost me a third job last year by pretending there is no record of my ever having worked at Abbotts. (Four, if you count the Royal Mail job I did not take to join Forterra)

Now that it's convenient for you, you and Shaun Smith choose to confirm that I did. One must also ask how you got my address if Jane Ingram is telling the truth and there is no record of me ever working there?

You have totally undermined her.

The irony of the location

Of course, although my recent meeting with the vile Shaun Smith at Sainsbury's was a chance encounter, I shop regularly in Wantage and this is our first meeting in many years.

My encounter with Linda Shaw after my dismissal was anything but. I was at the cigarette / paper counter, saw her watch me from the exit doors, walk quickly into the shop then hurry to leave right next to me from a hiding place in the first aisle, with no attempt made at a purchase. Then when I told my wife who I had just seen, she points out that the evil one is kerb-crawling just yards from us, then she speeds off when I clock her. You were informed of this, too, but only react with exaggeration against me, ignoring every bad deed I endure without exception, because you are corrupt.

Being straightforward and honest

Why don't you just be honest and state what the words allegedly used by me allegedly were? Don't let Shaun Smith gild the lily. I'm still waiting to hear what the alleged breast comment I allegedly made actually entails, as it failed to occur in either of Linda Shaw's two contradictory statements.

Then again, why don't Abbotts present genuine documents at tribunal, or ever address Linda Shaw's contradictions that prove she was lying, or her paranoid, impossible assertions that I'm psychic and in three places at once each morning whilst I'm obviously in a fourth.

Her evidence is clearly the demented ravings of a complete nutter, and that's even before she gets on to fantasising about heavy breathing phone calls. The nuisance phone calls to my children started immediately after Linda met my much younger, much prettier wife and miraculously ended when she went on holiday for three weeks. Wake up!

If you want to say I called Shaun Smith 'a fucking shit' in your words (with asterisks), I'm OK with that. I'm grown-up, so am not going to get over-offended that you want to attribute that to me. So if it makes you happy, go with it. He deserves it anyway. However, I don't confirm it. But as I said before, I reported the use of other colourful language in my report and under normal circumstances abhor it. You want to attribute me with calling him a shit, go for it, or call me in and I'll call him it myself.

In the great scheme of things I regard my language as less of a crime than bullying, hounding, intentionally targeting and attacking one of your best employees for no reason. I've been nice for so long and suffered so greatly something, sometime has to give.

Mine was the reaction, not the main event. I feel no remorse as there was 8 years of justification.

How would you react to your wife being called a liar, and Abbotts supporting cruelty to your children and a murder attempt on myself? If I got in my car and lay in wait and deliberately drove at someone head on, on their side of the road, forcing them to swerve behind a parked car, then I would call that attempted murder, as the police do. I would also expect Shaun Smith to act accordingly at my disciplinary hearing, knowing this happened, and not just try to silence and dismiss me.

If Abbotts had morals, they would call me in for the lie detector test on this very serious charge. You can't just pretend it never happened, just as I can't be expected to think it's OK when he won't even apologise for his evil.

How would you react if in light of the above factual paragraph, Abbott directors not just cost you your job but attacked your marriage, your home, your family life, your sanity, in fact, absolutely everything; and over an absolute overreaction to a total non-event that was reciprocated with interest by my accuser, in public, subsequent to the non-event causing such unbelievable offence months later?

Yet Abbotts ignore the elephant in the room and defend the person they know to be a **serial fantasist and troublemaker who had a similar issue at a previous Abbott site in Abingdon**. My record was spotless.

Bias and total lack of professionalism
As with at Sainsbury's, quoting Shaun Smith as genuine, Abbotts are again reaching a verdict before hearing both sides to an event, and one outside your jurisdiction also.

Linda Shaw publicly kissing me was a month after the hug and there were up to 30 or so potential witnesses, none of whom you questioned, and none of the 30 potential witnesses from my shift who saw the hug were questioned either. Not one of these reacted as if anything remarkable happened at the time. You do, however, question Linda's neighbour and close personal friend whose story does not add up at all.

My wife sends a four-page signed, dated, handwritten account of the night Linda Shaw publicly kissed me. This is inadmissible and no witness from the night out is questioned. My wife is clearly called a liar as her evidence is shunned. I later prove this to be true by lie detector, too.

Also, I had no disciplinary previous and another who hit a female with a metal ruler and sent vile texts to another, could not have had more. How is this racism allowed?

Also, punching a pregnant woman is fine, it's playful, but a public hug is assault, harassment, inappropriate touching and a neck grab, yet none of the 25-30 witnesses from my shift, all of whom saw nothing inappropriate at the time, were questioned. They all hugged that week, too. Of the hundreds or thousands of hugs that week one becomes sackable only when Shaun & Pat commit gross misconduct.

Also you are acting as my boss
Last week I was not an Abbott ex-employee, according to Jane Ingram. So if Shaun Smith and I have words on the way to the Sainsbury's exit past some checkouts and in the disabled bay immediately outside (all lasting less than 1 minute in total)…

What business is it of yours to be reprimanding me?

What does this have to do with Abbotts?

Why, when I have written of your misdemeanours for eight years, do I not get a reply? It is your job to right that wrong.

Why did you do nothing when Linda Shaw clearly stalked me and my wife twice at the same Sainsbury's in a premeditated act of following and kerb-crawling?

Why do you not address the ultra-serious stuff that happened on your premises concerning management bullying someone who was a member of staff at the time?

You're at it again in terms of blatant bias, racism and inconsistency

Since 2009 there has been the mother of all overreactions to every little thing I have done, all of which are at best molehills compared to the well-documented mountains that I have been the victim of.

I'll try

As a gesture of goodwill I will endeavour not to speak to the next Abbotts director I meet, even if it is Les, Shaun or Pat. Notice I use the word 'endeavour', not 'promise'. I talked myself into leaving Shaun's company 'tout de suite'. I don't really regret showing my displeasure with him or using an expletive, though. I think it is good for him to see the impact of his dishonesty on others.

I'm not sorry, but you should be

I'm totally unapologetic and still owe Shaun Smith 1,000,000 fold. He can sneakily give it out at work but is a bit of a wimp and cry baby in reality.

Don't back Shaun Smith or let his lies do me any more damage. I have paid a huge price already in terms of depression, anxiety attacks, the effects on my family, lost revenue, etc.

Don't back him; look at his conduct for my dismissal, then his lies to tribunal and do the decent thing. Think of my children.

I want to move on but the effects of your bullying are preventing me.

One important thing to remember is that I never chose this argument or declared war. I would much rather all this had no place at all in my life. It was unnecessary bullying. 8 years plus and counting have been wasted, or at least would be if I did not get justice.

I want to get on and concentrate on the positive in life, and am about as keen on an argument, or indeed on contacting Abbott, as I'm sure you are, me; but any decent human being will understand my frustration when I lose a third good job due to Abbott's lies (and a fourth where I talked of my dismissal at interview) and meet one I know to be a pure evil coward.

I have this absolute inbuilt desire to see the truth, and the whole truth, to triumph and for justice to be done, hence my overwhelming depression and anxiety attacks

You can help stop them, or at least give that possibility a chance.

It's indisputable I was set up and that Abbott and Linda Shaw were dishonest.

Look at her contradictions and letters (plural), not by the author stated.

Look at Les Muggeridge and Solicitor Wilcox's intentional perversion of the course of justice with the fake minutes they presented. There are some serious issues into why the judge let this go.

Look at Shaun Smith's lie about the reconvened hearing and his illegal holding back of vital paperwork.

Don't incriminate yourself!

There are enough at Abbotts up to their necks in it through their dishonesty.

A better way to get the facts

If you want the truth, just ask me every time. Don't quote Shaun Smith.

You don't need to send recorded delivery. If I receive a letter I'm always honest about it and always reply. Even Solicitor Wilcox will confirm that.

Judge Barrowclough was even so moved as to congratulate my honesty; sadly prior to his dutiful dishonesty.

This could all have been settled years ago, and sadly should absolutely never have happened in the first place. It's all so sad and so wrong, what Abbotts did.

....

In fairness to them and Jane Ingram they may have the menacing, intimidating presence of Les Muggeridge looming behind them.

I met a previous manager on one of my walks and told him of my fate at Abbotts. He referred to Les Muggeridge as 'a bit of a wide boy'.

Wouldn't it be good if all Abbott staff past and present got together and reported the UK HR Director for his bullying? I've had it face to face and on the phone and it's not low-key stuff. It is full on rabid berserk dog with a few nasty injuries stuff.

I could be the catalyst that makes Abbott a decent environment in which to work.

Chapter 38

So the Ball is Back in Andy Payne's Court

As you can see from the previous extensive letter quotes, Andy Payne of Abbott HR Witney/Maidenhead, another Abbott UK HR Director, is now fully aware of the facts of how a member of staff, i.e. my good self, was mistreated.

An HR Director with morals who has just seen my polygraph results, and my letter to him clearly explaining the company is chronically guilty of the most appalling bulling and racism towards me, would now surely act to right the wrongs, as it states in company policy.

Add to this the fact that Andy Payne has just proven his HR colleague Jane Ingram to be an utter liar beyond all doubt, not just beyond all reasonable doubt, and that he himself has shown himself to be an idiot by jumping head first to Shaun Smith's defence and threatening me.

Surely now Abbotts will finally say 'Sorry'. Logically it could surely not be statistically possible that I would meet yet another bent director or manager, having already encountered Nicky Albert, Shaun Smith, Amanda White, Pat Cole, Les Muggeridge, Miles White CEO (whom I eventually addressed as Miles Yellow due to his cowardice in dealing with my complaints) and more recently Jane Ingram.

On the subject of utter hypocrisy and inconsistency, all of which favours Abbott and all too conveniently. An HR Director Thug who should have the highest morals intimidates me in the loudest 'in my face' fashion possible and with utter pre-intent, and Abbott do nothing. I speak civilly and with due cause to another director and the kitchen sink is thrown at me again. It is a bit like comparing a kind hug to punching a pregnant woman. In denying I even worked there Abbott again showed they don't care about morals. They have none. They just care about protecting their own, regardless of right and wrong. Abbott HR have no morals except corrupt evil ones, and that's totally endemic company-wide.

Les Muggeridge should have to answer why he chose Pat Cole to chair the interview, having not opened my letter. From his intimidating, hate-filled talk it was 100% obvious that it was because he knew she hated me and wanted me gone. He knew with those two what the pre-ordained verdict would be too. He also felt above it being illegal.

Having worked in a betting shop after I left Abbotts and being very hot on statistics from my mathematics and engineering studies, if you were to make Andy Payne the eighth corrupt horse in an row in an accumulator then even if there was only a half chance that each was going to be corrupt, the odds would be over 250/1. Throw in all my appeals being ignored and the odds are in the billions. There has to be a common influence or influences like intimidation and institutional corruption. But then throw in that there is not a chance in a thousand that a ten-year-old could not see I was the victim of vindictive targeting and the state of the corruption at Abbott is infinitely more serious – in fact absolute.

Unless, of course, Andy Payne was to deal with my complaint and prove that Abbott did in fact have some morals.

But what did he do? Did he deal with my complaint? No, this ostrich of a director buried his head in the sand and blocked all online communication and went home crying to mummy.

Did he expect I would just go away? I had known for some time that Abbotts UK were a dishonest bunch of crooks, bullies and cowardly liars, and he has just absolutely proved it beyond all doubt.

Going international
Again I quote:

> It is up to each of us as Abbott employees to build our company and brand by holding ourselves to the highest ethical standards and by operating with honesty, fairness and integrity.
>
> Robert B Ford CEO (post–Miles White
> $1.6 Billion Abbott Depakote scandal)

Well, what a load of bollocks that is. It certainly was in my case.

These Abbott standards are international and perhaps one bad apple don't spoil the whole bunch. Perhaps just the UK was rotten, perhaps due to Les Muggeridge's iron 'dot-knuckled' fist engendering a culture of fear and intimidation among the specially picked, compliant, limited intelligence UK directors.

But luckily I can appeal elsewhere as Abbott have the highest international ethical standards.

As with sending my lie detector results to all I dealt with except the control freak bully, Les Muggeridge, who then immediately bullied me anyway, I could now send the details to all Abbott HR Directors worldwide excluding the Abbott UK bully.

So I then e-mailed the Abbott HR department of every major country on the globe. They received the same complaint Andy Payne received, my polygraph results and other relevant background information.

Surely every Abbott HR department in the world could not be institutionally corrupt and back the most deplorable bullying and racism behaviour of Abbotts UK.

Surely there were these highest international standards of ethics to uphold?

I suppose I should be flattered. One by one and within no time every international HR ostrich ran away from little old me, only to put its head in the sand, and block me. Wow!

Abbotts HR were now officially a bunch of bullying, cowardly, corrupt racists **worldwide!**

I was kind of surprised at the USA, but not because I had dealt with Miles 'yellow' White. This was the company headquarters.

I was even more disappointed in Abbotts HR Ireland. They turned a blind eye to all the racist IRA comments I received as well as all the other bullying and racial discrimination.

As a side note, regarding Ireland. Donegal Town was a place dear to my heart. One uncle has had a significant civil position in or around the town throughout his life. Another uncle was a very well-known and celebrated Donegal footballer, with whose family I spent a few summers in my younger years. He held on during his final few days to see the last time Donegal last won the all-Ireland championship. The captain dedicated the win to him on TV during the post-match interview.

The Ulster cup was at his wedding and the Sam McGuire All-Ireland cup was at his funeral.

On the one hand I hated the fact that there was now an Abbotts in Donegal knowing, from first- hand experience, how racist Abbotts were to those of Irish stock, but appreciated that it brought more employment to the area.

That's just coincidence that means something to me. Good luck to all at Abbotts Donegal.

Abbotts had now proven themselves to be a bunch of corrupt, bullying racists on a worldwide basis.

The $1.6 billion Depakote scandal just underlines how low that Abbott will go and their utter contempt for human decency and welfare when there is a buck to be made.

It also shows what a nasty, corrupt, intimidating bunch their lawyers are.

How can you treat families whose lives you have ruined in such a deplorable way? Silly old me for asking that question.

At least I'm forewarned of their tactics, which might result in a sequel as this lot are actually even worse morally than what I detail in this book.

Abbott could spend a few million less in apologising to and compensating me. Just a thought:

I've learned to live in hope rather than expectation.

But each time they try knock me down for good, to date I manage to get up and come back at them.

Don't play the victim again, Abbotts

I will say that if this book leads to legal threats to someone Abbott insist never worked there, proving themselves to be liars, I will not cower. I will publish all their intimidation, whatever the inevitable associated threats.

Evil occurs when good men do nothing.

This book is a last resort because of their lies, victimisation, intimidation and racism.

I am responding to my character being libelled by you and your lies and dodgy paperwork already presented to tribunal that clearly demands closer scrutiny.

That was all before you then pretended that I never even existed.

Enough said.

Chapter 39

Lie Detector Merits and Judicial Issues

Lie detectors and fairness

The wonderful thing about a lie detector is that it does not see colour, creed, gender, age, sexuality etc., the very first things an HR person sees, and the biggest influence on their decision making. It does not attend lodge meetings either or have ideological pre-programming or have emotions at all, so it can't have a conflict of interest.

It just sees whether someone is telling lies or the truth, with an accuracy far greater than a judge. I say this from genuine experience of both.

I am not accusing anyone specifically of freemasonry relating to the above. I'm just pointing out lie detector merits.

I've been on a jury at the Old Bailey, the case then moved to the Lord Mayor's court and have also attended an employment tribunal. Both times, thanks to the judge, the guilty walked away free. At the Lord Mayor's court the guilty walked free thanks to a technicality raised, that the jury ourselves were not even told about. I was then the one picked by the judge on our recall to pronounce the – in all probability – guilty person innocent.

How often does a case take forever to get heard, then a certain police officer fails to show or makes a paperwork error and the whole case is thrown out?

Mind you, with all my questions avoided, statements covered up, all the paperwork that's been lost, edited, destroyed, embellished and invented etc., the closing of ranks at billion-dollar American multinational Abbott's and at every judiciary and police level, would it be illogical not to have strong suspicions when instances like the above occur?

Again I emphasise I have no conclusive evidence of freemasonry, but there is so much unexplained intransigence and blatant unfairness that still stays unaddressed, and there seems no contrition or desire for justice from certain quarters, in plain sight. Most importantly every bit of bias and corruption has favoured one side only. The odds of this happening by chance are in the billions to one.

Dr Dolittle, if I could talk to the animals

As in Dr Dolittle, if I could talk to the animals. If only we could access directly the criminal mind and bypass the lying tongue…

Guess what … We can, but there is a whole raft of judges, police, freemasons, MPs, councillors and HR departments etc. who despise straightforward honesty as it would ruin them.

Think of the improvements of replacing judges with polygraph tests.

The obvious immediate answer is that we could finally get the justice we don't currently get. It would be fair, impartial and affordable to everyone, which it currently isn't.

What's not to love?

That's reason to celebrate unless you are a lawyer, judge, barrister or the like.

We could put an end to allegations of bigotry, racism, sexism, homophobia, ageism, etc. etc.

Judges and wilful unfairness

Let's face facts, the nation's tribunal judges are at the very least questionable in their judgement.

The first thing we do is swear to tell the truth, the whole truth and nothing but the truth, and decent people like me are totally hamstrung by taking this seriously. We must also contend with judges and solicitors constantly interrupting us when we try to utter the whole truth. It's a game to them.

Even when we appeal, telling them the truth in writing and point to the bundle where this truth is and where the inconsistencies and lies are, they simply ignore it. They certainly did in my case.

You then write to the regional judge who will not address a single point you make about the bent judgement and who then says you can only appeal to the ombudsman regarding her conduct only, but not the judgement, etc.

This is just blatant 'shithousery'.

We need a fair and just system that delivers justice.

Justice is supposed to be seen to be done.

Bonkers appointments

In the Law Society Gazette, a former deputy district judge Michael Rooze said the JAC and JACO are not fit for purpose and should be abolished, calling it a corrupt, self-serving closed shop. He advised that an independent body without judges or civil servants should recommend appointments.

He said the whole system was bent, 'top down'.

The JAC is the Judicial Appointments Commission and JACO is the Judicial Appointment and Conduct Ombudsman; that was Admiral Sir John Brigstocke KCB (RIP) in my case.

It is an indisputable fact, regarding my experiences, that every judge and police officer involved with my issues with Abbott has served Abbott at every corrupt turn without exception.

Let's simply get rid of all employment tribunal judiciary now, for the good of the vast majority.

The poor souls in the Post Office / Fujitsu Horizon debacle suffered bankruptcy, false imprisonment, and in some cases even suicides. In all over 700 prosecutions (usually without convictions, but all with ruined lives and characters). All these convictions, yet British justice, often in the High Court, got it wrong every time and never saw a link between all the cases. British justice was, here again, proven to be unfit for purpose.

After my tribunal hearing I was supposed to trawl through similar previous cases to present legal precedent to the judge. Hardly fair when representing yourself against the legal might of a multi-billion-dollar company.

The Post Office knew there were a great many similar cases but did not tell the postmasters this. The judicial gravy train chugged on without questioning the sheer number of similar cases. Or were these similar cases used by lawyers in summaries to get further convictions? I obviously don't know the answer, but it is a pertinent question.

Abbott know they have done a great wrong, then years later did me a great wrong again even after my polygraph test. Did they do this because they felt empowered and emboldened by a previous bent verdict in their favour, courtesy of a tribunal?

I know those at the Post Office would be very sceptical at technology being brought in after experiencing Fujitsu, but I can promise them that polygraph tests would have shown their innocence. They know, for sure, that the British justice system is unfit for purpose.

Morally my case should have never been conceived in the first place and is utterly flawed procedurally. Upholding the decision, after legitimate complaint, brings shame on the judiciary. It could have been nipped in the bud had a polygraph option been present at work in the first place, as my polygraph answers showed.

I have personally shown we have a better, just system that is fit for purpose.

Is that why I'm so hated and persecuted?

The bamboozle

To quote eminent scientist Carl Sagen re. bamboozle theory:-

'One of the saddest lessons in history is this. If we have been bamboozled long enough, we tend to reject all evidence of the bamboozle. We're no longer interested in finding out the truth. The bamboozle has captured us. It's simply too painful to acknowledge even to ourselves that we've been taken. Once you give a Charlatan power over you, you almost never get it back.'

In law, don't be bamboozled into thinking we can't upgrade the all-too-often corrupt, expensive pig trough of a tribunal system we have today.

We have always had this system so it must be right, we can't change. So say all the bamboozled.

I suggest we scrap the tribunal system and bring in lay people, like in the jury system and polygraph tests asking understandable questions in plain language.

We could have a system with no pre-bias that is affordable, open to all and which treats all fairly. Above all else it can reach the correct verdict and deliver justice, the type all those who wrote to Sir John, in vain, wanted. What's not to love about it?

The polygraph vs the combined minds of the police and judiciary.

For brevity I'll just give a few examples to illustrate my point.

Rape cases – intent and consent

If you are the victim of rape there is a far less than 1% chance you will get justice and, I have read, a 1.6% chance of the case occurring. The experience and cost in getting this justice or not will break you forever in a double whammy. There is every prospect you will be a financially ruined emotional wreck and you may not even see justice.

Generally in a rape case it is agreed or proven that the penetrative act has taken place.

The question is that of intent and consent and proving this. The lie detector can do this.

The only exception I can see is if one sees a green light and another sees a red. Even then, the honesty of both will still be shown.

This will also mean more genuine cases of rape are brought forward with a greater conviction rate, thus saving the next potential victims also.

It will also mean that the 'cry wolf' cases and innocent lives being smeared can be stopped.

The migrant backlog

Genuine applicants will have no worries and get faster resolutions, but bad news for the criminal gangs and bogus claimants.

Murder e.g. Stephen Lawrence

Questions that could have been asked in a polygraph test:

- Did you kill Stephen Lawrence?
- Were you present when Stephen Lawrence was murdered?
- Do you know who killed Stephen Lawrence?
- How much heartache and years wasted could that have saved? We could ask the exact same questions regarding PC Keith Blakelock.

Abbott, Pat, Shaun and Les

- Did you treat Michael Collins exactly as you would any other employee regardless of race, gender or religion?
- Do you believe absolutely that Michael Collins was guilty?
- Was your verdict motivated in any way by personal insecurity due to Michael Collins having the courage to raise necessary issues?
- Did you place your interests before the interests of the Abbott customer and shareholder when you dismissed Michael Collins? (This one might tempt a CEO.)

- Have you ever been a member of a secret society?
- Did you ever intentionally try to intimidate Michael Collins? Etc. Etc.

Don't let one of these machines anywhere near Linda Shaw, though. It might explode.

I would happily volunteer to take as many more polygraph tests as they like.

I do, however, insist question one is:
Did you have to take evasive action on your side of the road, when car reg: M888LAS was driven at you?

I wanted that to be question one last time.
Other questions might include:

- When you hugged Linda Shaw, was it in any way violent, aggressive or nasty?
- Was there a need to dismiss you to protect other members of staff (as Mr Muggeridge suggested to Mr O Morton at Jobcentre Plus, Southampton, that there was?)
- Did you find Les Muggeridge's behaviour at the gatehouse to be excessively nasty and intimidating?

Then we will see who the nasty one is. Then we will see who really deserved dismissal.

I fully volunteer to do this live with a screen behind me to show the graphs I produce.

We could make it a live charity event. Abbott like good causes. In fact I would insist on it being live. I know Les and Dodgy Documents.

I have often suggested that both Linda and I take polygraph tests relating to the driving incident.

If anyone has any doubts about my polygraph test, Contact Don Cargill. Ask yourself, 'Would I really send them to police, judges, the FDA, current affairs programmes, etc. if there was anything untoward?'

With regard the question I wanted asked first last time about the driving incident, I'm sure I worded it: 'Was car reg: M888LAS intentionally driven at you?' Don Cargill stated the obvious, that we couldn't do a Yes / No question regarding someone else's intent. Being slow off the mark and a bit excited and nervous, I didn't think at the time, 'Why don't you reword it so as it reads whether you had to take evasive action on your side of the road with this car being driven at you?' I had plenty of other reserve questions lined up too.

The benefits are seemingly endless

Jimmy Savile. The grooming gangs. So many cases could have been solved with simple standard questions and evaluated by a machine incapable of prejudice, corruption or discrimination.

Other questions

- Have you really changed gender and are now a woman, or are you pretending? Especially before sending men guilty of rape to women's prisons.
- Generally: Did you really take offence at that? Did you mean to offend that person?

I could save Abbotts tens of millions

I tried to save Abbotts a lot of money in my time there, suggesting improvements that were totally ignored.

They still persist with a flawed system which costs tens of millions to this day. Their woke, over-bloated, often unnecessary HR industry, that my case proves is totally useless and racist.

We could get rid of the whole twisted HR industry everywhere and reinstate the personnel officer at work. Woke is killing fairness and as a result, society's morals.

If all staff knew that in any work complaint they, or the one they accuse, had the right to insist on a lie detector test, we could eradicate the fake complaint whilst encouraging the genuine complaint.

The 'cry wolf' fantasist would not win. **I know a 'cry wolf' fantasist who actually won at tribunal without even having to turn up, and without ever having had to tell the truth.** How shit is that?

My case proves how utterly useless and totally unfit for purpose the tribunal system is. The same could be said for Abbott HR staff, and on a worldwide basis too.

To this day, 15 years on and counting, it is forever to the shame of Abbott that not one of Abbott's HR staff or directors has had the decency to apologise or admit the truth.

Peer pressure, self-preservation and the fear of rocking the boat leaves them clinging desperately to the HR bamboozle and their lies.

Their egos will not let them say, 'I'm sorry. I clearly got it wrong,' in fact, 'The whole system is wrong and does not work,' except, that is, when it works for the odd corrupt director or fantasist.

Then when, years later, Abbott are so wrapped up in their web of lies that they will even deny my very existence because the truth is so hard to face, that they start my torment all over again with yet another shocking lie, when again, I place the irrefutable evidence before them, surely then someone at Abbotts must say, 'Enough is enough'. Or someone should say it for them.

Still, to this day, nobody has even said sorry!

But then when the following year they start lying again and insist I actually do now exist after all when it is convenient for them, and I then inform them of their lie the year before, you would think they would finally say sorry. I've never heard that word from them once.

You would think that in the face of such 'shithousery' there would surely be a public body to which I could report them, who would attend to such an issue, and protect the public interest.

Or do certain individuals at Abbott now feel that due to their influence and getting away with what they got away with they are simply above the law and can tell any lie with immunity?

After my complaints in vain to Maidenhead police about this, too, it 100% looks that way.

Concluding

Nobody's perfect and we all have some skeleton somewhere, but we can get the big calls right.

Let's get the utterly useless dross of this world, like certain judges and police chiefs, and put them out to pasture for good, for the sake of justice and tackling crime.

Think of the billions we could save, too.

With polygraph tests, affluence and influence would then no longer be able to buy justice as it so clearly is now.

How can 'Represented billion-dollar company' vs 'Unrepresented me and my depression and complete lack of legal knowledge' possibly be fair?

Finally, with lie detectors everyone can then be treated equally regardless of their differences and not differently because of them.

That counts for differences in finance and influence, too.

Remember me saying that sentence about everyone being treated equally, Judge Barrowclough?

The judge supported me wholeheartedly when I said that, too.

Was this just an outward act of sheer hypocrisy? Looking at his summary...

Chapter 40

Meeting Shaun Smith Again in Salford

Moving forward to July 2022 and an event I'm looking forward to, My son's Covid -delayed graduation ceremony at the Lowry Centre, Salford, just across the ship canal from Old Trafford and the Coronation Street studios.

We had a lovely evening before in Cheshire and it was then wonderful to see my son again on his big day.

At the Lowry Centre it was ridiculously hot, one of the hottest days on record, so we were outside. I went in before the ceremony to answer the call of nature and, coming out, who do I walk past? Shaun Smith.

I say to my wife, 'You will never guess who I have just bloody seen? What are the chances of that?'

She reminds me, 'It is our son's day.' I assure her I know this is the case, but at the same time you can appreciate that his presence does not bring me pleasure.

We have Linda making an issue of our wedding, Abbotts costing us our honeymoon and now today of all days, there he is!

We go into the theatre and, bearing in mind there are many presentations that day at different times, guess where our seat is? We are about three rows behind the SS with his head directly in our eye line to the stage. He is even in some of our photos and videos, it is so unavoidable.

I did reflect that I also promised Andy Payne that I would endeavour to ignore or be polite to the next Abbott director I met, even if it was Les; Shaun or Pat.

I still keep to my promises.

Well, after all, Abbott have always been so good to me. Yeah, right!

My wife says, 'Don't let it get to you.' I said, 'I'm not, but I'm entitled not to like him.'

What was I supposed to do?

Give him a hug?

Looking back, it was just as well I didn't. Could you imagine that I had even said 'Hello' to him and shook his hand? He would probably have been off crying to Andy Payne again and I would probably have got a letter accusing me of a grab and intimidation.

The world we live in.

Chapter 41

Cutting Off Your Nose to Spite Your Face

What I'm about to tell you may just be coincidence, or it may even be karma for some very inept one-trick pony directors.

I was alerted watching TV, to some rather dodgy baby formula produced by Abbott. No, this time it wasn't all the beetle parts and eggs like before, this time it was bacteriological from another badly run Abbotts site.

On looking up the recall using key words I noticed that there was another Abbott recall. This was a recall of a product made in Abbott Witney between January and May 2010, according to Abbott spokesman Scott Davies.

The scale of this recall: 359 million test strips at a cost of tens of millions of pounds or dollars, let alone a shocking hit in terms of Abbott's reputation. I care about this because I worked hard to produce high volumes of quality product up until my dismissal in December 2009, the month before they started churning out defective rubbish.

Funnily enough I joined the company just after another disaster. Staff had been coming in for months just reading a book as there was an issue that debris from one process was appearing at the next stage, causing the basic circuit system to give false readings or not work. If memory serves me rightly, they referred to this as silvering.

I'm not saying that, just because I was there for a time of excellent quality and productivity in between two total disasters, all the good stuff is down to me. There were four shifts and many staff.

But what is true beyond doubt was that when there was an issue I was the one at meetings who did not just have the courage to raise that issue, but invariably offered a constructive solution, too.

What I did represent was a conscience and talent. If I saw an issue I would raise that issue. I would often think about resolving that issue and I always worked hard with my eyes open in the best interests of the customer. Because of that I was seen as a threat to the new, insecure management when, in fact, I was a great asset. I put my ideas forward and if they were rejected I accepted defeat but did expect the courtesy of some feedback for my efforts, and was hated by Pat Cole for mentioning this at a shift meeting.

The thing was, as well, that although I did a lot of overtime to earn extra, I always give value with my output. Any work on my ideas was in my own time, totally free of charge, and not a threat to anyone. I wanted nothing in return either.

If you see Chapter 13, my 'Good management, bad management' chapter, you will see what I mean.

On reading about the 359 million-strip debacle a few thoughts came to mind of how, if viewed as an asset, I could have helped the company and the customer.

Meeting two former colleagues outside Asda and M & S in Hayden in Swindon after my polygraph test I had heard how nasty the atmosphere had become at Abbotts. The chap said, 'It used to be a nice place to work; it is anything but, now. There is a climate of fear.' I mentioned how I had been treated and that I had taken a lie detector to show Linda Shaw was lying, too, but didn't believe that was the real reason for my dismissal.

Perhaps that nastiness mentioned was the reaction to whatever went wrong with the recall of so many strips and the embarrassment factor to Abbott Witney.

Perhaps it wasn't the staff that were to blame for all the garbage made, rather it was the culture engendered by an insecure management who were totally out of their depth.

We had previously for years made good product on the exact same machines. Something changed.

Staff would surely have known, as I was called up for an interview upstairs and disappeared thereafter, that if you ask questions the same will happen to you as happened to Mick Collins.

Many, for example, were convinced that the CCF election for which I stood was a fiasco.

They would have seen an exceptional, diligent worker named and shamed wrongly and vindictively on the weekly ER notice board incorrectly for weeks on end.

They would now know that he was stitched up in a false flag operation for a hug with Linda Shaw, just like all the hugs they all gave, and many would have seen Linda publicly kiss Mick.

When you have a management as out of their depth, insecure and cynical as Abbott now had, you wouldn't say anything for fear of being the next Mick Collins.

Basically to keep your job you keep quiet, just as to get to the top you kissed the right backsides and, no matter how immoral, you did what they wanted you to do, as my totally unfair, wildly disproportionate dismissal illustrated.

The canary in the coalmine

As you sew so shall you reap. If you engender a culture of fear then, when there actually is an issue, you won't hear about it as staff will be too frightened to raise that issue.

There are a lot people in North Korea goose-stepping to the Emperor's tune in public through fear but, in reality, they are among the poorest, unhappiest people on earth.

Abbott were now in a situation where they had the same processes as before, but had got rid of so much key talent and experience. They had people who could not stay awake on the nightshift getting priority on dayshift overtime, Sleeping Beauty and possibly Mr Magoo doing final inspection and Laurel and Hardy, aka Pat & Shaun, upstairs in charge. Standards would inevitably drop now that Abbott were no longer on the side of those who were on the side of quality and the customer.

The one who was protected by management for not doing a single visual inspection for at least two whole batches with blatantly visible, easily correctable defects ignored and who punched pregnant women was still there. The one who got told off for flagging this serious error to management as per company policy who publicly hugged a woman who later publicly kissed him, had been removed.

Coincidence, maybe, but the month after I'm gone and there are other forced and voluntary redundancies Abbott start making defective product for months on end, to hit the nail on the head. You can be sure that if there was an issue or obvious problem I would have raised concerns and in all probability offered a possible solution.

I had an OND in Electrical and Mechanical Engineering and Maths and had previously designed four wave-power systems and built one that worked perfectly first time. So I was a potential asset. I had a scientific mind and also worked full-time on the machines. More importantly, though, I could and would logically communicate.

What were the reasons they made all this crap in 2010? It could have been a problem with the ambience, which is one excuse I saw offered up. It may have been a material issue, or even just coincidence that things happened at this time. But for sure, it happened and nobody noticed anything or, if they did, nobody raised the issue – perhaps in a spirit of self-preservation.

I'd like to think that if I was there I would have smelled a rat and raised the issue, if something was obviously wrong. That would be me, being positive again. I would, of course, been sacked if I had.

But I did think back. I thought of a few occasions where I tried to help with my ingenuity and the courage of my convictions.

Shot down in flames

If you want to avoid a technical bit, move on to the Laurel and Hardy section of this chapter.

As said before too, when training I made sure the trainee had hands-on experience and repeated the process numerous times to show they understood. I offered encouragement, clarity and the assurance that questions were unlimited. Many others did not want to help with their 'look see, I can do it, bye and tutting' attitude.

I have told you all about my Norwegian Cross idea to improve printing, so will mention two others.

The next process after printing was the insulation tape laying. This was the process where I was falsely awarded fame and notoriety on the weekly ER notice board.

When I made this mistake, it was identical to what another colleague had made just before, although he was of course not named and shamed, as they were just out to get me.

I submitted a report into the psychology and potential optical illusion involved in making this mistake. I concluded it was due to the over-reliance and trust in the microscope alone, instead of using your eyes to check the bigger picture first.

This was me being conscientious and writing a 'corrective action, preventative action' aka a 'CAPA' report in my own time. I'm not sure Abbott had ever heard of CAPA reports, nor had I back then. This was just my initiative and natural concern for the Abbott customer.

What we were looking for was a white continuous thread laid by the machine, like that from a cotton reel. It could drift out of place from on top of a white background on to a darker background. However, a snapped non- existent thread did not show on this darker background, thus not triggering the brain to see an error that a simple visual inspection would see.

I likened this optical illusion in my report to the triangles you can google with 'I love Paris in the Springtime' which the eye computes as 'I love Paris in the Springtime'. The reader does not initially notice that the word 'the' appears twice. The eye automatically corrects this.

What I did was to assess my error, evaluate it and then make a positive suggestion to stop the next person making it and, as always, did this report in my own time to help others. This type of behaviour is welcomed by good managers and seen as a threat by weak ones.

This same mistake had already happened before, so it was an issue.

Another process where I tried to constructively help

There was another process after this where the cards are cut into six rows of strips and reject rows disposed of.

This penultimate process was called 'row converting' and this was another process where I was stupid enough to try to input positively.

I was 'numero uno' on this machine bar none. In both quality and output, and often for 72 hours a week. It was later deemed safe only to work 6 hours on these machines and I have no doubt my eyesight and posture has paid a heavy price for my hard work and diligence.

On nights, another 'former sex on-site production manager', who was now a company man, wanted a meeting with two row convertor operatives from each shift with a view to improving these machines. I was naturally the first asked on our shift and came up with a report with six major changes that could dramatically improve this process, both in terms of operator health and product quality to the customer, and could improve production, too. What's not to love?

No doubt after talking to either Laurel or Hardy, or both, there was a change of tactic. This manager spoke only to a couple of ladies on days who thought the process was OK.

This process basically cut the strips down to their final width and they were then visually inspected before the final testing, individual cutting and packaging process. Crucial to this visual inspection was a check that the blood fill area of the diabetic testing strip was present, adequate and in good condition along with the visible area of the circuit.

The inspection conditions were lamentable, to put it mildly. Some less diligent staff often failed to notice that vital blood fill areas were completely missing altogether.

Firstly there was an issue taking these strips out of the machine collection pot in the first place. These were just thin, multi-dented metal collection jugs in shocking condition. The jugs stuck in the machine and the product stuck in the jugs, meaning employees often yanked these strips out with force, causing the strips damage.

The inspection tables were flat. Some tables were even placed around pillars in the building, and the lighting was whatever you got from the ceiling above. This naturally led to eyesight, neck and posture issues in order to inspect these strips.

Some staff kept ahead and rarely let these collection jugs/bins fill up, so did not have to prise the strips free and were skilled with the hands, spreading these strips like a Las Vegas card dealer.

One row convertor would routinely pull the strips at an angle to the cutter, hence we had mis-cuts, and some eradicating the blood fill area altogether.

So I designed a system that cut strips to the same width each time, giving a consistent full blood fill area. These strips were then to be deposited horizontally into two clear collection receptacles that worked in tandem with each other due to a fill sensor mechanism and the strips were deposited horizontally in a correct sized container to avoid jamming and therefore not being extracted by force.

I devised for inspection a system where we had an adjustable angle and height inspection table, like a cross between a draughtsmen's table and a pulpit with a lip at the bottom to prevent product hitting the floor.

I then suggested three weaker-powered or yellow fluorescent tube lights above the operator to their front and sides in a cubicle, to minimise reflection and eye damage whilst improving inspection results. The reflective strong ceiling light above was to be blocked out by the cubicle, too.

With the adjustable table the operator could either sit or stand and the uniform, non-single source, slightly weaker light from both sides and front, would prevent bad posture and eyesight issues whilst enhancing inspection quality through less light reflection whilst highlighting key areas more.

This wouldn't have cost the earth and could have improved quality and production whilst saving space.

Perhaps with the light changing from an unfit for purpose, badly positioned white to possibly a dimmer yellow we could have named the cubicles after a CEO at the time.

This would not have cost $10s of millions like a CEO or product recall, and would have been so much more professional.

But, of course, this goose laid another golden egg, just to be ignored completely.

Laurel and Hardy

What we must ask though is why, when we know the bar for dismissal was set so low in December 2009, were Laurel and Hardy and, in fact, the three Amigos counting their guru Les, still employed by Abbott as far as I am aware?

In 2010 Abbott Witney made shit product. In 2009 Pat, Les and Shaun dismissed Abbott's fail-safe, the company conscience, and the customer's best friend.

It may just be coincidence and some product ambience issue, but could my dismissal be their most costly mistake of all? Had there been a culture for encouraging talent rather than destroying it, might things have been a whole lot different?

Perhaps if it was a product ambience issue it might have helped, too, if the store room doors were opened less often and used just for product storage rather than sexual encounters.

Dictatorships don't always work. Along with the stick, the carrot of encouraging and nurturing talent is also advisable. People don't flag issues to dictators, they hide them.

Ironically, when these bullies needed to use the stick they were just so weak. When I was gone the good for nothing, worse than useless nuisance texter, the pregnant combatant, her sparring partner and brother-in-law Sleeping Beauty, and useless directors, were all still there.

You now had night shift staff, who were not just useless and fit for nothing when doing unnecessary overtime on day shift, thanks to Pat Cole's genius, they were then useless fit for nothings when returning to their own shift, too, due to working illegal, unsafe shift patterns. Many were also working illegally under unchecked pseudonyms – another fact management were alerted to but ignored.

Many also knew that there they were above being disciplined as the racist, woke, useless HR department and directors only disproportionately targeted innocent white males, especially the Irish. This was a fact I also pointed out at tribunal, quoting specific examples rather than race. I was not allowed to use race in my statement as the judge said it was a protected characteristic. This insane wokery prevented what was also very much part of the whole truth being told. My family have feelings too.

Ironically; I believe in 2011 when I met another former member of staff in Witney; I was told about the 'night of the long knives' in Abbott Witney when nearly all the African staff had been kicked out overnight. Putting one and one together now, was this a result of the mass recall of strips? Let alone were Abbott making defective, useless strips in an error flagged in 2010, they were also making them using many workers with bogus identities, making the product illegal, too. If the FDA (US Food & Drugs Administration / Federal Agency) were to look into things.

The FDA might want to finally look at this now they have been given this information again.

One who had specifically benefitted time and again from Abbott's woke lunacy, our texting friend, or friend with alleged texting wife, pointed out to me the unfairness of positive discrimination, so knew it was unfair and knew he was a beneficiary. Abbott couldn't or wouldn't see it themselves.

After these identity checks and the night of the long knives, the African staff clearly carried the can after the disaster. It should surely have been HR and the directors. Even if this product had been good and the FDA had done a proper job it should have been illegal due to the bogus unchecked signatures of the staff who made them. The HR staff, managers and directors who facilitated this debacle with their slapdash approach surely had to go for this, too.

Naivety, bullying and ambition over ability

With hindsight and a pinch of honesty, some at Abbott might conclude that it would have been more financially prudent and wise to employ intelligent, capable directors rather than the easy-to-control, compliant one-trick ponies who when told to jump ask, 'How high?' rather than ask, 'Is that wise, necessary or the right thing to do?'

Perhaps another parallel is comparing Abbott to the Jimmy Savile case at the BBC and Philip Schofield and the woke protection at ITV, is when bullies become empowered and beyond questioning as everyone is fearful of their gravitas, then things inevitably go disastrously wrong. Good people get their lives destroyed and ass-kissers benefit from being part of the gang.

Surely the corporation has a duty to its staff, customers and shareholders to engender a culture where issues can be raised?

Pat and Shaun's first full year of leadership in financial and general disastrous terms can best be compared with Liz Truss and Kwasi Kwarteng in the UK. It was morally bankrupt too.

This was a legendary cock-up. But somehow, at Abbotts, Laurel & Hardy are still there.

In 2010 they tried to destroy the reputation of one of their best staff, including intentionally lying to Her Majesty's tribunal, only to finish the year finding out that they had made so much defective product for half the year.

These bullies didn't just illegally gamble with my reputation, they destroyed Abbott's by putting the customer last. Abbott backed these charlatans at tribunal when they should have been backing me.

It is often said 'The proof of the pudding is in the eating,' and Abbotts were left with a complete dog's dinner, egg on their face and had to eat humble pie after I left.

Abbott's hierarchy should say to Pat Cole and Shaun Smith, 'That's another fine mess you've gotten us into.' Their bullying and incompetence is still unpunished and illogically even rewarded to this day.

If you are getting the big bucks and such a disaster happens on your watch and the bar for dismissal is so low, then surely you have to walk the plank. I have complained officially about the bullying and intimidation of Pat, Shaun and Les more than once but, like the time Abbott lied about me even working there, this was all swept under the carpet.

As with ITV and the Schofield saga, when you have a toxic culture and anyone with an opinion gets heaved out of the door, when there is something wrong that everyone knows about, i.e. Phil's unwise relationship, because he has the favouritism from his bosses in a toxic environment nothing is reported as the penalties are too severe, and the ultimate penalty is inevitable. So the useless, overpaid bosses continue to ruin the company. Sound familiar?

Everyone should be equal in the eyes of the law although some directors, judges and legal experts are conveniently and intentionally blind to the obvious.

Some are clearly a lot more equal than others.

Chapter 42

The Wisdom of Solomon

You must conceal all crimes of your brother Masons...and should you be summoned as a witness against a brother Mason be always sure to shield him...It may be perjury to do this, it is true, but you're keeping your obligations.

Ronayne
Handbook of Masonry, **page 183**

Most of us know the story of King Solomon and the two alleged mothers and the baby.

It was obvious from both mothers' actions when King Solomon said, 'Cut the baby in half,' who the real mother was.

It would be obvious to anyone possessing even a grain of wisdom who, between Linda and myself was telling the truth.

It would be obvious, too, to any outsider when I went to the police to get the calls traced, or by taking the case to tribunal, appealing to judges and the ombudsman only to face the circling of the wagons, and then taking a lie detector test, who was telling the truth.

The freemasons will try to convince you that they are not just an anonymous community. They are a respectable, enlightened bunch of selfless, charitable, caring individuals. Enlightenment seems to be their theme and King Solomon is an important character to them. But are they the exact opposite? If they were not, human nature would suggest that they would not be so anonymous.

I tried to enlighten the – in all probability – masons and their peers as to the error of their ways in backing their friends at Abbott.

I can't say for certain who is a Mason and who is not. I am just going on the premise that if it looks like a duck, waddles like a duck and quacks like a duck, then logically it's a duck.

Abbott's, In particular Les Muggeridge, have always behaved as if they have 'Teflon immunity' and are above the law and consequences. I can't cite an example when this did not seem the case.

Using the wisdom of Solomon you would think that, especially after my lie detector results are presented, if Abbotts were a just and fair employer they would reopen the case, not engage their friends and puppets, the police, with spurious claims of harassment when ironically Abbott have done all the harassing.

Eventually Jane Ingram's lie about me never working at Abbott, and their subsequent own goal going after me again as I was then once again a former employee, were to underline unequivocally that my assertions about Abbott's utter dishonesty and confidence in their immunity with authority were correct all along. There were no consequences for this blatant law-breaking either.

Although this episode was law-breaking in itself Thames Valley Police, who issued me a harassment warning for emailing my polygraph results, claimed that Jane Ingram's genuine law-breaking was a civil matter and outside their remit.

What would King Solomon think of all this? Would he judge on my side or Abbott's?

Justice is purely and simply the rewarding of right and good and the punishment of wrong and evil.

More today than at any other time, there is a need for good, honest people to stand up for the truth.

We cannot trust the church, the police, the crown, the judges, the civil service or our MPs. In fact virtually everyone in public office.

The church and the crown

One person in the UK is the figurehead of both (at time of writing), King Charles III.

A family member, the Duke of Kent, has been head of the freemasons for over half a century.

I remember telling my son at Prince Philip's funeral, 'Just you watch. That coffin will enter the church at exactly three minutes past three.' It duly did, and to the very second. Thirty three is a sacred number to the masons. The Duke of Kent was of course in seat 33 at the Queen's funeral.

The new mouthpiece of the freemasons UGLE chief executive, Dr David Staples, was keen to advertise Philip's freemasonry in the aftermath of his death in 2021. According to his BBC interview, 'The freemasons is all about fun and becoming a better person' 'Philip would have had a lot of fun (especially on Thursdays, perhaps) and learned how to become a better person.'

He then says about the ceremonies Prince Philip went through, just like everyone else.

'The first ceremony teaches you how important it is to respect other people, particularly those less fortunate than yourselves,' like those clearly shafted by Her Majesty's judicial system, perhaps.

'The second degree ceremony teaches you the importance of improving yourself through education,' The judges I wrote to refused to be educated or address a single irrefutable point.

He then says, 'The final lesson in freemasonry is to make the most of your one life. Live respected, die regretted.' 15 years of my **one life** have been wasted through my innocence not being **respected**. I'm now making the most of my remaining one life in **educating** people through this book as to the unscrupulous nature of the establishment that has scant respect for justice.

In defending UGLE in 2017 Staples said that the masons raised just over 33 million pounds for charity last year. That number again. What he didn't say was that according to news items, much of that went to masons' charities like paying school and health fees for hard-up brethren.

I know from my childhood in the Catholic Church that you can also claim back the tax on charitable donations, giving the self-helping brotherhood another huge windfall.

Staples was on a huge PR exercise offensive at the time. It was the brotherhood's 300th birthday. They placed full-page ads in *The Times*, *Guardian* and *The Telegraph*, calling gross misrepresentation of his members 'discrimination, pure and simple.'

If he wants to know about real discrimination he can read this book and see how I have suffered compared to others. He can then openly disclose the details regarding all his members and where they work, to see if I have been the victim of discrimination by any of them.

Call me a cynical cunt, but I am a real Doubting Thomas who believes that the primary function of the masons is to gain an unfair advantage over non-masons, i.e. to discriminate. I see the charitable, more decent human being stuff as a facade.

I'll happily call myself a cunt if he can prove me wrong beyond all reasonable doubt. If he can prove me wrong in anything I have said here, having morals, I will openly apologise. Abbotts have been proved wrong so many times, and so unequivocally, and have to date shown no contrition.

Oh but of course poor David's brethren, in his own words, don't want to divulge membership for fear of discrimination.

Page 183 in the Masons' Handbook I quote at the outset of this chapter clearly encourages discrimination among the brethren.

Back in 1982 the late Sir Kenneth Newman, Commissioner of the Metropolitan Police, in his 'little blue book' of police ethics for his officers advised: *'The discerning officer will probably consider it wise to forgo the prospect of pleasure and social advantage in freemasonry, so as to enjoy the unreserved regard of all those around him.'*

I have experienced the most peculiar loyalties in Thames Valley Police and the judiciary which at the very least suggest a lack of impartiality. Could there be unprofessional conflicts of interest involved?

Surely if I report a criminal offence to Maidenhead police that warrants police action, such as Jane Ingram lying about my ever having worked at Abbott or Les Muggeridge's intimidation of me, and the police do nothing, but are the same police who issue a ridiculous harassment warning against me, which is not their duty, and at Les's behest, after e-mailing my polygraph results, Surely I should have the right to know if Les and any police at Maidenhead belong to the same lodge?

Surely you can say the same for when the police at Wantage refused to act on the nuisance caller who had already been traced by TalkTalk or didn't act with regard Linda driving at me deliberately, and in a premeditated act, as soon as they speak to Les on the phone.

I could say the same with my case being moved from Bristol to Reading and jumping the queue somewhat. Then there are the judge's alarming oversights, all of which backed Abbotts, without exception just like the local police in Maidenhead.

The society has admitted that around 200 judges and policemen are practicing masons. That is 200 too many in my opinion. That is, of course, if those figures are even remotely believable.

Some might criticise my cynicism with regard the masons, but something incredibly sinister keeps happening to me again and again, and I can't find a single establishment figure with the will to stop it. So I deserve answers, especially as these figures are paid by us to be fair and honest.

Conversely Abbott get away with everything again and again, up to and including attempted murder.

Unless, of course, someone can provide some alternative logical explanation for what I have experienced: We are way past the remotest possibility of entertaining coincidence as a possibility.

Some secretive self-serving clique has been screwing me for years at every turn, and the list of suspects is not exactly infinite.

It is long past time that the pretence, the discrimination and the secrecy all stopped.

Why do the angels on the UGLE crest have goat legs and hooves and so many grand lodges' crests have pentagrams, many having both? To me this is just openly satanic.

A classic case

Just how did freemason Sir Cyril Smith not just get let off the hook after being 'caught red-handed' and arrested for his boy-buggering exploits, but then subsequently get and accept a knighthood?

Still a mystery, that one.

Would your King Solomon say that my hug was infinitely more serious than all Sir Cyril's serial buggering and all of royalty-connected Sir Jimmy's crimes? Our establishment clearly says it is.

You say, Mr Staples, all brother masons are under a masonic and moral duty to report inappropriate behaviour. Did any report Sir Cyril?

Dare I ask David Staples how many masons innocently, of course, visited Kincorra and Bryn Estyn?

Enlightenment

I have always seen it as my Christian duty to fight Satan and all his evil works, hence I took the Catholic Church to task as I believed paedophile priests could not possibly perform the consecration, the act at the centre of the faith. I was disgusted that the Vatican sought to defend and cover this up. My view has not changed.

I did the decent thing.

Standing against the satanic is a lot more difficult and dangerous that reciting the same stuff parrot fashion on a weekly basis, but is actually, morally, what is required.

After all, didn't Jesus himself lead by example, overturning a few tables in the temple?

David Staples would welcome new brethren to his flock with the bullshit promise that membership would enlighten, leading you to 'live your life well', a bit like Abbott's bullshit, and be a better community member. Would this community be the one that members must then exclude, have unfair advantages over and keep so many secrets from?

I can enlighten and lighten you, David. Remove the cumbersome yoke of secrecy from your conscience and replace it with openness and honesty. You will be a better, more enlightened person for it. This advice is free and open and you do not have to join a secret society to get it.

As the masons so enlightened Sir Cyril Smith and, I would suggest, protected him to the detriment of innocent children, I say, 'To hell with your enlightenment; it does not make you better human beings.'

To the masons, apparently their guru Albert Pike's Lucifer symbolises enlightenment and knowledge and not evil. It's a call to seek light and wisdom, a core masonic value, according to masonic scholars such as Dr S Brent Morris.

Where we might both agree was that Cyril Smith, as a true mason, obviously sought the light of Lucifer.

Go on, David, make my day. Explain how the masons made Sir Cyril a better person.

The parallels with Sir Cyril

Much as I wouldn't accuse Les Muggeridge of having the same sexual preferences as Sir Cyril and can't confirm that he is a mason, the parallels between them are all too striking.

What we have in both cases is a vile, nasty, intimidating, controlling ogre who seems to have, or has had, total establishment immunity surrounded by kowtowing cronies who assist them in presenting a false image that these are genuine, trustworthy, wholesome characters and real people's champions.

Both, indeed, seemed to have alarming sway with the establishment.

All evidence relating to Sir Cyril's misdemeanours was hurriedly and aggressively destroyed.

Destroyed documents and the omission or covering of evidence, there's another parallel.

Lessons were going to be learned after the Sir Cyril scandal.

Now the establishment has the perfect opportunity to prove those lessons have been learned.

Has anyone apart from me tried taking Les to account?

Or is there more chance that, as well as enjoying establishment immunity, Les will eventually be honoured by said establishment too?

Abbott's conduct and the subsequent lack of consequences shames the establishment. So why do they still defend this shameful behaviour?

We need to make all discrimination illegal. To not do so is discrimination in itself.

Profiling

As with Linda Shaw and getting an expert in to see that her letters are indeed seldom from the attributed author, the wisdom of Solomon would smell a rat straight away.

Profiling Les, there can be no doubt that we have an utter bully without conscience who wants and uses every tool available to him, including the intimidation I suffered on more than one occasion, to get his way and screw people. He is a thoroughly nasty and evil, utterly manipulative control freak. This was illustrated when I sent my polygraph tests to all but him, his subsequent control over the police and the unethical use of his puppet, Pat Cole, at my appeal hearing, that he will stop at nothing to achieve his desired result.

Dare I say, one such as this who likes to control people and enlist them into his web of deceit would surely see the allure of the masons too hard to resist. What would Solomon think?

Who did give the idea to Jane Ingram to say I never worked for Abbott, in the full confidence they would be immune from police action? She didn't know me at all, and subsequent events proved that Abbott did have my personal records. Who would Solomon suspect would be behind this?

As with Solomon opening the windows to let the bees go to the scent of the real flowers, lifting the lid on these cover-ups could lead us to the something that really stinks. I smell a rat.

Perhaps others, and particularly scared others, who kowtow by default for an easy life, might say, 'Aren't you overreacting with all this freemason stuff?' Well actually, what would Solomon say about the police who intentionally ignored someone intentionally driving at me and beyond doubt, as well as ignoring intimidating nuisance calls that had been traced, but who saw fit to issue me a harassment warning at Les's behest for submitting polygraph results and defending my innocence?

This is not a community police force in action, and these are not proportional reactions by Les and his minions. What would Solomon say about the delayed, mother of all overreactions to just one employee's hug but not all others, yet turn a blind eye to punching pregnant women, sending poison texts and driving with intent to maim or kill, and all the rest of what went on? (Again – sorry to the reader for the repetition.)

Surely you would think the unhealthy sway, in fact the absolute influence that Les and Abbott have with the establishment detailed in this book, would merit a very thorough investigation by the police and the judiciary or, better still, an independent, outside investigation.

I won't hold my breath.

I'm surprised that the freemasons in these organisations, who have learned to be better community people than the rest of us, have somehow not picked up on all this already, after all my complaints.

For the good of all, let's grow up and stop this ridiculous game of pretend.

I'm in little doubt about the nastiness that could potentially come my way for being brave enough to write this book and especially this chapter.

Whatever – this book absolutely needed to be written. More so than Albert Pike's book ever did.

Perhaps I won't be the first Michael Collins to sign his own death warrant.

C'est la vie. Well, for as long as it lasts, anyway.

If I can make some sort of change for good and justice that will be an acceptable legacy.

Chapter 43

Window Dressing

Smile for the camera

If you look at Shaun, Pat or Les on LinkedIn or any other page, they will like some Abbott charity event or something and all the ass-kissers will like their likes, or what they like, etc. #abbottproud and all that bollocks.

Wonderful Abbott will sponsor the London Marathon and other sporting events.

Good old Abbott with their freestyle gentle Butterfly logo and their 'promise for life' and 'living life well' and the rest of it.

It's simply bullshit, window dressing, a big lie. A glossy veneer to hide the filth lurking underneath.

Hypocrisy

Like I have said before regarding bullies, would they be proud if their family could see how they act?

Shaun Smith, Pat Cole and Les Muggeridge are all bullies who should have been sacked 15 years ago.

If Abbott want to live life well and are an equal opportunities company with the diversity conscience they so falsely seek to promote, then prove it. Shaun Smith, Pat Cole and Les Muggeridge should have no place in their company.

Fifteen years on and the problem is still there.

I have had fifteen years of mental health hell. No contrition, and no doubt there have been more victims since.

Stand up for quality product and the Abbott customer and see what you get.

Abbott USA are no better.

The Depakote scandal

Don't ever be fooled into thinking that Abbott are a caring company that place any value on human life and decency or have any respect for it.

In the second largest-ever fraud settlement, $1.6 billion, involving a drug company, Abbott misrepresented the drug Depakote, falsely promoting it to control agitation and aggression in elderly dementia patients and also to treat schizophrenia. Neither use was approved by the FDA and Abbott's trials had failed.

Basically Abbott salesmen were trained to promote the off-label uses of this drug, targeting particularly the elderly and secondly children, the two most vulnerable groups in society.

Between 1998 and 2006 Abbott violated medical ethics with aggressive marketing with sweeteners, of a drug that basically turned grandma and grandpa with certain behavioural traits into compliant zombies. Care homes could and did give this stuff to patients to save on staff costs.

This case was eventually heard in 2012. In the years prior to that Abbott did not take too kindly to whistle-blowers, and four of these received a very healthy sum as part of this settlement. Was there a policy or even a purge of anyone in the company with a customer conscience and the courage of their convictions who, when they saw wrong practice, would challenge it around this time?

Will they ever learn?
Whistle-blowers feature again in the latest Abbott scandal regarding their baby formula and bacteriological issues. In 2022 Abbott recalled Similac and other products due to bacterial infections caused in infants.

The FDA on inspection cited some catastrophic procedural errors such as cracks in vital equipment and, believe it or not, a basic lack of adequate hand-washing. Who knows, perhaps staff were having sex on site there too, where they shouldn't have been. Trust me, it happens.

Abbott learned of the issues through a whistle-blower complaint in 2021, but the shelves were only emptied in 2022 because Abbott did not disclose them until an FDA investigation into child illnesses.

A 'National supply shortage' and blind panic, even from the White House, and the pharmaceutical- funded FDA agreed to the re-opening of this plant in Michigan.

It now emerges that there had been a number of cases over the previous decade where Abbott had employed the most ruthless, nasty, 'big law scorched earth tactic' lawyers to basically destroy poor families who also had the double whammy of brain damaged, incapacitated children to look after for life, too. Is that what Abbott mean by 'a promise for life?'

I hate bullies. Isn't it about time that bullies like Abbott and Jones-Day were simply banned from trading, in the interests of good and decent people? As it stands, evil occurs and the good can do nothing.

Let's just get rid of these ultra-expensive, anti-justice, life-wrecking parasites like Jones-Day and for the good of justice replace them with polygraph tests. Justice, in many cases, just like Abbotts baby formula, should not be a commodity that is for sale.

Meanwhile, back in the UK

People can die or suffer serious medical issues if diabetic strips produced by the million don't work. I stated that it was not a wise policy to have 'Mr Magoo' and 'Sleeping Beauty' as your final inspection team as well as not having bodily fluids and final product in the same store rooms.

I also then suggested, also providing tabular evidence, should there be any doubt that if 'Sleeping Beauty' can't stay awake to do inspection on night shift he sure as hell should not be getting priority overtime over alert workers on the day shift.

I certainly should not be sacked within a week or so because Sleeping Beauty can't even turn up for this crazy overtime, just because an egotistical, insecure director is arrogant and vindictive and has been proved unequivocally wrong.

I would still like an apology from Pat Cole, Shaun Smith, Les Muggeridge and Judge Barrowclough. I did the right thing by the customer.

The real Pizzagate (I'm not talking Arsenal and Man Utd either)

But there is even worse from Abbott. As mentioned before, I had designed a printing system method that was superior to what Abbott had, that could have resulted in better strips for the customer. An out-of-her-depth insecure director saw this wonderful gesture as a threat because it came from me, instead of welcoming initiative as a good director should.

Abbott printing staff also conducted their own scientific experiments. They didn't just eat on site, they cooked on site, too. They used to bring in pizza and cook it under the ink drying heaters. Cooked cheese tends to bubble and spit a bit. Abbott product used to follow the pizzas under the heaters. Diabetic testing strips at that, were probably contaminated with cheese drippings.

'Sex in the store rooms boy' was not the type to wash his hands; I saw this myself. I have no doubt that on returning from the car park after the blow job and fingering that he boasted of and his partner confirmed, he would have been sniffing his fingers. He probably tucked into a bit of pizza after that before handling the product, too.

Perhaps they will come after me again

Now the book is out I know what certain directors' first instincts will be, and they will try to get the company to pay the legal fees to go after me, too as they don't like staff who put the customer first.

The Abbott CEO should put the customer first, get rid of this nuisance and apologise to me.

Am I not now finally due an apology and some contrition?

That's not a difficult question either.

#abbottproud and all that bollocks.

Abbott should think and be civil

Although Abbott, having played the victim in a false flag operation, cut off my communication to them through influenced, unmerited harassment warnings and blocking all my e-mails, I have never blocked them.

This book became a necessity in the public interest, after the farcical judgement, and is my only remaining avenue of communication. From a personal viewpoint, it is a necessity in the interests of my mental health, too.

The aim is to provide cathartic closure but the possibility of further bullying and intimidation is very real, as this is all I have experienced thus far.

I'm now advertising my innocence and how Abbott have targeted me, and this is long overdue!

But I'm still here and still fighting the good fight.

They did ruthlessly go after the families with the brain damaged babies.

They might win the case going after me, especially as I may not even defend myself in His Majesty's bent legal system, but will the publicity be in their interests and do the great sponsors of such wonderful events really have the morals they like to portray, or indeed any morals?

Proof of the pudding, and all that. We'll see.

Chapter 44

This Paddy Never Let Britain Down

Although at my workplace at Abbotts I might be greeted with, 'Hello, Michael Collins and how's the IRA?' comments, I never complained at the time and always did a good job, giving 100% to the customer. Attendance, punctuality, productivity, quality of product – all boxes ticked.

Perhaps I had the attitude, like another infinitely more well- known individual, whose origins are from the Emerald Isle, when he said, 'Think not what your country can do for you, but what you can do for your country.'

Those I've mentioned knowing, before regarding honours and whose work involved Her Majesty, were of Irish descent too, one with origins from the same town as JFK.

Of course JFK also had the courage to speak out honestly and openly against the secret societies shortly before he was bumped off. Ooops!

Better just mention that I currently have no physical health issues, have never taken drugs, have parental filters on my PC and will never have the slightest inclination to transform etc. Just in case something suspicious happens to me.

This Paddy never let Britain down in her time of need
Like the day of JFK's death, there are very few people in the world of whom it can be said that most people at the time remember exactly where they were and what they doing when they heard of that person's death.

One such person was Princess Diana.

She, like JFK, left us far too young and in tragic circumstances.

At Diana's funeral it is well remembered that Elton John changed the lyrics of his hit *Candle in the Wind* from being a tribute to Marilyn Monroe to being a tribute to Diana.

Naturally, with Diana's charity work and public demand there was an inevitability that this was to be made into a charity single. It was obvious, too, that it was going to sell 'shed-loads'.

Back at the time, I used to manufacture CDs. Our factory was one of the very first to volunteer to mass produce this on a non-profit basis.

To basically explain the CD production process:

The manufacture of compact discs involved a production line integrating numerous processes. Firstly there were twin injection moulds that dovetailed via a robot arm-assisted production line, integrating the processes of high DC voltage Anode/Cathode/Target aluminium cloud deposition, followed by centrifugal lacquer deposition, followed by high temperature curing then finally camera inspection.

Four sample discs at regular intervals then underwent 17 further tests for potential failings with data and graphs produced for each test.

The completed CDs once passed then went on to a six-colour silk screen printing process before being individually packed.

We worked on a four on-four off 12 hour day/night shift process.

On my last shift I helped set up all the moulds to manufacture the *Candle in the Wind* CD. The production lines would then be basically flat out making only this for the next 'as long it takes' number of days or, as seemed more likely, weeks.

I felt a real buzz as there had not yet been official confirmation that this was going ahead and you wanted to do something good. You wanted to be part of doing something to help, such was the mood all around at the time. Well for me, anyway. Not so much for the two due in on the next four nights, as they phoned in sick.

Living just around the corner and being Mr Forever Reliable I came in to do what I could to replace this 2-man shift.

During the day the four engineers joined in on the shift and about 46,500 discs were made. They wanted to see how many discs our machines could make at maximum output. With no job changes, this was the opportunity. They said to me as I came in, 'There's no way 50,000 was possible.'

Red rags and bulls
The next morning they came in to find I had made 51,500 discs.

There were various on-the-job tweaks to speed up production whilst ensuring the quality was just as good, if not better, for example if the mould cooling time is reduced slightly, without compromising pit depth (pits are what the laser on the CD player reads) so that more discs can be made.

Another way, albeit with some risk, is to regularly change the robot arm suckers 'on the go' instead of letting discs pile up and wait as you change these suckers. When discs pile up some discs will cool and bow away from new hotter discs and may be rejected by the cameras.

This did involve a risk, like getting your arm smashed if you tripped a robot arm sensor, but more discs and better quality discs were made this way.

So, to cut a long story short, I made 12 hours of quality discs without taking a break, especially as I knew why these discs were being made. Also, I would have the hassle of starting everything up again from cold if I took a break.

Then the next night, I suppose it being a weekend, the other two were sick again. I came in and made 53,711 discs (I can still remember the number). My adrenaline was through the roof as what I was doing was like plate-juggling, keeping everything going. Then at the end of the shift when I stopped there was so much adrenaline that I felt seriously light-headed, like I was on a high and floating.

I explained that what I had done was not safe or to be recommended, but there was a buzz like a bit of a high everywhere at the time and it was great to do your bit to help. Monday morning, the first of these were heading for the shops.

I can say without doubt that it would have been impossible to work any harder both mentally and physically than I did that night. I truly gave 100%.

I believe, though I cannot prove it that, as that was by far the biggest selling single of all time and we were one of the first and last places to manufacture that particular CD until demand died totally and we had three twin moulds, i.e. six new modern moulds running constantly, and that I did 12 hours every day, doing the work of two, I can surely claim to have manufactured more of a particular single than anyone else ever – not that there ever would be a world record for such a thing. It can, of course, never be beaten now with the introduction of online music.

The nation expects once more – Paddy turns up again.
Years later in a new and altogether different millennium, and facing a national emergency, I find myself facing a brand new challenge.

Moving the clock forward a few years to 2020 there is a worldwide Covid pandemic declared following the first outbreaks in 2019.

By now I'm the other side of my spell at Abbotts and am doing final-stage testing on Anaesthesia machines before they are shipped to and installed in operating theatres worldwide

Final test of Anaesthesia machines was a responsible position. Rigorously checking the machine worked over a process and being able to identify and repair all issues was vital, as my work was the final stage before the machine became operational in a hospital operating theatre.

Machine functionality and the various gas percentage readings, for obvious reasons, had to be right.

Much as we were not the world's busiest place, although every order still seemed to be an emergency, our skill set, suppliers and experience made us the obvious people for the government's ventilator challenge.

Our company was the first indeed to design and produce a working ventilator to meet with the criteria the government demanded.

There was a frenzy around the place with TV news cameras, etc. turning up, wanting to know what we were going to do and how we were going to do it, etc.

We had been told at work that it was not compulsory but there were to be six eight-hour shifts working four-on four-off, making these machines with about 30 outside volunteers or workers coming in to assist on each shift, and our experience would be invaluable at this time.

There were two of us on final test. The other chap, who had a vulnerable partner who also worked there, refused to be part of this after confirming details regarding Health and Safety procedure and what would happen in the event of a Covid infection outbreak on the premises during this time. We did not know back then how dangerous the pandemic was or how long it would last. He also helped his nearby elderly Mum & Dad regularly.

I don't blame him at all, and fully understood him for refusing to take part.

There were also two on penultimate test and general assembly whose skill sets were better than mine in certain areas. I do feel that our floor manager loaded too many eggs into one basket, her shift, and could have spread us out a little better. Some shifts had none of us allocated at all, and it showed.

Anyway, like with the CDs back in the day, it was all hands to the pump and we integrated with a good many companies to get the show on the road. Ford's in Dagenham, like many other companies, were doing their bit and the input on certain shifts from the Williams and Renault F1 teams was excellent, as well as a couple of their former workers who I believe worked voluntarily.

Even before we got properly up and running, I felt my experience could input a lot. I noticed that the child lung testing equipment was giving readings on average over 10% out so, before the serious output started, I went around one day and tested all of them and the adult lungs for comparison and, with my results, got the criteria changed. The original, incorrect results criteria was going to make most machines failures, not because they were not working but because of these readings.

Then, once we were up and running, we then had an issue with the monitors on most of the systems, locking the user out after the settings had been locked in by the operator, rendering them unusable.

Had I obeyed the '5s instructions' from months before I would have destroyed a copied document of an email sent years earlier with vital documentation on unlocking these frozen monitors. There were right from the outset a very high percentage of these 'locked-out' machines.

I said to our manager, who was not supposed to be there as he had a very vulnerable wife, 'I thought I had to save this information, in case of a rainy day' (against his advice). 'Now it is absolutely teeming down.' How fortunate it was that I had such foresight.

The only other chap who, I knew, had this information was now at home. This production director who was not now directly involved with manufacture should have been at home, too.

But he had his ego and had had his TV moment. I said to my colleague who stayed at home, before his mind was made up, 'I bet old ego boy can see an honour in this.'

This manager insisted on coming in against all medical advice, as he himself said, as his wife was very vulnerable, but he was so insecure and fearful of missing anything.

The first day he was in the corner of the factory doing paperwork, well away from everyone.

In no time, he was in on all three shifts, breaking all the company's own isolation rules and national Covid rules.

He had by then, on numerous occasions since the Covid outbreak, publicly hugged the shift manageress as 'their shit don't stink.' The rules of Covid did not apply to them. You couldn't make it up. Do as we say, not as we do.

All shifts had thorough cleaning at the start and end of shift and a break between shifts to stop infection spreading between the shifts . This was rendered useless by his insecurity and arrogance.

He also came in every day across the next three shifts, on their four shifts on rota. Yet again, his shit didn't stink. He had, in the past, referred to himself as God.

If he had caught Covid all six shifts would have had to stop and for all we knew at the time he could have killed his wife, too. Leading by example.

But anyway, when the hard work all got going, I loved it. I was so busy going around everybody, at as safe a distance as I could, helping and answering questions and things were starting to go really well. You didn't really put the health risk to yourself at the top of your priorities.

We didn't have PPE. Then again, I'm sure our environment had far less worries than the nurses and care home workers faced.

A red flag: or was it a chequered flag?

An issue then occurred on the other shift which annoyed many. This was, after all, a pandemic and an emergency, assuming what all we were told on TV to be correct.

I was later told that the first lot of machines ready for shipment were delayed for two days whilst people nationally were dying. And why? 'My shit don't stink' boy decided we needed a photographer and massive F1-style chequered flags that had not yet arrived, and the New CEO present in order to wave the first machines off.

Yes, people were stood in front of the lorry six feet apart, arms raised for the camera, celebrating the intentionally delayed despatch of what was hoped would be vital, urgent life-saving equipment.

If he wanted these pictures so badly, surely he could have done these photos with the second or third batch rather than delaying urgent items.

But a lot of good stuff was happening and things were getting more efficient. I believe we got 11,700 finished in 12 weeks before anyone else really got started.

I don't think more than a handful of these machines were ever used. Probably just as well, because with the government's revised guidelines these things had the capability to ventilate a cow. Human lungs may have suffered irreparable damage with these machines in the wrong hands.

Like so much during the pandemic, things started to go a bit pear-shaped. F1 was given the green light to resume and we had a load of new workers to train again, with varying abilities.

Before they came to us they were to be given special instruction on what to do before they arrived. Whoever had been picked to teach them entered the room and said,' How do you turn the machine on?' 'No, seriously: how do you turn the machine on?' He had absolutely no idea.

It was then decided that all data was now to be entered by tablet, so there was to be another presentation out in the refreshments marquee. Only problem: no one turned up to present anything. An hour passed by and IT boy failed to show.

After a couple of weeks another issue then arose with a couple of workers given overtime on our shift, and the risk of cross-contamination that this brought. I must confess that by now I, too, was a little blasé, perhaps a little hypocritical, questioning how serious this pandemic was, and thought to myself, the extra know how these two could bring was potentially more rewarding than risky. Others were not so happy. But surely that horse had already bolted with the first rule breaker?

Snouts in the trough

Nationally we all eventually learned, in time, that during this pandemic some very dodgy government contracts worth millions were seemingly handed out for stuff such as vital PPE to companies, shall we say lacking in experience and suitability, in fact seemingly any experience or suitability.

In our production establishment we now had a situation, with the new influx working on ventilators, that different individuals were earning varying amounts for the same work, too.

On my shift, compared to the outside world, I was earning less than £10 an hour whilst others were sat at home on full furlough pay that I was paying tax for.

I was also instructing 30 or so people who were earning £25 per hour and on full furlough also.

I was then to learn afterwards that on another shift others were earning £50 an hour and in two cases £100 an hour, plus furlough, whilst those who instructed them earned as I did.

But I must admit that throughout, although I could see it was unfair, it was not my top priority and those who I knew at the time were on £25 an hour plus furlough didn't curb my enthusiasm. I just thought at the time, 'It is what it is, good luck to them.'

I avoided all the photos, however, and am in none of them, and there are absolutely loads of photos that are still in your face everywhere, I'm told.

I always saved my breaks for these moments when all the staff were called out for the photoshoot.

I was here to instruct and get product out, so during the photos was the perfect time for a break as there was no one who needed my help.

To me it also had shades of North Korea with all forced to smile, hands aloft, spread out like a Michael Jackson video shouting the company's name. Not my scene at all, as I said at the time.

Retrospectively

I was positive throughout and happy to help, and six of us subsequently got awarded by our peers for our outstanding input.

There has been a lot of bitterness since I left, so I'm told, as the CEO who was only seen by most for photos got an MBE and the one who did the public hugging (a sackable offence in non-Covid times for some) who could have killed his wife and shut down all six shifts with his egotistical negligence, who then delayed the first shipment for two days, eventually got a BEM.

I heard there was particular dismay at this from those who went and helped set up the Nightingale Hospital at the O2 arena, who had real expertise and absolutely put themselves out.

BEM boy, his arrogance and his ego were legendary. He was in many ways quite childlike and always wanted attention. He would often come in on a ridiculously loud motorbike, revving it furiously and totally unnecessarily, whilst reversing it with his feet.

I just thought, when I heard, that the whole thing with the honours was hilarious and vindicates my theory with Her Majesty's honours, once again.

There were the ass-kissers who would go over in wonderment to admire his motorcycle each time he rode in. These are the same ones who religiously asked each Monday morning how his weekend went.

These were also the same lucky few who got a bar of chocolate each after his 50th birthday. His tightness was legendary and he was shamed into buying bars of chocolate by upstairs colleagues but, on the shop floor, only handed them out to those whom he liked, those who kissed his backside and nobody else. What a great piece of management that was.

One older chap who brought loads of sweets and cakes for everyone weekly, including BEM boy, did not get honoured with a bar of chocolate. He did not grovel enough to the boss.

I suppose in a way it was an excellent piece of management. He made everyone happy. All those who got a bar of chocolate were delighted, and all those who didn't were also delighted. It was a badge of honour to not be amongst the chosen ones.

I don't even have to guess which arse-kissing minions would have 'voluntarily written' in on his behalf to get him honoured by the establishment. I'm sure they all like chocolate and were especially grateful for one particular bar they received. Pass me a bucket.

There are some you work with, and we have all met them, whose primary goal at work is to incur favour with the powers that be. They tend to be over-reactive and underhandedly nasty and backstabbing to their colleagues, too. I always thought that if such as these put the same effort into helpfulness and doing their job the world could be that bit better. I think what I'm trying to say is if they set goals and competed against themselves instead of seeking advancement at the expense of others and through backstabbing, vindictiveness and crawling…

You could now argue that I'm being a hypocrite criticising them, though not by name, writing this book, but the point needs making.

Only a hug? Try telling that to Abbotts

Ironically, with 'My shit don't stink, ego boy' here was someone who should have been sacked for a hug, in fact numerous hugs, during the pandemic, for which I reprimanded him, and his floor manager for so doing, at the time. 'But you've got to have a hug, haven't you?' they say to me of all people, with hypocritical arrogance. So now in this job my bosses tell me, 'You've got to have a hug!'

Their 'do as we say and not as we do' arrogance was on a par, and at the time of the pandemic, with Boris Johnson and his cronies and their gatherings whilst forbidding many from a last goodbye to Mum and Dad.

Another comment I made at the time was when this 'you've got to have a hug' hypocrite told us all to stay two metres apart, then said, 'How do we best visualise two metres?' I said, very appropriately at the time, 'Why not think of it as the length of an adult coffin?'

The penny still didn't drop. To think I was sacked for a hug in normal times, our floor manager here had a 20-a-day + hug habit. At the daily morning meetings, she was literally hanging off the other managers.

Many didn't like her or appreciate her hugs as the next minute the venom could kick in. You never knew where you stood.

No one died, and they were just hugs. But at that time someone could have, for all we knew.

No one lost their jobs or was officially disciplined over this either.

There was also the issue at this company of serious, daily homosexual harassment including the likes of tongues in ears, involving one individual targeting, in particular, another individual who put up with this rather than causing a fuss. This aggressor was a nasty piece of work, as was his wife, with both prone to temper tantrums and both, also, competitive nasty ass-kissers and grasses who knew how to keep certain weak bosses on side. The filth, from this 'outwardly gay-obsessed' individual went on for years and, I'm told, still is. Other staff have left due to his wife's unpunished nastiness.

I'd love someone to explain the rules of harassment at work to me, and the rules regarding hugs!

I'm glad I'm out of the place. What a world we live in.

The BEM award does make me laugh, however!

I'm so glad our friend managed to contrive an 'I'm better than you' award. It underlines the total farcicality of the system. Again, apologies to the deserving.

Power not just corrupts but attracts those least likely to utilise it correctly, in my experience. This applies to the work place and the establishment.

I left the place as soon afterwards as I could, waiting until after my dad's drawn out but expected death.

I couldn't really start a new job with his death imminent but did not let it affect my help during the Covid emergency.

Statistics and context – a corrupt establishment
So there are our pilot friends whom the likes of me are instructing. As said, I've been reliably informed they were earning £100 per hour and that is before furlough, which was no doubt an extra £30K per year on top of this.

Some of us were the canaries in the coal mine, possibly risking our lives from the offset and were the skilled ones in this, but were on less than 10% of their wages with no furlough payments.

Much as I never kicked up about this, I'm mentioning this again as, in regard to this, there is another very striking argument regarding the establishment that is well worth a mention.

I would think that these pilots on £100 per hour had more than £7-8K in savings. When I was unemployed, because of my hard-earned honeymoon savings earned on 12-hour nights I was put on 10p a week that I had to travel over 15 miles to sign on for, at my expense.

At my 10p a week from the establishment, assuming I had no outgoings like, for example, the journey to sign on, and the need to eat, then it would take me 770 years at that rate to earn what the £100 an hour pair each earned in a week. And that is before they then got their £30K furlough on top of this **regardless of their savings.**

Their furlough alone was nearly six thousand times as much as what I got whilst unemployed, and not through my own fault or choice. How can this be justified?

The socialist in me is coming out.

This all stinks of jobs for the boys, like the PPE contracts.

The good news is I'm not totally excluded from this equation. No, my taxes will go to pay off their furlough dividend. The same can be said for the care home workers' and nurses' taxes.

How many students who start life with a 50K debt they have to repay?

Surely those who benefitted from furlough should saddle the furlough debt, not the likes of care home workers.

I also think that care home workers who tried so hard, only to helplessly watch the frail die, and in particular the two excellent former Williams & Renault F1 guys who worked voluntarily on our shift during Covid, would be a lot more worthy of honours than those who most only saw for photo opportunities, and those whose arrogance both delayed shipment and could have had all six shifts shut down. Just my opinion.

Stepping up to the plate

Both in my efforts making the CDs and in working whilst not knowing what we were risking during Covid whilst all were safe at home, like the NHS and care workers, I did my bit.

When the time came I stepped up both times and never let the country down.

The police, the judges and Abbott sure let me down, and totally.

Much as I would neither want nor accept an award from this corrupt establishment…

I would like some fairness. I would like justice.

I have yet, after thousands of times trying, to even get acknowledgement that my treatment was even a tad harsh compared to others.

Much as I didn't care at the time, and have long since written it off, people were not treated with fairness and equality during Covid either.

Like in a previous chapter, I did not want to mention all the Abbott sex-on-site issues. I didn't really want to mention this company and left on good terms. But it is essential to give context with regards the hug I was sacked for and to also show how trustworthy and fair our establishment is – or perhaps isn't.

PS Another thought

Perhaps those who receive four star accommodation and legal costs at the expense of the taxpayer might also be given a debt similar to that which our students have to pay for their accommodation and tutorial fees. This can then be removed from their wages once their asylum claim is inevitably accepted.

That way they can show their gratitude for the help received in saving their lives, helping them escape these brutal regimes, as anyone would surely be only too happy to do in such circumstances.

Chapter 45

Morals, Honesty and Grown-up Behaviour

In this modern politically correct world we strangely once again find ourselves back in middle ages in the days of the Witchsmeller Pursuivant, in terms of lack of intelligence, gullibility and a submissive flock mentality.

In this new moralistically upside down, tail wagging the dog, crazy woke world it pays to cry wolf.

We are in the days of fake victimhood since PCHR became an industry.

I could say to Pat, Shaun, Les and Linda, 'Grow up, it was only a hug.'

But things are a lot more nasty and sinister than that.

To put it bluntly Pat, Les and Shaun behaving like the nastiest, most spiteful children ever in their wilful overreaction to an act of kindness was evil and shocking. That's if you are gullible enough to believe there was no ulterior motive on their parts.

To destroy someone's life, to destroy their livelihood and attack their marriage with the accusation of harassment, to threaten their home, their family life, their sanity and also destroy all their future prospects in the mother of all overreactions is simply evil. All this whilst intentionally ignoring so much real serious shit.

The Abbott directors can be likened in their priorities to Inspector Clouseau in the *Pink Panther* film, interrogating a blind accordion player regarding his monkey's finances, whilst an armed robbery is going on in the bank behind him. He fails to notice the robbery, even picking up a bag of loot which the robbers dropped, then passing it to them before bludgeoning the bank manager who tries to stop them.

Was Inspector Clouseau, demoted to Officer Clouseau in this case, trained by Thames Valley Police?

'Zose polygraph test results you e-mailed constitutes harassment. Nuisance calls and intentionally driving zee car at you with intent to harm or even kill are not. Under section B100DY11AR5: Zat is zee low.' It's bloody low alright, an incredible low, beyond all reasonable doubt.

Surely some action should be taken against Nicky, Shaun, Pat and Les for genuine harassment by targeting and bullying, as I have insisted to Amanda White, Miles White, Jane Ingram and others.

Even legally, dismissal is supposed to be an absolute last resort when there is no other option.

On Facebook I might finish a message to girls I've known for decades, 'Love Mick x,' or send or receive a heart emoji, especially after key life events. We are grown-up enough to know this does not represent carnal intent. I have also called girls I had crushes on a number of decades ago 'former goddesses'. Lock me up and throw away the key! The alternative, of course, is just be grown-up.

I would happily take a polygraph to show that I have been monogamous this last 30 years. How many can say that! Perhaps Linda and I could both take this test too.

At weddings and funerals and other events I'm a regular hugger who is also regularly hugged. It's just a spontaneous, natural, kind human reaction.

In a recent job the manageress was a 20+ hug-a-day person who still publicly hugged during the Covid pandemic. At meetings, most days, she was literally hanging off other managers. Nobody had their life ruined because of this. You could rightfully argue that during the Covid pandemic this did actually represent a genuine serious disciplinary issue regarding a hug.

Dare we mention again serious matters regarding actual, hour-long in duration, shouted boob comments with exposure thrown in, that a room full of police officers actually ignored.

Whilst Abbott, in total contrast, enacted their Inspector Clouseau policy, bludgeoning zee victim of zee fake boob comment conflicting stories.

Zat is not finny if you are zee victim.

As sarcastic humour with underlying relevant moral points is the theme in this chapter: Here is another thought I had.

Going back to the sex on site at Abbott chapter and the flasher having acceptable characteristics for dismissal. The Kenyan girl who was on the receiving end of this told me the story in full but found Indian boy's unpunished prolonged aggression and intimidation and subsequent texting far more distressing.

I was imagining the scenario had our Indian friend with the 'Wife who miraculously texted anonymously from his phone' had flashed at this girl.

His explanation might have been like a scene from Little Britain.

'I dropped my phone as my wife texted me (so she has her own phone then) and as I was bending down to pick it up, the elastic in my underwear and track suit bottoms both gave way simultaneously exposing my sack and crack.'

'Then I slipped on something propelling me, sack and crack first in the direction of the young lady's face.'

'This was extremely embarrassing and distressing for me and I now sincerely hope that this is now the end of the matter.'

Pat Cole would surely have accepted this explanation and no doubt asked how he was coping after this unfortunate trauma that had just befallen him.

Well this is no more ridiculous that the crap this 'creditable witness' in his own words, told the judge about his wife texting this same victim and turning a genuine fists and all assault involving a pregnant woman into playful waving.

Hang your head in shame Judge Barrowclough. Creditable witness, my arse, as another would say.

Chapter 46

The Weak Authorities
Who Look the Other Way

After 15 years of trying, apart from this book there are no more avenues to try.

Sadly I can say with complete honesty that I could not find one good person in the police, the judiciary and the Ombudsman's office, never mind at Abbott Worldwide who would even address a single point I made.

I believe the points I made were always legitimate, relevant, and fair.

I was honest throughout, too.

This book justified insults and all. It truly was my last resort.

The influent and affluent

I was so clearly the victim of a vindictive witch-hunt yet it seems impossible to find anyone in authority with the will to act on this.

The case against me was undeniably bent, procedurally flawed and illegal.

Justice should be for all, and it should be the reward of right and the punishment of wrong. It's that straightforward.

All the cases at the Post Office / Fujitsu Horizon scandal were all initially judged in favour of the guilty. Innocent people went to jail and others died before seeing justice.

I've seen enactments of the Hillsborough Trials. It can fill me with rage, tears or hopelessness?

Prime Minister Rishi Sunak, with the opposition in full agreement, confirmed to Parliament how utterly bent and untrustworthy the entire British Establishment is in the wake of the infected blood scandal, and the shameful arrogance of all the 'unfit for purpose departments' in delivering justice, putting the institution before integrity. Tell me about it.

I have only encountered justice when taking a polygraph test. Of course, the unjust ignored this.

Referring again to the CAPA corrective and preventative process principles:

In this book, having shown the clear discrimination that was fully enacted against me, I showed the way we can fix it for all, treating everyone equally by using a method that can't discriminate.

I demonstrated a process that can't see colour, race, creed, gender, age or sexual preferences, etc. It simply shows if someone is telling the truth.

I know this system gives the correct verdict, and have twice seen a judiciary that doesn't.

To cut a long story short

Someone intentionally drives at me.

I'm then sacked for a harmless, reciprocated kind gesture to this person.

The police refuse to trace nuisance calls to my family with the evidence waiting for them.

The most blatantly unfair dismissal both procedurally and morally is upheld at tribunal.

Years later, this same company then costs me another job with more blatant dishonesty.

All this is done, seemingly with knowing immunity. Otherwise it surely would not be attempted.

It's as if these people know they have an evil guardian angel.

I will no doubt be crucified and cast as the bad guy for suggesting this angel might have hooves.

Evil occurs when good men do nothing.

I have at least tried to stand up for what is right.

The moral of the story

When you spoil a child and refuse to reprimand it when it does wrong, supporting this wrongdoing by intentionally ignoring or excusing it: (as the police and judiciary did in this case) *the child will just want and expect more. You will invariably end up with a vile, bullying, obnoxious monster that always expects its own way and hasn't the conditioned deterrent or the morals to care about the impact on others.*

'As you sew so shall you reap,' to quote another well-known saying.

Years later Abbott went on to illegally destroy me again in the secure knowledge they had total immunity from any consequences.

Chapter 47

The Ball is now in Abbott's Court

Much as an overdue apology would be welcome, I know of at least one who would like to threaten me again with all sorts of action.

Let's face it, though. Abbott's credibility is in tatters after they illegally denied I ever worked for the company, causing me even more mental anguish and another ruined start in life. Then later, when it was once again convenient, in trying to remind me of my responsibilities as a former employee.

They are simply proven liars who, like all liars, totally tripped themselves up.

Perhaps they should then consider that, out of convenience, or desperation, they backed someone known and shown to be a proven liar and fantasist or, as they understatedly put it, 'dramatic'.

I'm sure they know in their hearts who really was the victim of a bullying campaign of rumours, who took evasive action to avoid the culprit, only to be then bullied again with the ultimate sanction from an extremely vindictive management.

I'm even then accused of harassment for taking a polygraph test.

Did anyone from this company ever consider that I might have feelings?

They know, too, how alarmingly different my treatment was to others.

They know, and would be better people if they now admit, that the whole procedure against me was just spiteful vindictiveness with an ulterior motive that should never have happened in the first place.

They should bear in mind that they were very fortunate at tribunal as their evidence does not stand up to the proper scrutiny that a competent; and fair legal panel would have provided.

There were so many procedural and paperwork inconsistencies, too, like the three month less one day rule being ignored, directors judging themselves and a pre-written letter of dismissal brought to a falsely alleged reconvened hearing, etc.

Perhaps they should consider that any further action against me would result in further, far greater publicity and scrutiny, and there is so much that Abbott would not like a spotlight to shine on.

I didn't instigate, want or deserve all that has happened.

Abbott should remember, should they want to set the pack hounds after me again, that it was their lies and unfairly targeting me, and the psychological damage caused, that was the primary reason this book had to be written. This book is also now my last available option.

Perhaps they could just finally admit their behaviour was disgraceful, consider the consequences over the last 15 years for my family, and make amends to an excellent employee.

Chapter 48

Tangents and Sticking to the Subject.

Towards the end of writing this book, just close to the finish line I got to that point, that overwhelmed feeling, perhaps even a breakdown. I'm not totally certain what one is. Perhaps I've never had one. Perhaps I've had quite a few.

Questioning myself I again turned to so much stuff I had decided to leave out. After all my pruning I started adding again.

Although there is plenty repetition in this book, I have really pruned down, for instance, the chapters involving the tribunal and the appeals which inevitably involved repeating the events that I had already written about.

I had also deleted so many chapters where I went off at tangents into subjects with personal relevance but not wholly relevant to this book.

There was a chapter about my upbringing and good role models during that period. There was another involving morals, values, the church, etc.

Being someone who probably identifies as 'stuck in the 80s London Irish,' there were two related chapters there, too.

One involved Ireland, the famine and the prison ships, etc. and the discrimination previous recent generations had to contend with, without perhaps complaining as much as some others.

There was another inspired by memorials to the fallen in so many places I visit in Britain. The war that would end wars: how terrible it must have been: basically, thoughts illustrated so well in the song *The Green Fields of France*.

I thought of the two sides both fighting for St George and one of Victoria's grandchildren and thought of the futility of it all. I then questioned, 'What would the fallen, many just teenagers, think of the country we inhabit today?'

As I'm mostly on the offensive in this book I wrote a few self-critical chapters for balance, addressing my demons, failings and negative sides. I then tried to address the psychology and reasons for this.

I then drifted into other near-death and scary experiences, of which there have been many. I could quote three in Fire Brigade training alone.

All these would be another book in itself.

But this isn't an autobiography and I'm not planning a sequel.

I sincerely hope that my debut as an author coincides with my retirement as one, too.

Emotionally this has just been too costly.

I have never wanted to write any book, let alone this one.

Chapter 49

How to Finish the Book

Another of my great failures has been my song writing exploits.

Only once ever, well knowingly, anyway, did I ever put my words to someone else's tune.

The song is a well- known Irish standard of yesteryear, 'The Spinning Wheel' and although author unknown it is believed to have been written by an English Lawyer in Dublin in the late 1800s.

Much as I loved the tune I never cared much for the lyrics.

One day I added my own.

Looking back at this book, I have to summarise somehow and I think that these lyrics I wrote so long before these issues began kind of sum up life and what was to come.

It is called 'Keep your heart's fire burning'.

KEEP YOUR HEART'S FIRE BURNING

A child as it grows up is clothed with affection
Treasured and loved in a world of protection
And he'll learn there's a world full of sunshine and gladness
But all he will find is a world full of madness

From boyhood to manhood through changes of season
Sees man torture man, what he'll not see is a reason
The world that he saw as a child was deceiving
The world he sees now is without make-believing

Now violence and mind games make people of wrong minds
Believe they are heroes, believe they're the strong kind
And never a thought to the one who's left crying
The young child's illusion left furthermore dying

The sorrow and heartache as lives they are shattered
And some walk away as if it never mattered
A mind can be scarred and the scar kept from showing
But seeds of despair once planted keep growing

There's many will stop you, you must never let them
Do what you must do, so you can forget them
And never let no one destroy your desires
Don't ever let no one put out your heart's fires

Now life is a long road with many a turning
And along that road you will always be learning
But never let no one stop your heart from yearning
Hang on to your dreams; keep your heart's fire burning.

As you have got this far:
Thank you from the bottom of my heart for reading this book.
Truly appreciated

Chapter 50

Postscript: Appeals

Who did I correspond with? It's a pretty extensive list.

Judge Latham, President of the tribunals of England and Wales. Baljit Ubney, Chief Crown Prosecutor, The Crown Prosecution Service. Kenneth Clarke, Home Secretary. Judicial Ombudsman Admiral Sir John Brigstocke KCB. Chief Constable Thames Valley Police. Dame Sarah Thornton DBE QPM to begin with.

Also MP for Witney, former Prime Minister Rt. Hon David Cameron and the MP for Maidenhead. Former Prime Minister Rt. Hon Teresa May and my MP. Former cabinet minister Ed Vaizey.

I write exhaustively to Miles 'Yellow' White Abbott CEO and the 'Independent' Police Complaints Commission (IPCC) which became the IOPC Independent Office for Police Conduct but still maintained its lack of independence and total uselessness.

I write to the FDA, British, American & Irish newspapers, relevant current affairs TV programmes. Basically I write to everyone and anyone. You get the gist.

I could publish volumes of books containing only my correspondence. This book is the last resort in the line of my attempts to get justice. I would love closure with justice. I'm mentally shattered as I write this and reflecting on all that time wasted does not help at all.

I will close, highlighting one face-to-face appeal – my arranged meeting with MP Ed Vaizey, a cabinet minister at the time, at his surgery in Faringdon.

I now refer to him as Mr E Vaisive. As I was clearly banging my head against a brick wall, so to speak, there came a point during his one-sided barrister waffle that I just upped and left.

I later said to the now 'Lord E Vaisive' in my correspondence…

You may well have had temporary relief and smelled victory the other day as I upped and left.

There was a simple reason for this; my pure disgust at your misplaced loyalties and total unsuitability as an MP.

What is the point of articulately transmitting my genuine issues to a person whose receivers are intentionally switched off? There are none so deaf as those who refuse to hear.

I had by this time met too many of those.

Tel: 0800 077 8560
Fax: 020 7376 9231
E-mail: don@nadacgroup.com
www.nationalpolygraphs.co.uk

NOTE.....AN EMBOSSED NADAC COMPANY SYMBOL SHOULD APPEAR ON EVERY PAGE
OF THIS REPORT TO ENSURE THAT IT HAS NOT BEEN ALTERED IN ANYWAY

The address of NADAC Ltd. and the examiner are not shown due to security
reasons. Details of NADAC Ltd can be found on the above website.

POLYGRAPH REPORT

Date of examination:	25/09/2011
Type of examination:	AFMGQT
Polygraph examiner:	Don Cargill

Subject name: *Michael Collins*

Date of Birth:

Examination Address:

ARRANGEMENTS:

Arrangements were made by the named person above and he was examined at the
above address.

ISSUES:

The issues under examination were covered in the relevant questions listed below.

Michael was given a pre-test interview in which he was explained the nature of the
test, in detail, as well as the operation of the polygraph instrument.

During the interview, Michael was read the questions that would be used during the
testing.

Michael consented to the polygraph examination and its questions, and did sign a consent form. He also provided proof of his identity.

The technique used in this detection of deception procedure involves the scientific identification of emotional reactions to control, relevant and comparison questions, with these reactions being represented by measured physiological changes in the blood pressure, respiration and the electrodermal activity.

Michael was given a detailed presentation of the polygraph instruments and a number of comparison questions were discussed in detail.

Michael was very co-operative throughout the test and was checked to ensure that there was not any use of countermeasures to affect the results of the polygraph test.

Michael clearly understood every question asked of him and was given numerous rehearsals of the questions to be asked of him before the actual test itself.

RELEVANT QUESTIONS:

The subject was administered one (1) polygraph examination consisting of a series of polygraph charts in which relevant, comparison and control questions were used. For information purposes only 3 relevant questions can be asked on a polygraph test.

Question 1. **Have you ever made a remark to Linda Shaw about her breasts?...NO**

Question 2. **Have you ever made a phone call to Linda Shaw's mobile or home phone number?... NO**

Question 3. **Did Linda Shaw kiss you on your right cheek in front of your wife in July 2009?...YES**

The Polygraph charts were scored using the very latest computerised polygraph software as well as being manually checked by the examiner.

OPINION AND CONCLUSION.

Based on the test and during the examination and interviews, it is this examiners opinion that **Michael Collins** should be classified as showing:

NO DECEPTION INDICATED in relation to the questions numbered 1, 2 and 3 listed above.

Respectfully submitted

Don Cargill APA BEPA
NADAC Senior Examiner
Chairman and Full member of the British and European Polygraph Association
Full Member of the American Polygraph Association

COMPANY PROFILE

NADAC is the largest privately owned Polygraph Company in the UK, with offices based in London and Manchester. In addition NADAC provides polygraph services throughout the UK and on an International basis.

We specialise in providing highly confidential polygraph testing for the Corporate sector, Government and Private individuals.

Our examiners are fully conversant with the most up to date techniques for testing, analysis and interview.

EXAMINER DETAILS

Don Cargill is NADAC's Managing Director. He is a member of the British and European Polygraph Association (BEPA) and the World Association of Professional Investigators (WAPI). Don Cargill is also the British and European Polygraph Associations' current Chairman.

He qualified with straight "A" grades from The International Academy of Polygraph in Fort Lauderdale, Florida and has conducted hundreds of tests in most market sectors for a multitude of different issues.

He is also a full member of The American Polygraph Association (APA).

The APA is the largest Association of polygraph examiners in the world. Membership of the APA and BEPA is strictly regulated and controlled.

Don also has passed additional polygraph examinations to test post convicted sex offenders (PSCOT)

Don is also the resident polygraph examiner on the Trisha Goddard Show which is shown on Channel 5

EQUIPMENT USED AND ACCURACY

NADAC use the very latest computerised systems and the most up to date software polygraph scoring systems. The equipment used on this test was the Lafayette LX4000, which is the preferred choice of most professional polygraph examiners in the World.

The American Polygraph Association has conducted more than 250 studies into the accuracy levels of a polygraph test.

Their research concludes that the accuracy of computerised polygraph is in the range of 95-98%.

3.37 PM 4/02/2010.

Time and date of my submissions, written
in Les Muggeridge's own handwriting.

REASONS FOR APPEAL

I wish to appeal against the Company's decision to dismiss me as of 11 December 2009
and set out my reasons for appeal below.

Timing of Linda Shaw's complaint

Post-it note arrogantly left
over text by Abbott solicitor.

One has to question the timing of, and indeed, the reasons for Linda Shaw's complaint.
Linda has been gossiping and colluding with associates for 5 months from ᴿ nights in an
attempt to exaggerate a simple brief hug, since the event took place on 1(*This is the*

Had there been any genuine excessive physicality or inappropriate beha\ *split*
would have complained at the time and had a whole shift as witnesses (i
Linda has a renowned history of complaining, and if what she said happ *Who do you want*
happened then this would surely have taken place at the time, *↙: - ?₁ me to send to?*

The timing of the official complaint is questionable and it arises when Linda was
heard that I have been complaining about the stories she has been telling, and, using the
same medium, i.e. the grapevine, that she has been using for years to subject me to false
accusations and slander. In order to rightly defend my character from this slander I have
merely responded in kind. *Did not consol with Ltd. With Birdwright should have also
detect on my behalf.*

It would seem fair to conclude that Linda, in sheer panic, knowing all that she has said
about me has decided to submit an official complaint, through fear of being finally
complained about.

The hug from my point of view

Although I was initially a friend of Linda Shaw I have seen the relationship deteriorate
since the time I first said I was intending to get married. I had tried to forgive a lot of
slander, for example, her saying I made a pass at her, then that I followed her to her
house, all of which I found particularly hurtful, as it was at around the time I was getting
married.

I turned a blind eye to many things including Linda driving her car directly at me as I
feared for her mental and emotional state. In spite of this I wanted to patch up the
friendship, so as to leave the night shift on a good note with Linda. The public hug was to
show clearly that I harboured no bad feelings as I said my goodbye that night.
The hug was an innocent kind gesture and could have been viewed as such by any of the
people present. Linda did not pull away or give any inclination that she was not
comfortable with the situation.
↗ July 09.

I am further confused by the allegations made against me by Linda Shaw in light of the
fact that a couple of weeks later at the farewell evening at Cumnor Cricket Club, Linda
publicly kissed me on the dance floor, in front of my wife, and her husband.

1

I worked tirelessly, condensing my notes, e-mailing them, and even hand delivering my comments re the investigation notes of others, all by the Wednesday before the meeting.

On Thursday I e-mailed some new evidence and was told to come in the next morning, Friday, for the outcome..

I am of the opinion that the evidence I produced was wholly ignored. Was the fact that I was also handed two new interview statements after dismissal, that I was given no right of challenge to, or to even read; proof beyond doubt that the outcome was predetermined?

I was dismissed it seems primarily because of a letter and then, a hug which took place 15 months later, with a complete disregard for the change in circumstance during the intervening time, and also a complete disregard for the fact that Linda Shaw had consistently ignored my letter of the same time regarding parking.

My treatment at Abbots 2009

I believe that there has been an effort on the part of the Company to remove me from the business. At open meetings, when questions were invited, I would oblige. I see that my dismissal was perhaps an indication of how the Company treats those employees that ask questions and raise issues with senior management.

The last calendar year has seen me involved in a number or incidents that together make a compelling case that lead me to suspect that there are those who, in spite of me having been one of the Company's most reliable, honest and productive workers do not altogether appreciate my presence, and would have preferred for me not to work within the business.

When the night shift merger was first put forward, we were told individually or in groups of 2 or 3, because in a group meeting the 'same people' always ask the questions, a clear dig at me. I raised the point that the strip manufacturing units had no representative at CCF level, and that a CCF rep in cartoning did not represent us and was not easily accessible. Did this lead to CCF elections, that were unwanted upstairs?.

Pat Cole sitting in judgement of herself.

Soon afterwards when, one morning after night shift, I informed Pat Cole by telephone that I had an idea for the night shift going forward. I informed her that I was standing in the CCF elections that night. On arrival that evening Pat Cole went straight to the area in which I was working, but deliberately ignored me and spoke at length to the three other people in this area,

I was one of four employees standing, later that night, for the post of CCF Rep, but was, for some inexplicable reason, the only one, not told the election result by management, but instead had to hear it through the grapevine, via a shocked member of staff who believed that the outcome of the election had been pre-determined.

"A Parking fix"

5

On questioning the management, I was denied the opportunity to know the final count and was simply told that the election was fair (a matter I had not questioned) and then told, when questioning further, that I did not even come close, in spite of many telling me they had voted for me.

The events of these 12 hours left me feeling extremely intimidated and victimised by the management.

I was then publicly made an example of when my first ER was granted the honour of bearing my name and being left on the weekly notice board for 3 weeks. This is in direct contradiction to the company's 'no blame policy.' Once more, me as a diligent and meticulous person has been singled out and given the 3 week name and shame treatment, which caused me great professional embarrassment. It turns out that the error was not even technically an ER. *Raised with Team Manager: Deellege Stephens: Harriet Eley.*

I then rightly addressed the issue with particular regard to Health and Safety of the sudden and strange decision to give night shifts overtime on days. I highlighted also management spin, with regard to withholding overtime for night shift workers for the last few months of A and B nights, through to the time when days were being questioned about doing overtime on nights, as their daytime overtime had been cut to prioritise accommodating nights, *Raised with Duncan Stephens: Did not raise it with Held 14.*

I even presented a table to show the excessive hours now being worked by some on the night shift, but was told that Shaun Smith would not entertain the idea as Pat Cole wanted things to go ahead as they were, and would not wear it.

← Pat Cole sitting in judgement of herself.

Immediately after I found I was no longer entitled to basic health and safety equipment. I was not allowed to be issued with ear defenders that are issued to other flat melt operatives, as they were 'too expensive and could not be just be given to everyone.' *Kim. Regular flat melt op. For 9 yrs.*

I was then dismissed for a kind gesture made five months earlier, without my evidence even being heard, in fact, it being deliberately ignored, even more suspiciously so, at a time when further voluntary redundancies were due to take place. My excellent long term work history was also completely ignored.

<u>Institutional Sexism and Racism at Abbotts. A Personal Vendetta?</u>

Kowtowards

Kowtowards of this nation, make headway kissing arse
In their imagination they'll view this act as class

Kowtowards of this nation will run off like a hare
When there's a situation about which they should care

Kowtowards of this nation, they'll jump on words you say
But grooming gangs or knife crime, they'll look the other way

Kowtowards now hate Savile, the vile disgusting thing
But when they see his best mate, Hurrah! God save the King!

Kowtowards of this nation, they're all too blind to see
The great discriminations, woke and freemasonry

Rose tinted specs and blinkers and heads deep in the sand
They're our commissioned thinkers – God help us in this land

I had a page to fill.
Two minutes of inspiration whilst recently on a walk.
Perhaps I've invented a new word in the process.